ART OF
THE
WORLD

ART OF THE WORLD

THE HISTORICAL, SOCIOLOGICAL

AND RELIGIOUS BACKGROUNDS

'NON-EUROPEAN CULTURES'

INDONESIA

THE ART OF AN ISLAND GROUP

BY FRITS A. WAGNER

McGRAW-HILL BOOK COMPANY, INC.

NEW YORK · TORONTO · LONDON

Translated by Ann E. Keep, Dr. Phil.

← Bas-relief from Borobudur, Gallery 3, North Side. Shailéndra dynasty.
Approx. 800 A.D. (Central Java).

© 1959. HOLLE & CO VERLAG BADEN-BADEN
COLOR PLATES PRINTED IN GERMANY
TEXT PRINTED IN HOLLAND
LIBRARY OF CONGRESS CATALOG CARD NUMBER 59—13943

When Holle Verlag asked me to contribute the volume on Indonesian art in the series "Art of the World", I hesitated for some time.
For I had first to consider whether it would be possible, within the
framework of a book which naturally had to be limited in length, to
give a sufficiently clear and profound picture of an art such as that of
Indonesia, with its immense diversity of modes of expression, techniques and styles. For the history of this region, which commences
with the emigration of the Indonesian people from Yunnan in South
China between 2500 and 1500 B.C., is the history of an archipelago
of vast expanse, which, moreover, by reason of its location has lain
open to all the important cultural and religious influences of the
Orient, such as the Dong-Son culture, Hinduism, Buddhism, and
Islam; in several districts, too, Chinese influences may also be traced.
Furthermore, in the course of the last four centuries the West has
exercised an ever-increasing influence upon the historical development of Indonesia, which has also led to some fundamental changes
in the cultural field. Since sea-borne trade naturally opened up the
way to penetration by cultural influences, certain areas — Java in
particular — were especially exposed to all the influences mentioned;
whilst other islands, or parts of islands, on the other hand, were either
so inaccessible or so unattractive to traders, (or both), that the tribes
which had settled there were able to lead an almost isolated,
existence until very recent times. Between these two extremes there is
to be found almost every conceivable degree of direct or indirect
cultural influence. Thus there is hardly any other area in the whole
world which has experienced so many cultural and religious impulses
of such diverse kind and force and of such enduring effect. This most
varied cultural development is reflected in the art of the Indonesian
peoples, although the basic aesthetic conceptions of the indigenous
culture which crystallized there in the pre-Hindu era have of course
remained more or less formative.
Naturally one has to set oneself limits when dealing with such diverse
material, the more so as the art of the Buddhist period will be treated
in a separate book. But on the other hand the picture to be drawn
must not forfeit any of its clarity or scholarly accuracy. Within this
framework space must be set aside for all the important artistic achievements of mankind in Indonesia. Whilst preferential treatment has generally been given to the particularly striking architecture and sculpture of the Hindu-Javanese period, in this volume, on the other hand,
no undue attention will be given to any one particular aspect of art.

I was never in any doubt that this would not be a simple task. But my decision to undertake this work was greatly influenced by the fact that Holle Verlag enabled me to supplement the text with some 60 photographs in colour and some 30 drawings. Photographs explain more than long descriptions in words ever can. Apart from this practical point, I was also motivated by a consideration of a more idealistic kind. Although an enormous amount of literature has been published on every possible aspect of Indonesian art, no attempt has yet been made to present it in its entirety. And this I regard as a particularly important and useful task at the moment, when, with turbulent developments taking place in almost every field, a great deal of beauty which at one time signified the wealth and happiness of a people has either been lost or is threatening to disappear, and when every innovation is often over-rated in a striving after the utmost modernity.

I am especially indebted to Doctorandus R. L. Mellema of the 'Koninklijk Instituut voor de Tropen' in Amsterdam, who obtained for this book the 48 coloured illustrations of *objets d'art,* which are gratifying to the specialist and at the same time excellent both from the technical and artistic points of view. These were kindly made available by the Cultural and Physical Anthropology Department of the Institute. I should also like to express my thanks to Miss Nel van Dam, who prepared the maps and drawings and undertook a final critical examination of the text. I also owe thanks to my son-in-law, Johan Smit, who spared no effort in supervising the taking of the original coloured photographs in Java and Bali. Finally, I should like to express my gratitude to many of my colleagues at the 'Instituut voor de Tropen' who rendered me every possible assistance, to L. Langewis, the textile specialist, who gave me many valuable hints, and also three of his magnificent fabrics for reproduction, to Dr. Jaap Kunst, an expert in the field of music, and to my colleague J. A. Mulder.

I hope that this work may contribute to better understanding and mutual appreciation between the peoples of the world.

Haarlem, Christmas 1958

FRITS A. WAGNER

PLATES, FIGURES AND MAPS

LIST OF COLOURED PLATES

LIST OF FIGURES AND MAPS

CONTENTS

At this point I should like to express my gratitude to the 'Koninklijk Instituut voor de Tropen' in Amsterdam for their kind permission to reproduce the finest specimens from their unique collection. The selection was made by the author, who has been associated with the Institute for many years, but all coloured photographs of objects were taken expressly for this work by Doctorandus R. L. Mellema. The outdoor photographs in Java and Bali were taken under the supervision of Mr. Johan Smit, except for that of the cliff tjandis of Tampaksiring, which was made available by Mr. B. Ph. Groslier. The figures and maps are by Miss Nel van Dam. To all who have collaborated in the production of this work I should like to express my special thanks.

I. THE NEOLITHIC AGE

Out of the mists of the distant past indistinct images have been located upon the radar-screen of time. The work of prehistorians and philologists has made it possible for us to penetrate into the life of prehistoric man. In this way we are able to chart the course taken by important cultural movements even though the limits of time and place frequently remain vague and blurred. Stones which have been discovered bearing traces of working by human hands have enabled the prehistorian to investigate these cultural movements and to define them more precisely, at least within certain limits. No doubt further individual studies will confirm scientifically much that at present is merely conjecture. Comparative philology has also yielded valuable results.

Cultural movements

The cultural movement which was of greatest importance to Indonesia emanated from Yunnan in South China. Various groups and tribes emigrated to Indonesia from this region, where the upper courses of the great rivers Hwang-ho, Yangtze-kiang, Mekong, Salween, Irrawady and Brahmaputra are not far distant from each other. These emigrants first proceeded from Yunnan to Further India, and then moved southwards into the Malayan peninsula. From this southeastern tip of the Asian continent they embarked upon their great enterprise: in their river-craft, which they rebuilt for the purpose — slender vessels with curved bow and stern — they sailed out into the unknown towards the islands of Indonesia.

This migration must have proceeded very gradually, probably over the course of some thousand years, since large groups will hardly have been able to leave at the same moment. In view of this long duration, cultural influences will probably also have made themselves felt at various stages of the process. The prehistorian R. von Heine-Geldern puts this movement at between 2500 and 1500 B.C.

Rectangular Axe (Neolithic)

Despite their different development in other respects, these migrants were in the normal neolithic stage of civilization. The material objects characteristic of this period are chiefly ground and polished stone axes, which are to be found in various shapes. Typical of this culture is the rectangular axe, so called because of its long rectangular cross-section.

R. von Heine-Geldern considers that the centre from which the rectangular axe culture spread was Yunnan. Axes of this kind have been found not only in this region but also throughout Further India, as well as in the Malayan peninsula. They constitute, so to speak, the sign-posts on the path taken by the Indonesians towards the south. The fact that these types of axe have also been found further to the west indicates that a similar cultural movement took place in the direction of India. But since this is of no significance, or at least no direct significance, so far as Indonesia is concerned, the problems which this raises will not be considered here.

Spread of rectangular axe

In the Indonesian Archipelago rectangular axes have been found in central and southern Sumatra, Java, Bali and the other Lesser Sundas, Borneo, Celebes and the Moluccas. Particularly amongst the finds in southern Sumatra, Java and Bali, one comes across specimens of fine expert workmanship and exquisite shape. They are amongst the most magnificent artifacts ever found.

It is beyond all doubt that neolithic man lived in permanent settlements. There must have been special reasons for the migration from Yunnan to the Indonesian islands, but these can only be guessed at, not ascertained with certainty. It is thought that the Indonesians were expelled from Further India by Austro-Asiatic peoples, amongst whom were the Khmer in Cambodia and the Mons in southern Burma.

Neolithic man is generally thought of as barbaric and scarcely civilized. It is hard for modern man to detach himself from his own world, in which technology has opened up possibilities for advance hitherto undreamed of, and to appreciate adequately the progress achieved during the neolithic era.

Those migrants who came to the Archipelago were no longer nomadic. They built rectangular houses supported on piles and developed the planting of rice in artificially irrigated fields. They kept pigs and cattle, but owing to the lack of suitable pastures cattle-raising was of insignificant importance over vast stretches of the Archipelago. They made articles of clothing from the bark of certain trees and receptacles from clay. But as there existed many kinds of bamboo, the canes of which could easily be worked into wooden vessels, pottery was restricted to the so-called coiling technique: the clay was coiled upon itself in concentric rings until the desired shape was obtained. A potter's wheel was not employed in this technique. For the firing of pottery, naturally, only a fairly primitive process was known.

Whether these tribes were versed in the art of weaving cannot easily be ascertained, although this is probable, since ancient receptacles

14

Spread of the rectangular stone axe from Yunnan, so far as this is ascertainable.

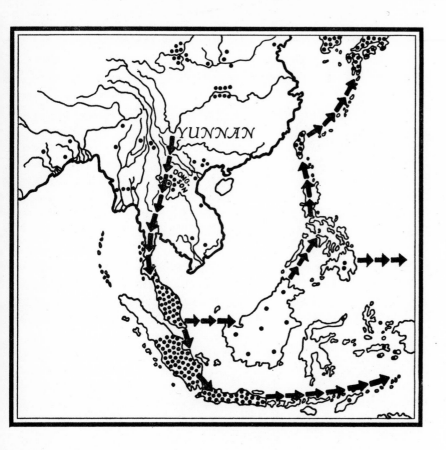

have been found which still bear the imprint of plaited work and woven fabrics. However, it has not yet been possible to date these remains with absolute certainty. Besides the rectangular axes already mentioned, the largest specimens of which were undoubtedly used in agriculture as hoes, one also finds adzes — axes used for the purpose of working wood. This follows from the manner in which these stone implements must have been secured at the haft. These kind of quadrangular axes, which have come down to us in various sizes, testify to the fact that the Indonesians of the neolithic period must have been fairly skilled in the working of wood, as is shown by the finds of small adzes which can only have been employed for woodworking of a more delicate kind.

Detail of woman's cotton skirt. Pattern woven by *ikat* of the warp and supplementary warp weaving technique. Design: ancestral figures, tree of life, birds. A multi-coloured band of beads *(katipa)* with a bird motif is sewn on to the lower border. (East Sumba, Lesser Sunda Islands). *Collection of J. and L. Langewis.*

As is only to be expected, objects made of such non-durable material, or remains of such objects, have not been preserved. But artistically worked objects in stone — beads and bracelets, evidence of various stages of technical development — have been found. From this it follows that people who could master technical difficulties in producing magnificent artifacts of this nature were certainly capable of making beautiful objects from wood, which was so much easier to work.

Grooved axes

The question arises as to where neolithic man found the hard types of rock which he required for his implements. Excavations at many sites have brought to light whole collections of stone implements which have only been partly worked. Only the rough primitive shape had been hewn out; no ground or polished pieces are to be found, or remains to show that these sites were inhabited. In all probability these are workshops dating from the neolithic period, since they are always situated where there are plentiful supplies of the appropriate kind of stone, silicated limestone. One may presume that the stone implements were only worked upon provisionally here, so as to reduce the weight of this heavy material as much as possible before transport. The grinding and polishing, on the other hand, required much more time, and could be carried out more easily at the place of destination. At the same time it should be borne in mind how dangerous it must have been for these men to stay away from their homes for a long period of time.

But the finds in Java also point in another direction. Workshops have been discovered here where highly skilled stone-cutters have apparently been at work, for the same kind of implements are to be found over and over again. The stone-cutters may have carried on their craft here, and the semi-finished pieces brought by means of barter trade to those villages where the hard stone required was unobtainable.

Spiritual life

All this enables us, perhaps, to visualize the material culture of the neolithic era. But it is not so easy to form an adequate picture of spiritual life at that time. The only means of doing so is by way of analogy. For in our own day communities exist which are still in the neolithic age. The question remains wether conclusions can be drawn from the spiritual culture of such communities with regard to the Indonesia of the neolithic period.

Amongst the many stone implements found there were also some which were clearly not used for any immediate economic purpose.

These were not only made from magnificent semi-precious stones, but were also not worn at all, which indicates that they were not in everyday use, but served other purposes of some special kind.

Such beautifully-worked implements are also to be found in neolithic communities at the present day. They have, as we know, a sacral significance, and are used in religious ceremonies. We may assume that cultures in which implements of this kind apparently served a similar purpose were themselves of a similar type.

But one can go further. There exist in Indonesia groups of people who, up to the latter half of the last century, remained virtually unaffected by the cultural influences which reached Indonesia during the course of the last two thousand years. Amongst these peoples, too, implements for the performance of religious rites were used, and frequently are still in use today, whilst the civilization of these groups resembles that of the neolithic cultures which still exist.

The significance of this becomes all the more apparent when we consider that the culture of those groups mentioned which remained independent for so many centuries is rooted in the long since extinct neolithic culture of Indonesia. A strong and persistent tradition has apparently kept alive the characteristics of neolithic culture as it developed thousands of years ago. The neolithic cultures which still exist, together with the cultural phenomena of the groups of people referred to above, enable us to obtain a rough idea of the spirit and essence of neolithic culture in Indonesia.

Types of community Neolithic man formed village communities and lived chiefly from agriculture. Genealogical communities, clans, are to be found in areas where agriculture remained extensive, as was the case wherever *ladang* cultivation alone was practicable: i.e., where rice was planted in dry fields, and where hunting and the collection of roots, fruit, etc., still helped to provide the barest necessities of life. Here the community is held together by common descent, or merely supposed common descent, from the same ancestors. On the other hand, territorial communities were formed in areas where the soil was tilled intensively and where rice was planted in artificially irrigated fields. These agrarian communities feel themselves bound by a religious tie to their communal land. In addition there also existed hybrid forms, in which — within the village as a territorial community — a division into genealogical groups is met with.

Whatever the outward form of these communities, the inner bond is always one of sacral nature, which finds expression in mythical tales and images. These reflect the way neolithic man conceived the world about him.

Each community is, so to speak, a world of its own, an entity modelled on the universe: everything is connected with everything else. The medium of this mystic union is a living force, generally referred to as *mana*. It is an indispenable prerequisite to gain control of *mana* if one is to obtain those guarantees which, it is believed, will ensure the continued existence of the community. But control over *mana* and influence upon it require an external sign.

The actions and symbols with the aid of which man believes he can influence *mana* or obtain certain things he desires can be summed up in the term 'magic ritual'.

Magic ritual

It should be made perfectly clear that the ritual means used can vary greatly, although the basic idea of men who practise magic is everywhere the same. For all this great variety, one point stands out in relief: *those expressions of men who think and act magically and which can be termed 'artistic expressions' were originally firmly rooted in magic ritual.*

This is why L. Levy Brühl, writing about Australian art, could remark: "le dessin ne les intéresse que par la participation mystique qu'il réalise". This also applies to man of the neolithic era, with regard to music, dancing and games in the same way as to architecture and sculpture.

Neolithic man regards the material things he creates, and which the Westerner habitually terms 'artistic expression', in the final instance simply as a means of attaining a particular aim, of achieving something he desires, in an irrational way. In his case "art springs unconsciously out of collective perception, out of an irresistible mystical impulse, a primitive demonic urge to seek fellowship with the powers that encompass him, the powers which he cannot comprehend, by means of magic. He is driven by a strong impulse to give expression and shape to feelings of his which are outside reality, to very complex metaphysical and emotional sentiments, such as fear, or the desire to obtain protection from some tutelary power in order to ward off unpropitious spirits, etc. This kind of creation is a sacred act." [1]

It is easy to imagine that social conditions within the community are likewise determined by this myth-enshrouded outlook. Thus, for example, clan elders infer their social function of being *primus inter pares* from the office which they perform of supervising the observance of the sacral prescriptive right, *adat,* which is rooted in myths

Outlook on life

19

and sacred traditions. Unwritten laws have to be observed — and, indeed, observed extremely strictly. For the mythical deified ancestors who have made these laws are watching carefully to ensure that they are obeyed exactly. Thus these ancestors occupy a very significant place in the universe as neolithic man imagines it. They are regarded as *mana* bearers of highest rank, and are at the centre of the actions whereby living man hopes to gain influence over *mana* by magic means. Ancestor-worship is thus also a sublime 'confirmation' of the living group. A special position within the community is also held by those magicians, medicine-men, and shamans who, because of their special talents, are qualified to practise magic rites, or to lead the community in performing them. These men, it is believed, are capable of influencing *mana* by means of concentration and outward signs. The means applied are of many different kinds, as are also the effects which it is hoped to achieve. Accordingly those who possess strong magic powers have very varied functions.

The creative artist, too, as might be expected, is firmly rooted in this social pattern. It is he, after all, who creates those objects which have their indispensable role to play in the customary rituals. Since social relationships are in the last instance based on the same mythical and magic basic concepts as the veneration of 'works of art', the latter are also closely connected to the social framework.

Communities of this type are always strongly influenced by tradition. "Tradition is unshakable; strictly speaking, it is not permissible to touch it at all. Constant repetition is significant as a confirmation of continued activity." [2]

Artistic achievements in particular are exposed to the influence and pressure of sacred traditions for the very reason of their pronounced magic character. Here, too, pressure for constant repetition manifests itself very clearly.

Not, of course, that changes are ruled out altogether. They can result from external cultural influences. But in essence the spirit of the old traditional culture remains unaffected. A kind of assimilation will always ensue, whereby the stylistic elements introduced, though not changed, are nevertheless organically integrated into the inherited totality of traditions.

Persistence of magic ideas

Changes are also conceivable without external cultural influences, but the process is then extremely slow. Moreover, in this case they will affect — to a far greater extent, if not exclusively so — the external shape of the artistic work concerned, and not the magic idea behind

Detail of cotton fabric, ornamented with human figures woven in by pilih-technique (Iban Dayak, North-west Borneo). *Collection J. and L. Langewis.*

it. For the art of neolithic man serves a practical purpose, and is thus always ideoplastic, a rendering of ideas. Ideoplastic art is not implicitly bound to any particular form. But there probably originally existed, and in many cases there still exists, a convincingly identifiable connection between some particular form taken from nature and the magic idea symbolised in it.

Thus the human figure is frequently the starting-point for three-dimensional, as also for purely ornamental, works of art. In the course of time the human figure can undergo changes, and can finally become so 'estranged' that its original prototype can hardly be recognized. By this it is not, of course, implied that the functional significance of the work would also have to undergo a change.

1 Drs. P. W. van Milaan: Indonesische Kunst. Oosthoek's Encyclopaedie. Utrecht, 1950.
2 Prof. C. T. Bertling in 'Sociale werkelijkheid bij de primitieven', 1947.

II. MEGALITHIC CULTURE

As has already been mentioned above, during the neolithic period there came to Indonesia not only stone implements for immediate economic use, but also beautifully shaped stone axes which served a sacral purpose. Both types were, however, tools according to their shape and purpose. The former were used by all in the performance of their everyday tasks in agriculture, tree-felling, hunting, etc., whilst the latter, the 'irrational' implements, were in the hands of those who performed certain sacral actions, such as sacrificial slaughter of animals.

But other objects made of stone also play a considerable part in neolithic culture. They represent something special in so far as they have not the slightest connection with the term implement as such. They are to be found practically everywhere in the world where civilization has developed. Colossal and mysterious, they exite the imagination of the observer of today. Thus in northern districts of the Netherlands we find tumuli, and in Brittany table-shaped stones and tall upright monumental stones, as silent witnesses of a neolithic culture long ago extinct. And the Breton terms *dolmen* and *menhir* are employed by archaeologists when referring to similar objects the world over. These megaliths, i.e. large stones, are so widespread, and are so much alike, *'Large' stones* that it was even thought that they had been brought to far distant parts of the earth from Egypt, the land where megalithic culture developed on the most grandiose scale.[1] Be that as it may — and the last word has by no means been said on this theory — the fact remains that, apart from the single exception of Australia, megalithic culture has existed throughout the world, and here and there is still in existence even today. In Indonesia, too, megaliths are to be found in many places. In most cases they bear witness to civilizations which have ceased to exist. But on Nias Island, on the other hand, an island off the west coast of Sumatra, megaliths are still venerated objects, whilst on Sumba and Flores in the Lesser Sunda group stone sepulchral monuments are still being erected at the present day.

But it should not be supposed that megaliths are necessarily always stones of considerable size, although the term 'large stones' might lead to this misconception. On the contrary, smaller stone objects must also

Detail of woman's cotton skirt woven by supplementary warp weaving technique. Design: stylized female and animal figures. Artistically knotted fringe on both sides. (Sumba, Lesser Sunda Islands.) *K.I.T.*

be classed as megaliths,inasmuch as they were evidently made with some particular sacral purpose in view, and have no connection with implements in the ordinary sense of the word.

In Indonesia these are to be found in many shapes and sizes: dolmens, menhirs, and terraced burial-mounds, both unworked or worked only superficially; large stones, upon which human beings and animals are often depicted with surprising realism, as the specific shape of the stone permits; stone cist graves, sarcophagi, and troughs in which skulls were probably buried.

R. von Heine-Geldern distinguishes at least two groups among the megaliths found in Indonesia. To the oldest group, the monumental, belong primarily the menhirs, dolmens, and terraced burial-mounds. These date from the neolithic period, an era when polished rectangular axes were also known. Examples of the more recent group, the dynamic, are to be found amongst the worked stones mentioned above.

Groups of megaliths

The oldest megaliths undoubtedly date from the neolithic period. Several megaliths, however, have been found in regard to which it can be ascertained with certainty that they were not made until a time when metal had already been known in Indonesia for some centuries. Thus iron implements were found in a stone sarcophagus in eastern Java beside glazed Chinese pottery. This even made it possible to date the sarcophagus: it must have originated in the ninth century A.D. at the earliest. Iron objects were also found in various stone cist graves in the mountains on the south coast of central Java. Metal, after all, had already been known for a long time on Nias, Sumba and Flores. On the basis of the above it can be said that megalithic culture did indeed originate in the neolithic period, but that it continued in some places to form part of the living culture at a time when the stone age had given way to the age of bronze and iron.

It was, no doubt, in the making of implements that metal first took the place of stone. This can be taken for granted in view of the better results achieved by using metal implements. Probably this improved result was attributed to the fact that metal was more heavily 'charged' with magic. If one follows up this line of thought, it becomes apparent that ceremonial implements were also made of metal, even when no material reason for this existed. The sacred tradition which consented only with reluctance to the acceptance of anything new in matters of magic ritual, would otherwise probably have opposed the change of material. On the other hand, it was difficult to replace the megaliths by similar objects made of bronze or iron, owing to their size, which was usually considerable, and the fact that metal was very costly. These stone megaliths therefore continued to exist, and were accorded a firmly allotted place amongst the sacral customs that were observed. But bronze urns have been found which must have served as ceremonial objects, as is clear from the decoration upon them.

The importance of megaliths in neolithic culture can perhaps be assessed by studying the megalithic civilizations which still exist at the present day.

After-life The construction of stone cist graves, sarcophagi, etc., is indisputably connected with worship of the dead. Neolithic man believed in an after-life. The dead were interred with a special ceremony, and objects such as weapons, implements, etc., which were deemed indispensable for the life to come, were placed in their graves.

Megalith memorials were certainly not erected for every person who died; this will have depended upon the social, and consequently the magic, functions of the deceased.

The erection of menhirs and dolmens, etc., obviously served the purpose of honouring the living as well as the dead. Thus chieftains and other important men in the community erected them as memorials of a consecration ceremony, an investiture, or as monuments to their own rank and dignity. This event was usually accompanied by great festivities; the person in whose honour the stone was erected was obliged to distribute precious gifts, and cattle or pigs were sacrificed. Other ceremonial customs will also have played a part, head-hunting not excluded. Where stones of this kind were dedicated to the dead, it was as an outward sign of the connection between the existing community and its ancestors. When certain ceremonial actions were performed, it was believed, the spirits of the dead descended upon the living.

Megaliths are to be found in particular profusion at a site in the Pasemah country of southern Sumatra. Here, in addition to menhirs, dolmen, stone cist graves and terraced sanctuaries, there are also huge stones which have been carved into the shape of human beings and animals such as buffaloes and elephants. The variety and skill with which the single figures have been incorporated into the whole are both surprising and impressive; they are, moreover, valuable for us since the sculptured figures carry swords, and wear helmets, necklaces, anklets and bracelets. These megaliths have consequently been erected at a time when metals were already known. It is especially noteworthy that some stones are to be found with figures of men holding objects

Small basket with lid plaited from veins of lontar palm leaves. Design: small human figures in black and red. (Kisar, Lesser Sunda Islands.) *K.I.T.* (Height 12¼ ins.)

on their backs which may be identified as bronze kettle-drums. On the basis of these drums it is possible to establish a date for these statues.2 Before we go further into the questions which are suggested by these figures, we have to cast a glance at the cultural movement whereby bronze and iron were introduced to the indigenous culture of the Indonesians.

1 Perry, The children of the sun.
2 Tom. à Th. van der Hoop: Megalithic remains in South Sumatra.

Detail of decoration
on a kettle-drum
of Hanoi

III. DONG-SON CULTURE

If the Indonesians had developed the technique of working bronze on their own, bronze axes would undoubtedly have been found which would have greatly resembled ordinary stone axes in shape. For one can hardly imagine that in so vast an area, once the technical difficulties of metal-working had already been overcome, a sudden deviation would have been made from the traditional shape, and a transition effected to an entirely new shape of axe, and yet one which had the same shape wherever it was found. But the bronze age in the Indonesian archipelago did not apparently produce any rectangular axes in bronze, but only so-called socketed axes, and these most accomplished in their manner of execution. The shape of these socketed axes is very different from that of the rectangular axes dating from the stone age. The most essential innovation is that they were fixed to the haft in an entirely different way: for with the socketed axes the haft is inserted *into* the blade, and no*t vice versa*, as was the case with the stone axes. From this the conclusion must be drawn that the working of bronze did not develop locally, and that the socketed axes were brought to the islands from somewhere else; the technique of bronze casting must have become familiar in Indonesia at the same time.

This cultural innovation also came to the Indonesian archipelago from South-east Asia, in particular from the area of Tonking and northern Annam. Here, close to the village of Dong-Son, such an abundant variety of artifacts has been found that prehistorians regard this area as the cradle of bronze culture throughout South-east Asia and Indonesia, so that the site of these discoveries has given its name to the whole culture as such.

Certain finds show that the Indonesians were able to give an individual touch of their own to this new addition to their culture — although this was not the case with the socketed axes, which were used in everyday toil, because the shape of this implement was determined by considerations of practical utility, and in this respect the socketed axe could not be surpassed. But there have also been found bronze equivalents to the stone axes mentioned above which were used for ceremonial purposes, and in the case of these 'implements' the function which they performed was completely different: since it was irrational,

Bronze-working

Socketed axes

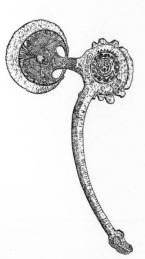

Ceremonial axe (Roti)

29

the shape acquired characteristics of its own. Although the axes used for ceremonial purposes which have been found in Indonesia correspond to a certain extent with those from Dong-Son, both types being asymmetrical, in the case of the Indonesian axes this asymmetry is striking, and often touches upon the bizarre — in contrast to the axes from Dong-Son.

FIG. P. 29

In addition to the above-mentioned axes, other bronze objects of great importance for the history of Indonesia's cultural development have also been found: the kettle-drums mentioned in the last chapter, which have been found both in Indonesia as well as in Further India and some other areas of South-east Asia. But it is difficult to decide whether these bronze drums were actually produced in Indonesia, or whether they were imported from South-east Asia. In order to appreciate the complexity of this problem, one has to know how these drums were made.

Kettle-drums

When casting bronze objects, one can either use and re-use stone moulds, or else apply the so-called *à-cire-perdue* (waste mould) process, i.e. as follows. Upon a core of clay wax or other grease is moulded to form the shape desired. To form the outer covering a fairly thick layer of clay is applied, in which the necessary funnels are left open. With the application of heat the clay becomes solid, the mould melts away, and is removed. The molten metal is now poured in through the funnels; when cool, the outer casing is broken away. Thus the mould goes waste. Whether this process was applied can be established by the existence of irregularities in those parts of the object adjacent to the funnels. Thus it is obvious that whenever the *à-cire-perdue* process was applied

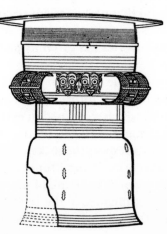

"Moon of Bali" (Pèdjèng)

it can hardly now be ascertained whether the object found was really made in this area, since the original mould has been destroyed. This was also the case with a particularly fine kettle-drum, 'The Moon of Bali', which was found near the village of Pèdjèng on the island of Bali. Prof. T. P. Galestin remarked in this connection: "it is clear that some drums were imported, and, in the case of a few of them at least, it is assumed — and attemps to prove this point have been made — that they were cast in Indonesia either by means of the *à-cire-perdue* process or by means of stone moulds. For in the neighbourhood of the village in question fragments of one of these stone moulds of tuff have been found, which, to judge by its decoration and general appearance, was designed for a drum similar to the one found in Pèdjèng, but smaller. One thing is in any case certain: the drum in Pèdjèng is the largest kettle-drum in the world, and is one of the most magnificent masterpieces ever created by man. Whether this gem of bronze casting — the surface implies that no moulds were employed — originates from Bali is of course quite impossible to prove." 1

"Moon of Bali".

And he goes on to say: "If the drum was brought to Pèdjèng, possibly from Java or an area to the east of Alor (where smaller specimens dating from more or less modern times were used in bride purchases, and where some of them were imported by the Chinese at a comparatively recent date) then the opinion expressed above about the old drums is valid with regard to both districts. The assumption that the 'Moon of Bali' may have been brought to Pèdjèng in historic times, that is to say, in the course of Hindu-Indonesian history, cannot be entirely dismissed."

This does not mean that it is *ipso facto* excluded that ancient kettle-drums found in Indonesia were also made there. It should merely be stressed that one cannot be certain about this point. The use of these drums on Alor Island, north of Timor, referred to in the passage quoted is a clear example of the persistent way in which certain ceremonial objects have remained in use to the present day. Their use on Nias Island, where megaliths still play an important role, has already been noted.

It is worth drawing attention to the representation of figures on certain drums from the region in which the Dong-Son culture originated. Victor Goloubew has examined these in his study 'L'age du bronze au Tonkin et dans le Nord Annam'. On the drumhead of a kettle-drum preserved at Hanoi are represented strikingly attired figures, apparently performing a dance. Amongst them are men with axes of asymmetrical shape. This depicts a ceremony at which drums were probably also used. The most interesting thing is that the typical decorations permit comparison with a very similar dance which is still performed today on the Mentawei Islands off the west coast of Sumatra.

FIG. P. 174 Other figures are playing a kind of mouth-organ, which has a resonance box. Instruments of this kind are still met with among certain Dayak tribes in Borneo. An instrument of this sort is also to be found depicted on a stone relief at Borobudur, the Buddhist monument in central Java, which can be dated to the middle of the 8th century A. D. The mouth-organ, therefore, was still a familiar instrument amongst the population of Java at that time.

So-called 'ship cloth' of cotton woven by floating weft technique. Design: ship of the dead, stylized human beings, animals and birds, tree of life. (Kroë, southern Sumatra). *K.I.T.*

Particularly worthy of note are the designs on the upper rim of the drum-shell. These represent flat-bottomed ships and human figures attired and adorned in the same way as on the drumhead. One can also identify various objects, such as oars, a shield, a ceremonial axe, and a kettle-drum; the animal depicted is presumably a pig. FIG. P. 28

This is a so-called 'ship of the dead', which plays a part in 'transition rites'. The belief that the souls of the departed go to the land of souls by ship is still current among various peoples of the archipelago. Comparable designs are to be met with even today amongst certain Dayak tribes in central Borneo; and the Kroë country in south Benkulen, south Sumatra, is famous for its magnificent textiles, on which such ships are portrayed. PLATE P. 32

In the bronze age axes and drums were naturally not the only objects known. Other bronze implements, and in addition jewellery of all kinds, have also been found. The ornamentation on these objects has had an enduring influence upon the development of decorative art, which up to the present day has remained an important component part of the Indonesian artistic tradition.

1 Indonesië. Algemene Kunstgeschiedenis, Volume 6, Utrecht, 1951.

IV. GENERAL OBSERVATIONS
ON DECORATIVE ART IN INDONESIA

When one surveys the artistic achievements of the peoples of Indonesia, one notes their obvious predilection for decorative art — a partiality which in many cases is expressed with consummate artistry.

The techniques employed are of very different kinds, and naturally vary according to the material used: stone is cut, wood, bone and ivory carved, fabrics skilfully woven and dyed, metals cast, corroded, engraved, incrusted, chased and finished, parchment beaten, and so forth.

Variety of styles On closer examination we are very forcibly struck by the great variety of styles which are to be found in Indonesia, especially in the field of decorative art. One of the most important reasons for this phenomenon may perhaps be the diverse cultural influences from abroad.

R. von Heine-Geldern writes on these questions: "the 8th century B.C. was one of those periods of unrest which from time to time shook ancient Asia and Europe and during which large groups of tribes, torn from their homelands, migrated over the vast expanses of the Old World. At that particular period tribes from the Caucasian region, from South Russia, and from the lower Danubian countries moved eastward. Some of them settled in Central Asia, some entered China, while others branched off toward the South and by way of Szechwan and Yunnan eventually reached northern Indo-China. In China and Indo-China they were soon absorbed by the local population, however not before they had introduced various new forms of tools, weapons, and ornaments and, above all, their own style of art. The latter was a late branch of the Mycenean style which in their lands of origin had survived long after it had disappeared from Greece and the Aegean region. It was a highly decorative style, abounding in spirals, curvilinear designs, and meanders.

In China, where a rich decorative art had been flourishing for nearly a millennium, the western elements were transformed according to Chinese aesthetic ideals and integrated into the native art, thus producing what is known as the Late Chou or Huai Style. In Indo-China, where purely ornamental designs previously may have been practically unknown, those introduced from the West were adopted with

Woman's hat of veins of lontar palm leaves, leaf work. Decorated with gaily-coloured small pieces of cotton, snippets of paper and mica discs. (Southern Celebes). *K.I.T.* (Diameter 16½ ins., height 5½ ins.)

very little change. There, a new, bronze-using civilization arose, usually termed the Dong-Son Culture, from the place of Dong-Son in northern Annam, the first of its sites which has been excavated. It flourished from an unknown date, possibly the 7th century B.C., until Tonkin and North Annam became Chinese provinces in the 1st century A.D. Outstanding among its products are bronze axes, beautifully decorated bronze daggers and battle axes, belt-buckles, primitive bronze figures, and above all large, magnificent bronze drums, covered with decorative designs and with representations of boats, of warriors wearing feather head-dresses, and of festive scenes relating to the cult of the dead. Although the style of the Dong-Son culture and that of

Ornamented bamboo
(Toradja)

Late Chou China have many elements in common and thus are to a certain extent related, the former is by far simpler and lacks the more sophisticated and more typically Chinese motifs of the latter.

Both the Dong-Son and the Late Chou styles have deeply influenced the art of the Indonesian peoples. They were introduced in the archipelago in the latter half of the first millennium B.C., together with the art of casting tools, weapons, ornaments, and drums of bronze. As far as the present and still very imperfect state of our knowledge allows us to judge, they seem to have been brought to the islands not by large scale migrations of whole tribes, but rather by merchants, artisans, and small groups of settlers from the coasts of Indo-China and southern China. The culture of these groups must have been superior enough to impress the native population, but they were not numerous enough to impose their languages. The whole process may therefore be compared to that of the Hindu colonization which occurred a few centuries later.

The enormous success of the decorative designs of Dong-Son and Late Chou origin with the peoples of Indonesia was probably due to the fact that prior to their introduction purely ornamental art, as far as it existed at all, was of a very simple geometric character. In contrast to the commemorative and symbolic motifs of the original, monumental style of the Indonesians the creations of present day decorative art are to a considerable extent "art for art's sake". This does not mean that religious and magic ideas do not play an important role in Indonesian art. However, it is significant that motifs relating to ancestor cult, sacrificial feasts, head-hunting, or the magic propagation of fertility and wealth are in many cases derived from the older, monumental style." [1]

Three styles According to the above writer, there are thus three styles, which have each contributed something of their own to the formation of the multiform decorative art of the Indonesian peoples: the monumental style, connected with the original neolithic culture of the indigenous population, the Dong-Son style, and the late Chou style. As Heine-Geldern also explains, the Dong-Son style made its influence felt almost everywhere in the Archipelago, whereas the Late Chou style only penetrated to some islands, particularly Borneo.

Cultural influences which appeared later, such as Hinduism and Buddhism, will not be examined for the present.

Neolithic style The oldest of the three styles, hereafter referred to as neolithic, is characterized by conventionalized frontal-type figures of ancestors,

often of startling realism, as well as by magic symbols such as buffalo horns, human heads, various animals, renderings of the so-called tree of life, etc. In addition fairly simple geometrical ornaments are also to be found.

In the Dong-Son style the tendency towards decoration is accentuated. *Dong-Son style* A whole series of new motifs, in particular the spiral, and other patterns of curved lines, are added to the traditional basic design. At the same time this design tends to depict human and animal figures together with ornamentation, rather than on their own. Decoration is also present in the strictly geometrical segmentation of the entire surface; in the fields thus formed the individual motifs are repeated, set against one another, and varied regularly.

The two styles mentioned prefer symmetrical composition, both in *Late Chou style* their general design and in detail. The Late Chou style, on the other hand, stresses rhythm rather than material composition, and has no place for symmetry. Where one finds an asymetrical pattern, one can attribute this with certainty to the strong influence of the Late Chou style.

Considering the fact that the influence of the Dong-Son and Late Chou styles manifested themselves in various degrees, partly by immediate contact but in many cases only by means of the links existing between the Indonesian peoples themselves, it becomes clear that this inevitably led to a great variety and considerable differences in decorative art. Each tribe has left its imprint upon its ornamentation, and amongst many Indonesian peoples the characteristic features have not changed up to our own day. They are determined by the special motifs which are chosen, often (but not always) connected with the way in which they are integrated into the decoration as a whole, and also by the technique employed in working the materials, as well as by the dyes used.

In this chapter we will examine more closely a few examples of *Textile design* the textile design of those peoples which were not directly influenced by Hinduism or Buddhism, or were only influenced by them to a slight degree. This form of decorative art, which can be regarded as Indonesia's most varied and attractive artistic achievement, has several different characteristic features. Since tradition was particularly strong, the original character of their work has

Evolution of key-shaped figure

Gold-threaded fabric *(songkèt)* woven by floating weft technique. Design: *kembang manggis* and *tumpal*.
(Palembang, southern Sumatra). *K.I.T.*

been preserved in an extremely pure form. But Java and Madura, for example, will not be dealt with in this chapter, since the most important method of textile design, i.e. *batik,* developed much later, and deserves a chapter to itself.

I shall deal later with the question of the technical processes and dyes used. But some examples of bamboo work will be discussed here, since these are intimately connected with our subject.

On fabrics made everywhere between Sumatra and the eastern islands motifs are to be found which have a remarkable affinity with one another and which are composed of the same elements. The most characteristic of these elements is the key-shaped figure, combined with other geometrical figures, amongst which the rhomb occurs most frequently. The key-shaped figure most probably developed in the following manner. From the straight line, which with the dot is the most simple basic form, there developed hook- and key-shaped figures. Two of these key-shaped figures may then have been combined to form double key-shaped figures of various types. *Geometrical composition of motifs*

Two motifs may also be combined to form, for example, the rhomb- and key-shaped figure shown in the fig. on page 37. FIG. P. 37

The key-shaped figure may perhaps also have developed as a simplification of the spiral-shaped figure introduced along with the Dong-Son style. This is implied, in particular, by the fact that the key-shaped figure is so frequently to be found in woven fabrics in which, for technical reasons, only simple contour lines were possible. In this case its widespread distribution is connected with the fact that the Dong-Son style was able to penetrate throughout practically the whole of the Archipelago.

The combination of simple geometrical forms such as the key and the rhomb, sometimes with the addition of a straight line, an equilateral triangle or a square, permits an enormous number of variations: not only a wealth of motifs, but also stylized renderings of human beings, crocodiles, lizards, trees, etc. Various tribes have no doubt made use of such geometrical motifs and adopted them in their ornamentation. But it is easy to be tempted to read too much into them, and by exercising a little imagination to see in every rhomb- and key-shaped figure a human being or an animal. It is even more difficult to make out whether one is dealing with a purely decorative ornament or a representation of a particular object, since in the course of time the original significance may have been lost, by the form having become divorced from the content and having been subjected to gradual change.

Rhomb- and key-shaped
figure (Kantuk Dayak)

FIGS. PP. 40, 41

*Influence of Dong-Son
and Late Chou styles*

PLATE P. 16

PLATE P. 21

Dr. J. H. Jager Gerlings explains in this connection: "It has already been noted that the weaver feels herself limited by the ornaments traditional within her group, but this does not mean that she actually understands them or that she always copies them exactly. Thus with the passage of time changes also take place within certain groups. In general a tendency prevails to make the figures ever more complex . . . The original meaning of the simple forms which are the basis of the more complex figures are no longer comprehended at all. This is quite clear from the fact that the borders are often cut off in an arbitrary manner. Occasionally they are actually torn into pieces and then made up into new patterns.

In doubtful cases one therefore has also to consider first of all the part which the fabric played in the religious conceptions of the tribe in question before any conclusions can be drawn as to the nature of the objects represented upon it." [2]

The accompanying figures show the rhomb- and key-shaped combinations which are to be found on the fabrics woven by peoples often living at a great distance from one another. In each case the origin is indicated, and the area inhabited by each of these tribes is also shown on the attached map on p. 56.

On fabrics from Sumba Island the stylized human figure of the frontal type appears alternately, either as sole ornament or accompanied by other figures, in a regular pattern. The whole area is segmented in a very simple manner into uniform bands of different width. On textiles of this type the artistic motif is unmistakably the salient point of interest, and the planning of the whole area is of subsidiary significance.

The neolihic style exerts a strong after-effect upon the manner in which the human figures are represented, whereas influence of the Dong-Son style is apparent in the pronounced rhythmic decorative element.

The human figure is treated quite differently on fabrics woven by certain Dayak groups in central Borneo. The Iban Dayaks in northwest Borneo, in particular, have produced magnificent work of this kind. The conventionalized human figure is correlated to the decorative planning of the whole area, and in many cases the composition is more rhythmic than metric. One finds no trace here of the often extremely impressive representation of human figures on the fabrics woven on Sumba Island. The design is purely ornamental, and harmonizes with the rhythm of the whole. Even when human figures adorn the border, the treatment remains purely ornamental both in character and design, just as with the figures incorporated into the composition as a whole. The influence of the Dong-Son style is unmistakable. The manner in which the figures are fitted into the decoration as a whole, and the regular repetition and distribution of motifs in the border ornamentation, both point in this direction. If one compares these compositions with the artistic textiles of other Indonesian peoples, it is striking how much more animated the ornaments of the Dayaks are. This, taken by itself, does not suffice to infer the influence of the Late Chou style. But if we also take into consideration the style in which the Dayaks decorate wood, bamboo and bone, then I think it becomes clear that we are indeed dealing here with the influence of the Late Chou style. The plate on p. 58 gives an example of asymmetry in the motifs applied and in the manner in which details have been integrated rhythmically into the decorative ornamentation of a bamboo quiver. The motifs overlap one another as well as the principal lines of segmentation passing across the area to be decorated in a manner which one does not find anywhere else. A comparable arrangement of patterns is also to be found on Dayak masks and shields, but nowhere else in the entire Archipelago is there decorative work of such individual character, in which the influence of the Late Chou style is so clearly manifested.

If we now examine more closely individual textiles woven by the Toradja in central Celebes, we perceive how completely the rendering of human figures merges with strictly geometrical patterns. Only an accomplished expert is just able to pick them out from the interplay of lines. In this case the influence of the Dong-Son style can be clearly demonstrated. In the two most important centres of this type of art, Rongkong and Galumpang, very different means of solving the problem have been adopted. On textiles from Galumpang the basic motif does not stand by itself, but is integrated into the geometrical arrangement of the area as a whole, which always bears the same features. In Rongkong, on the other hand, it is precisely the basic motif, the so-called *sèkon* motif, which dominates the entire composition. This motif has developed almost wholly out of a single unbroken line, and only on closer examination does it become evident that we are dealing here with a rhomb- and key-shaped figure woven in two parallel lines. With its predominantly geometrical design, the Toradja style is basically static. This can be especially clearly seen in the bamboo work

PLATE P. 24

Rhomb- and key-shaped figure, *ragidup* (Toba Batak)

PLATE P. 58

Rhomb- and key-shaped figure (Timur Dayak)

FIG. P. 36 produced by this tribe, which differs markedly from the decorative bamboo work of all the other Indonesian peoples.

Out of the vast number of artistically woven fabrics we have selected examples which clearly demonstrate the various cultural influences of the pre-Hindu era. In the case of some of these, their place of origin can be ascertained without difficulty. The fabrics from Sumba Island reveal their origin by their prominent motifs, which have not been fashioned in a similar manner anywhere else, whilst the textiles from Rongkong also have the easily recognizable *sèkon* motif.

It is similarly not difficult to identify fabrics woven by the Iban Dayaks, inasmuch as human or animal figures (or both) appear in the ornamental pattern. These motifs are incorporated into the ornamental composition as a whole in a particularly successful way, and in this connection the figures introduced have been re-fashioned in a typical manner. Both these characteristics give these fabrics an indi- PLATE P. 21 vidual *cachet*.

But it is not so easy to identify the fabrics from Galumpang, since there is a close affinity between these and the fabrics woven by the Iban Dayaks in so far as ornamental designs and patterns are concerned. In cases such as this one has to examine the technical process employed and, where necessary, also take into consideration the dyes used, in order to ascertain their place of origin.

TUMPAL MOTIF

One of the most widely distributed ornamental designs is the decorated triangle, or so-called *tumpal* motif. This ornament is not only very ancient, but was even able to survive in regions where ornamental art was exposed to the lasting influence of Hinduism.

It can no longer be ascertained with certainty what served as a model FIGS. P. 44 for the development of this motif. Some experts interpret it as a human figure which has become unrecognizable owing to far-reaching stylization, whereas others have suggested that it is a stylized bamboo shoot. In the former case the magic character of this motif would be obvious: it is an ancestral figure. But the same would also apply in the latter case, for the bamboo shoot has an unusual vitality and grows rapidly; thus the *tumpal* motif could be a fertility symbol.

1 Introduction to the Catalogue of the Exhibition 'Indonesian Art', New York, 1948.
2 Dr. J. H. Jager Gerlings, 'Sprekende weefsels', 1952.

Masked dancer at funeral of a prince wearing chest ornament composed of strings of pearls fastened on a cotton backing with small brass bells (Timur Batak, northern Sumatra). *K.I.T.*

Ornamented bamboo,
tumpal motif
(Menangkabau)

Ornamented bamboo, *tumpal* motif
(Dayak, Central Borneo)

V. APPLIED ART
IN ISLANDS OTHER THAN JAVA
AND BALI UNTIL CIRCA 1850

At the beginning of the Christian era extensive areas of Indonesia embarked upon a path of cultural evolution which was to add new and very varied features to the traditional cultural scene. Hinduism, Buddhism and, many centuries later, Islam were to introduce new themes and techniques, but the original pattern still remained a major formative influence and may still be recognized amongst the new trends.

Those tribes that were scarcely, if at all, affected by the new movements retained their ancient culture, which had taken shape in the neolithic age, almost unchanged up to modern times.

Since tradition was very tenacious, we can assume that the artistic creations of these isolated tribes, which have been studied at first hand in comparatively recent times, have not diverged in essentials from the style developed two thousand years ago, which was formed under the influence of the Neolithic, Dong-Son and Late Chou styles.

R. von Heine-Geldern draws the following picture of the effect which this persistent tradition had upon the art of these isolated tribes, even upon those originating from areas which were exposed to the new cultural stimuli: "While the persistence of a style of art introduced more than two thousand years ago is a sign of the conservatism of the Indonesian peoples, the fact that they were able to develop it in an original manner, to create a large number of local styles of specific character and beauty, and to keep them alive and vigorous for such a lengthy period testifies to their deep aesthetic sense and their inborn artistic talent. When the Hindus came to the archipelago they found the various local styles of Dong-Son or Late Chou derivation already well established in the islands. There are many indications that such styles existed also in Java and Bali, and it is of them that archaeologists chiefly think when they speak of native influence in the development of Hindu-Javanese art."[1]

Java and Bali are thus especially important, for it was here that the effect of Buddhism and Hinduism was most persistent. On these islands, owing to various circumstances, art acquired such distinct characteristics that it will be treated separately here. In this chapter we shall examine the art, and in particular the applied art, of districts other than Java and Bali, emphasis being laid upon the artistic achievements of those areas which remained more or less isolated. Examples will also be given from tribes which were probably influenced by post-Dong-Son civilization. This will show that a distinct connection can be established with primitive conceptions and decorative techniques, in many cases both with regard to the ceremonial and/or social function of the objects concerned, the decorative motifs employed, and the technique applied in ornamentation.

If occasional reference is made to a work of art from Java or Bali and to the influence exerted by these islands upon other areas of the

Earthenware jar with decoration cut in the clay whilst damp. (Southern Celebes). *K.I.T.* (Height 6¾ ins.)

Archipelago, this is a consequence of the fact that they are treated separately here.

Of the great number of technical processes only the most important ones will be mentioned, and technical descriptions which the layman would find difficult or impossible to follow will be omitted. The place of origin of the tribes mentioned is shown on the map on p. 56.

This chapter is arranged according to the various materials worked. In conclusion it should perhaps be noted that especially in the present century many of the techniques described have fallen into disuse. The reasons for this will be discussed in the final chapter of this work.

Already in the neolithic era the Indonesian undoubtedly used vegetable fibres to make various everyday objects. The tropies yielded in abundance materials requiring little or no preparation and which could be worked into simple tools. Thus articles of clothing were produced from beaten bark and bast, and palm-leaves (especially from the pandan palm), generally several together in layers, were made into all manner of articles, ranging from head-gear to resonance-boxes for certain musical instruments. Plaiting was also practised; fibres and ribs of bamboo, as well as the leaves of the lontar palm being available for the purpose. Up to the present day leaves and bast are used in this way, predominantly amongst the isolated tribes; plaiting is generally known, and among the Menangkabau in central Sumatra plaited mats play an important part in family life even today.

USE OF BAST AND LEAVES; PLAITING

But it is not the method used that is really important so much as the attractive way in which these objects are decorated. The plaited basket from Kisar is a good illustration of this: knotting and simple human figures go to the making of a most appealing work of art. A Toradja hat made from leaves shows what beauty in form can be achieved even with simple means.

PLATE P. 27

PLATE P. 35

Although plaited work, in a material so excellently suited to such various purposes, can be put to all manner of uses, there is, however, one indispensable quality which it lacks, namely sufficient pliability, for articles of clothing to be made from it. One could make do somehow by making the strips of material thinner and narrower; but although fine plaited work can be very pliant, it nevertheless has its limits. Furthermore, plaiting is done by hand, and the finer the single strands used, the more difficult it becomes to keep them apart with one's bare hands. The need thus arises for some mechanical appliance, i.e. for a loom.

WEAVING AND TECHNIQUES OF TEXTILE DESIGN

Fortunately there was to be found in Indonesia the cotton-plant with its downy fibrous substance, the very thing needed to obtain in a simple way, *viz.* by means of a spindle, a thread of any desired length and of almost perfect pliability. Only if these prerequisites are met is it possible to produce a good-quality fabric. One must therefore make a digression, and examine the technique used in weaving.

The most simple fabric consists of numerous threads of a certain length running parallel, termed warp, crossed at right angles by another floating thread, the weft, which holds it together. The warp threads are made fast to the loom. In order to interweave the weft thread by means of a spool (or shuttle), a device is necessary to raise every second thread of the warp at the same time. Having raised the odd-numbered threads, — 1, 3, 5, etc., — and passed through the shuttle containing the weft thread, one then raises the other threads — i.e., 2, 4, 6, etc., — and allows the shuttle to slide back, and so on alternately. On both sides of the fabric where the shuttle is reversed, there remain on the edge small loops, or selvage, which holds it all together. When the fabric is finished, it has to be fastened along its breadth, so that it cannot unravel. If a fibrous substance is used for weaving, the selvage is bound to break — quite apart from the difficulties involved in extending the length of the fibres.

On the Sangi Islands north of Celebes, attemps were made to overcome these difficulties by using a fibrous substance for the warp threads, but cotton for the weft threads. Thus for several centuries a very fine fabric has been woven there, the so-called *koffo* fabric, which, however, was not pliant enough for articles of clothing to be made from it.

The floating weft   If one wishes to make a change from the regular crossing of warp and weft, in other words if the weft is to ride over several warp threads at once, the fabric loses much of its necessary strength. But if it is desired to work in a pattern by means of coloured weft threads, then there is no alternative. There are two ways of meeting this difficulty. One way is to pass the weft threads through the warp threads as described above by moving the shuttle from right to left, and then passing through the coloured weft threads afterwards, also from right to left. The first thread ensures that the fabric remains firm, whilst the second one merely serves to make the pattern. In order to be able to pass it through properly, there must be some means of raising the warp threads in certain groups. For this purpose each thread of the warp has an adjustable heddle, and by means of a shed-stick the weaver can achieve his object.

48

Cooling jar, earthenware, polychrome. (Kei Islands). *K.I.T.* (Height 7¾ ins.)

In various areas of Indonesia gold and silver threads are used to work in the pattern.

Sometimes the coloured weft thread is passed through the warp threads by means of a long spool carrier. The weaver must then take special care to pick out the warp threads which have to pass over the coloured threads. The fabrics obtained in this way — for instance those woven by the Iban Dayaks — are called *kain-pilih* (*kain* = cloth, *pilih* = to choose).

The foregoing merely gives an idea of the basic principles of the technique. There are, of course, still other methods of introducing a pattern, but these can be disregarded here.

In the last chapter it was pointed out that there is a striking resemblance between the patterns customary upon the fabrics woven in Galumpang in central Celebes and those on certain textiles produced by the Iban Dayaks. But these two fabrics differ greatly in the methods of manufacture. The Iban Dayaks employ the *pilih* technique just described, whilst the Galumpang fabrics are woven by the so-called *ikat* method (*ikat* = to bind).

Tattoo mark
(Makulit Dayak)
Ikat method

By this method the thread is dyed according to a special process before the weaving begins. For this purpose fibres are wound around small groups of threads at certain places, so that the tightly bound parts do not take up the colour when the fabric is dipped into the dye-bath. A single coloured thread would not show, and it would be much too troublesome to wind fibre round each thread separately.

This tie-dyeing process constitutes the *ikat* method, which came to Indonesia along with the Dong-Son culture. There are three ways in which it is possible to obtain certain patterns, namely by applying the ikat method to the warp, by applying it to the weft, or to both.

Ikat of the warp

As the warp has to be dipped into the dye-bath a second time after the threads have been tied up, the threads are not mounted from the beginning on the loom, but on a special frame, where they are tied by their ends. For the purpose of tying the threads, any substance can be used which does not absorb much dye, usually the so-called *agel* thread, obtained from the leaves of the *gebang* palm.

It is, of course, important to take the necessary care when tying the threads. If they are tied too loosely, the colouring matter will seep in, and the pattern will become blurred, thus giving a more picturesque effect.

There are various methods by which the required colours may be applied. The choice depends mainly upon the result desired. If one is content with just a simple pattern, a colourless motif on a one-colour ground, much less preparation is of course required than if one seeks to obtain more complex patterns in several colours.

Tie-dyeing of the warp is general amongst those Indonesian tribes living almost isolated from external influences. The Bataks weave fabrics by this method with a simple arrowhead motif; the Dayaks, and in particular the Iban Dayaks, weave textiles with magnificent and fairly complex patterns; the Toradja decorate shrouds with the motifs already described. Amongst the various fabrics tie-dyed on the warp to be found in the islands in the south-east of the Archipelago, those from Sumba are amongst the most precious works of art woven anywhere.

PLATE P. 16

Ikat of the weft

This method is rarer and almost entirely limited to southern Sumatra. For this purpose the floating weft thread is wound round a vertical circular frame, which rotates round a horizontal axis, and the circumference of which corresponds to the width of the fabric to be woven. It stands to reason that the thread must be wound round absolutely uniformly, as only then can the pattern desired be brought out. The method of tying together in groups, winding round with fibre, and dyeing is otherwise exactly the same as in the previous method.

Ikat of warp and weft

In this case the two methods described above are combined. The utmost accuracy and care must be taken, for when weaving the coloured groups of warp and weft must coincide in the right way in order to obtain the desired pattern. This difficult technique is only practised in the mountain village of Tenganan Pagringsingan on the island of Bali.

Significance of textiles

As is the custom the world over, textiles are used to make articles of clothing, in particular clothes worn on festive occasions both sad and gay, for ceremonies, as well as clothes worn to identify the wearer as a member of a certain class or as holder of a certain rank.

But what makes these textiles so immensely significant is the special part they play in many ceremonies and customs in the life of the Indonesian peoples. Certain fabrics have a sacral and/or ceremonial function to fulfil at birth and death, at important events such as circumcision and filing of the teeth, in customs connected with marriage, as well as in certain rites observed when planting rice.

The Indonesian envisages not only the world of nature as male and female, but also the whole cosmos, including material objects. Sun and heaven are the masculine counterparts of moon and earth. Textiles represent the female element, whereas weapons, on the other hand, represent the male element; when both are combined (with the weapon generally being a spear, or its harmless substitute, a long stick), this becomes a symbol of the universe as a whole. The carrying of flags and pennons, which is generally considered as merely a festive ornament, or a means of expressing joy on some special occasion, thus acquires a symbolic significance in the truest sense of the word.

Such significance attaches to the textiles not only of those peoples relatively unaffected by later cultural influences, but also to those strongly permeated by Hinduism, e.g. on Java and Bali. On these islands certain textiles are still especially esteemed, in particular the old calico cloths produced by the tie-dyeing process, which are deemed to possess special magic powers.

After what has been said above, it need hardly be pointed out that the patterns of these fabrics are, or at least originally were, connected with the magic or ceremonial role for which each particular one is designed. In this respect the motifs on the fabrics have much affinity with the tattoos still in vogue among several tribes, including the FIGS. PP. 50, 54 Dayaks and some tribes on the Lesser Sundas and the Moluccas. This, at least, is so with textiles worn as articles of clothing. In many cases, of course, the pattern has changed so much in the course of time that it is hardly, if at all, possible to discern the magic or ceremonial purpose for which it was originally designed. At the same time it should not be forgotten that the ornamental patterns were also held in high esteem merely on account of their beauty. The religious significance of these textiles is also indicated by certain ancient customs: for instance, in Pekalongan the weavers keep awake and burn incense throughout the night before commencing work on a new fabric; the Sundanese women were not allowed to marry until they had woven a *samping*; and the Toba Bataks accompanied the dyeing of the thread with sacrifices and the prayer, "Come, Spirit of the Father, bless my work!" Apart from those actually engaged in the work, no one was permitted to be present; no one might speak of death, pregnant women were excluded, and so on.

We can only examine here a few of the vast variety of customs for which these fabrics were used.

The Toradja *ikats*, i.e. the textiles from Rongkong and Galumpang mentioned in the last chapter, play a tremendously important part in the customs observed by these tribes when burying their dead. Thus in many areas the Toradja wrap these fabrics around the bodies of the deceased, calling them 'cloths of the dead', and in one particular district

Riders on a mount, earthenware (Macassar, southern Celebes). *K.I.T.* (Height 10¾ ins.)

the fabrics from Rongkong are also referred to as *pepewao* — 'that which serves to clothe the spirits'.

But these sacral fabrics are also used for other ceremonial purposes.

Man's tattoo (South Ceram)

A dowry must without fail contain at least one piece. Elsewhere they are even used when murder or manslaughter are committed, and form part of the fine to be paid.[2] In these latter cases economic as well as magic reasons are involved.

The fabrics from Sumba Island mentioned earlier, with their human and animal figures, are likewise used in burial ceremonies.

Among the *ikats* of the Dayaks, very large pieces are often to be found which are not worn as clothing. They are used exclusively at certain ceremonies to mark out the sacral spot. Such cloths used to be employed by the Iban Dayaks to contain the heads which they took when head-hunting.

Such large-sized fabrics not used as clothing are also to be found on Java. They are produced by the process of tie-dyeing of the warp, are sometimes approximately twenty yards long, and are known as *kain kasang*. Their manufacture is exclusive to western Java, where they are hung up on ceremonial occasions. These fabrics are still in use at the courts of central Java, which shows that they are held in great esteem, particularly the ancient specimens.

PLATE P. 32
The ornamentation on the so-called 'boat cloth' from Kroë, a district in south-western Sumatra, clearly indicates that it was used in the death rites. The ornamental design has been made by the floating weft method. The main motif on such cloths is always a 'ship of the dead', such as we already came across on the bronze kettle-drum from Hanoi and which can also be found elsewhere in Indonesia — for example, amongst the Dayaks, who, however, draw it on bast, or ornament bamboo receptacles with it. The image of the ship is obviously intended to express the idea that the soul of a deceased person can only be conveyed to the 'land of souls' by ship. But the renderings of the ship of the dead are remarkably different on the fabrics from Kroë. There are all manner of subsidiary motifs, such as human figures, buffaloes, fish, birds,

Woman's tattoo (Lomblen, Lesser Sunda-Islands)

and trees of life. The human figures show a distinct affinity with the style of *wayang* figures in Hindu Java (cf. section of *wayang-purwa*). It is not ruled out that this indicates Javanese influence, exerted after the 14th century. This hypothesis is also supported by other motifs, such as the sunshade.

The textiles from the mountain village of Tenganan Pagringsingan on Bali, already referred to above, deserve special mention. The tie-dyeing method on both warp and weft is employed — a technique to be found nowhere else in Indonesia except in this one village. All the women participate in weaving these fabrics. At regular evening gatherings held in an appointed place the girls practise the arts of spinning, weaving and *ikat* work.

Already the name given to these fabrics points to the magic character ascribed to them. They are referred to as *gringsing* (*gring* meaning 'illness', and *sing* 'not'). Thus the name could be translated as 'illness-averting'. The importance attached by the village community to the weaving of these fabrics is apparent from the fact that the name of the village itself contains an allusion to *gringsing*.

These textiles are thought highly of everywhere in Bali and play a definite part in many important events and ceremonies. When a child has its first hair-cut, it is wrapped in one of these cloths, and when it has its teeth filed its head rests on one. At the marriage contract ceremony the young couple are enveloped in a *gringsing,* a brand-new cloth being used, in the shape of a 'quiver cloth': the warp threads are mounted on the loom by rotation, which has the advantage that the length of the loom need only be half the length of the fabric. The bride's mother cuts through the warp threads. After this ceremony has been completed the fabric can be used as an article of clothing; it is no longer preserved for any other purpose.

These cloths are also used to cover the dead, and are carried on long poles at cremation ceremonies. In several places on Bali they are also wrapped around the top of the cremation tower in cases when the deceased was a member of a caste (cf. the chapter on Bali).

In Tenganan much has been preserved which dates back to the pre-Hindu era, whilst on Bali Hinduism survives up to the present day — examples of the dogged persistence of ancient traditions.

Wherever tie-dyeing of the warp is employed, cotton is used as the basic substance, and no Hindu influence can definitely be traced in the designs. Apparently tradition is particularly strong and vigorous

Cotton as raw material

MOUNTAINOUS
AREAS

SOUTH CHINA SEA

MALAYAN
PENINSULA

ATJEH

BATAKS

NIAS

SUMATRA

DJAMBI

MENANG
KABAU

PALEMBANG

PASEMAH

MENTAWAI Is

NKULEN

KROE

LAMPONG

ENGGANO

B

CENT

DA

JAVA

CENTRAL JAVA

MAD

WESTERN JAVA

EASTERN JAV

THE ISLANDS OF
INDONESIA

Carved bamboo container with stopper in the shape of an elephant (Apo Kayan Dayak, central Borneo). *K.I.T.* (Height 15½ ins.)

in these places. Amongst these relatively isolated tribes tie-dyeing of the warp has therefore generally remained the only method of weaving textiles with designs on them. If in an exceptional instance a different technique is employed, the patterns diverge considerably from the usual ones. This, for example, is the case with the textiles of the Iban Dayaks woven by the *pilih* method, the patterns of which occupy a particular place of their own in Dayak art. The same applies to the so-called *ragidup* textiles of the Toba Bataks, who use the floating weft. On their fabrics, made by tie-dyeing of the warp, there is only an arrow-head motif, whereas the *ragidup* fabrics are ornamented with the most elaborate geometrical motifs.

The fabrics woven by the process of tie-dyeing of the warp from the Lesser Sundas to the east of Sumbawa and the South Molucca Islands are particularly attractive. Each island has retained its individual artistic style, motifs, and dyeing methods. Besides the Sumba textiles already referred to, those of Timor, Sawu, Roti and Lomblen must be mentioned.

Wherever silk is used as the basic substance, either tie-dyeing of the warp, the floating weft technique, or a combination of both methods is applied. But this is only the case in those areas where the post-Dong-Son period left its mark, such as southern Sumatra, the Padang plateau, and Atjeh (Achin). Considering that in general the population was economically better off in these parts, it can be readily understood why it was that gold and silver threads were worked into the fabrics.

Silk as raw material

PLATE P. 38

BEAD WORK

Already in the earliest times objects were decorated with dry fruit, and stones from fruit, which lent themselves to this purpose by reason of their colour and lustre; in addition flat polished pieces of various kinds of shell, called *nassa* discs, were also popular. But as well as ornaments made from natural substances, there was a vogue for beads made from other materials. Glass beads were held in particularly high esteem; they were originally imported from Venice in the 15th century, and later mainly from Germany.

With their pronounced sense of colour, the Dayaks more than any other tribe appreciate glass beads, and have used them in various ways. The Bataks also understand the art of working coloured beads into fabrics. Several methods of doing this are known. Easily recognizable are those on strings: the beads are strung, and then the strings of beads are fastened on to a backing. These beads have occasionally replaced *nassa* discs, and thus the magic significance which attached to the latter has been transferred to the beads. This is sometimes the case with those on strings. Originally the shells from which *nassa* discs were taken served the purpose of currency. Strings of shells were therefore used in trade, but in addition they were in their entirety deemed to be charged with magic of considerable effect. This accounts for the particular value attached to these strings of beads in the Batak districts, for instance, where they are reserved exclusively for persons of princely rank, and otherwise are only worn by the masked bearers who play a special role in the funeral rites of a deceased prince.

PLATE P. 43

POTTERY

The art of pottery has not flourished to any great extent in Indonesia. Although clay of high quality is available, the art of firing objects was not properly understood, and consequently the art of glazing could also not really develop. They resorted either to pouring sea-water on to the objects to prevent them from becoming too porous, and a deposit of salt crystals then formed in the material during firing, or else the pottery was sprinkled with pulverized resin, which then melted.

It was not regarded as particularly necessary to manufacture ceramics, as vessels could be made more simply in a different way, e.g. from bamboo, coconut-shells, etc. Moreover, pottery, and even porcelain, were imported by Chinese merchants in great quantities at a very early date, in any case after the eighth century A.D. These extremely beautiful objects were undoubtedly held in very high esteem. In this connection the *martavanen* should be singled out for special mention. These were vessels, often of stupendous size, which were highly regarded by the Dayaks.

PLATE P. 46

But here and there in southern Celebes, for instance, the natives themselves produced pottery striking in its ornamentation; before firing lines were drawn in the clay whilst it was still damp to produce decoration.

Excellent work is produced on the Kei Islands in the east of the Archipelago. Here the damp vessels are painted with a yellow colouring matter which turns to a reddish tone when fired. These objects are

PLATE P. 49

characterized not merely by their fine ornamentation, but often also by their exceedingly attractive shape.

In some areas, for example in southern Celebes, human and animal figures are formed from clay. Despite their simplicity these figures are rendered extremely pleasing by their general appearance, often very

PLATE P. 53

impressive, and the serenity and harmony which emanates from them.

BAMBOO WORK

Decoration on objects made of bamboo is necessarily limited by the nature of the material. However ordinary these objects may be —

flutes, pipes, receptacles for shuttles and other things — the decorative motifs, the elaborate work and the manner of working employed manifest such variety that we may say that this is a decorative art with a character all its own. Precisely because the indigenous element is so pronounced, we have referred to it in the previous chapter.

The patterns, which are frequently complex, are applied to the hard surface by scorching, engraving, hatching, dotting, and/or scratching, and finished with the aid of colouring matter, black wax, tinfoil or silver leaf. The general practice is to stop up the bamboo container with a circular piece of wood, through which a small ribbon is drawn; the Menangkabau place a cap of bamboo on top, the upper side of which is decorated with sumptuous silver filigree. Stoppers are also found, being occasionally embellished with small reliefs. The Dayaks PLATE P. 58 carve small human and animal figures on them. The Bataks make containers of a rather special kind: they have a curved foot at the bottom, and a large stopper sticking out made of shiny horn or polished ebony. In this connection it is striking that the Bataks and Menangkabau always, and the Dayaks generally, carve the tumpal motif on these objects, the receptacles of the Dayaks often being elaborated to an extent found nowhere else.

These decorations are greatly influenced by the Dong-Son and Late Chou styles. In the course of centuries on this basis a decorative art came into being, the motifs of which were evolved by various tribes according to their own taste, — motifs which have survived to the present day amongst both smaller and larger groups.

In Indonesia timber is both abundant and varied, and has therefore *WOOD CARVING* always been popular in applied art, as well as for the sculpturing of free-standing human and animal figures.

The most impressive wood carvings are in Java and Bali, especially on the latter island. For reasons already stated we shall consider the various types of carving on these islands later.

Decorative wood carving is applied in the most attractive way on the houses of the Bataks, Toradja and Menangkabau. These houses do not accommodate single families, but large genealogical groups, or clans.

The Batak house, in particular that of the Toba Bataks, is a wooden *Decorative* building of a particularly bold construction. Heavy planks form the *wood carving* walls, and the roof rises high and slopes inwards towards the centre. The façade, also of wood, is decorated with carving, in which the spiral motif is the dominant feature. In this case the influence of the

Fig. p. 65

Dong-Son style is clearly manifest, and colouring helps to enliven the general appearance of the building. In the case of the Toba Bataks the so-called *singa* figure is characteristic. This is a stylized head of a mythical being which is affixed to the house to ward off evil spirits. The houses of the Toradja likewise are imposing in their manner of construction. With the Toradja in particular the ridge of the roof rises high up both in front and at the back, culminating in a projection which juts far out and thus forms a sort of porch. This projection of the roof is frequently supported by a broad post and horizontal beams. Both this post and the façade of the house are decorated with coloured carvings. The arrangement of a great many motifs is strictly geometrical, not unlike those on bamboo objects. But in addition the spiral may also be found. Occasionally human and animal figures of a more naturalistic type are incorporated, thus accentuating the magic character of the entire decoration. On the stake referred to or on the façade a stylized head of a kerabau is affixed, for the East Indian buffalo plays an important part in the life of the Toradja tribe. The social status of the owner is determined by the amount of cattle he possesses. The sacrifice of these animals plays a special role in ceremonial customs, and above all in funeral rites.

A characteristic feature of the particularly fine Menangkabau houses is the saddle-backed roof, with high gables at either end decorated with buffalo heads facing downwards, probably also as symbols of protection against evil spirits.

These houses are often enlarged by the addition of annexes, which also have curved ridges beginning beneath the overhanging ridge of the main building. The Menangkabau style of architecture is undoubtedly the most magnificent in the whole of Indonesia. Incidentally, the technical college in Bandung was built in this style. The façade, i.e. the long side, of the house is generally of wood, as are also the walls of the annexes, if any. The effect of the wood-carving on these houses is accentuated by colouring in white, black and red.

But the motifs displayed on them are conceived in a style which differs considerably from that of the Bataks and the Toradja. Instead of the decorative interplay of lines reminiscent of the Dong-Son style, we have blossoms and flowers intertwined with tendrils. Thus we may note strong Hindu influence, which was able to survive in this very area of Sumatra longer than it could elsewhere. Yet the primitive motifs have not completely vanished, and thus the tumpal motif reappears in these carvings, though only very rarely.

Main post of an *adat* house with wood carving (Lampong area of southern Sumatra). *K.I.T.*
(Height 6 ft. 5 ins.)

Hampatong, or wooden figure to ward off demons, at entrance to village
(South-eastern Borneo). *K.I.T.* (Height 6 ft. 2 ins.)

Main post of an *adat* house with wood carving (Lampong area of southern Sumatra). *K.I.T.*
(Height 6 ft. 5 ins.)

Hampatong, or wooden figure to ward off demons, at entrance to village
(South-eastern Borneo). *K.I.T.* (Height 6 ft. 2 ins.)

In other areas, too, we often come across particularly fine and vigorous carvings as decoration on the most important parts of the houses, such as the main post of the supporting piles.

PLATE P. 63

Apart from houses, a great number of wooden objects are also carved. Sword-hilts, shields, and prows of boats, for example, are often decorated with traditional motifs of an unmistakably magic and symbolic character. This is particularly the case with the Bataks, who incorporated all manner of magic signs and fertility symbols into their decorations.

Sculpture in wood

Since the Indonesians have a special talent for the decorative arts, we shall treat this in some detail. Some attention deserves to be given to the manner in which the artists of the Archipelago have treated the free-standing human figure. Ancestor worship in particular gave rise to the carving of such sculptures. These statues were worshipped almost as though they were the ancestors whom they represented; this means of artistic expression was thus rooted entirely in magic. The form is largely determined according to the manner of identification. In this way expression was given to those elements believed to be especially powerful or effective. Thus statues were carved with accentuated genitals, excessively large heads, and so forth. This 'fixation' is sometimes so marked that the statue can hardly be recognized any longer as that of a human figure. There are statues in which the demonic spirit is expressed at times with startling realism (protective sculptures); there are others which give expression to certain abstract tendencies and aspirations (ancestor sculptures).

singa figure (Batak)

Amongst the Dayaks, for example, one finds the so-called *hampatongs* — figures designed to give protection against evil influences — roughly-hewn piles which no longer bear any resemblance to a human figure, and also statues with an intensely dynamic force expressed in an almost surrealistic style.

The ancestor sculptures on Nias Island occupy a special position. The stylized head-dress, the small beard 'stuck on' and the right ears with distended lobes, are certainly strange in detail, but the general impression is one of a sublime composure which enhances their value. In the case of ancestor sculptures carved in simpler fashion by tribes in the South Moluccas — almost all of which are shown seated, with the arms crossed and resting upon the knees — the expression conveyed of serene poise is often moving, and in keeping with the sacral function of these sculptures. The statues from Leti — a small island in the South Moluccas — are unique in shape.

PLATE P. 64

PLATE P. 67

PLATE P. 70

The plastic art in wood of the Bataks is characterized by a particular predilection for more complex compositions of human and animal figures. Sometimes carved in high relief, at other times free-standing, protruding from the ornamentation as a whole, this type of wood-carving is always close to plastic art. Amongst objects used for ceremonial purposes decorated in this manner, the 'magic staff' is often of a bizarre beauty. The figures and motifs are carved into a heavy stick of hardwood, and wrench themselves, so to speak, with the utmost effort towards the top, which is crowned by a free-standing figure, usually a human head.

The Bataks' excellence in wood-carving is also evidenced by their 'medicine horns'. These consist partly of a buffalo horn worked at one end only and plugged in front with a wooden stopper; this plug is in many cases beautifully worked. The *singa* figure already referred to is employed over and over again, usually in conjunction with human figures placed one upon another.

Also amongst the Dayaks sculptures combining human and animal figures in a curious composition are to be found. Work of this kind serves mainly to ornament areas of considerable extent, the individual component parts being joined by odd snake-like objects, the so-called *aso* motif, whose rhythmic movement gives the whole work its own particular cachet.

Wood carving in Indonesia is an ancient traditional art. But over and over again these works manifest to a surprising degree, within their limitations, the living artistic sense of their creators.

BONE, HORN AND
IVORY WORK

Bone has been used for various purposes since the dawn of civilization. Without having to exert much effort or change the shape much, many parts of the skeleton may be worked into daggers, knives, arrow- and lance-heads, whilst the larger hollow cylindrical bones can be made into receptacles and ornamental objects.

In Indonesia, too, the working of bone is one of the oldest crafts practised, but really artistic objects are comparatively rare. On the island of Timor carved receptacles are known. The carved sections are coloured jet black with a black wax, as in the making of bamboo receptacles. The motifs are stylized figures of animals, such as lizards, millipedes, etc.

PLATE P. 73

If we include in the category of bone the massive horn of the stag, the carved *mandau* hilts of the Dayaks are amongst the finest objects made of bone. Seen as a whole, they are very strange arrangements of *aso* motifs in high relief and in ajour technique, blended rhythmically. (If

Sculpture of an ancestor, wood. Typical of such statues are the headgear and distended lobe of the right ear. (Nias Island). *K.I.T.* (Height 20½ ins.)

the wooden sheaths are carved, we usually find repetitive motifs, set off against ornamentation of beads and plaited *rotan* in geometrical form). Of the above-mentioned materials, horn is the one most frequently employed. To work it is by no means a simple matter, and in fact demands great skill. This is why one finds many objects made of horn which are totally devoid of any artistic value. Amongst the Bataks and Achinese in Sumatra, for example, we come across powder horns which retain the original shape of the horn and are frequently ornamented with great artistry. Also worthy of note are the Karo Bataks' bullet-holders, shaped like a curved beak; the elasticity of the material is cleverly put to good use to keep the bullets in place. Some of the finest objects into which horn is worked are the Bataks' medicine horns referred to above.

Also in Sumatra, in Atjeh, the Batak districts and in Palembang, horn is used for hilts of striking and thrusting weapons, which are often adorned with the mask of an animal.

Of the eastern islands Timor and Sumba may be singled out on account of their delightful horn work, some of the artistically decorated spoons and combs being real masterpieces. A special point of interest is the wearing of horn ear-rings as a sign of married status in southern Celebes. Precious ivory is often used in ornaments of various kinds, but above all for the hilts of splendid ceremonial weapons, as, for example, in Sumatra, southern Celebes, Java and Bali. Among these weapons the kris occupies a special place, as we shall see later in the chapter on Java and Bali.

LEATHER AND PARCHMENT WORK
There is not much in the way of leather working in Indonesia. Since the art of dressing hides was not known, the leather always remained hard and stiff. Only shields used by the Toradja tribe made of thick and coarse buffalo hide are worthy of notice. They are slightly curved inwards, oval and broad, and the decorations on them resemble those on bamboo or bone objects. For the ornamentation is cut into the buffalo hide, the top layer of which is then pared down, leaving the desired figures. The smoother parts of the decoration are usually coloured black, whilst the rough ground is treated with red, reddish-brown and white dye. The large circles with the so-called kerabau eye motif are striking.

Although the various Indonesian tribes have not much to boast of in the way of leather work, they know how to make very good parchment. Apart from Java and Bali, it is primarily the islands in the east of the Archipelago which are distinguished for their objects of parchment, mostly shields of various shapes and sizes on which human beings and fish can sometimes be identified; on some islands, such as Flores, these are also painted.

But however attractive some of these objects may be, it is only the people of Java and Bali who have made full use of the opportunities presented by this splendid material and have created, in their *wayang* puppets, works of art of lasting beauty.

PLATES PP. 124, 129

METAL WORK

Iron work has in general been limited to cutting and thrusting weapons. Bronze is not hard enough, so the smiths were obliged to rely upon iron for this purpose. Otherwise iron was used only very rarely, when hardness was particularly called for. In southern Sumatra, for instance, we find wrought-iron receptacles for blacking, distinguished both by their shape and their excellent workmanship. These receptacles were formerly used when filing teeth, a ceremony at which the filed-off teeth were subsequently coloured black. These receptacles are shaped in the form of animals, such as cocks, stags, kerabaus, and snakes.

PLATE P. 76

Iron was also used for the manufacture of the so-called *pinang* scissors, for in this case very solid material was an essential prerequisite. The *pinang* nut, which is one of the ingredients of *sirih* quid, for which these scissors were used, has an extremely hard shell. There are some very fine specimens in Atjeh, where filigree is soldered on, as well as in southern Celebes, where these scissors are partly gold- and silver-plated. In Java and Bali, too, there are exquisitely wrought specimens to be found (cf. the chapter on Bali).

The armourer's craft flourished in many parts of Indonesia, and many sorts of weapons were known: swords, daggers, and lances are ubiquitous. The blacksmiths employed various techniques for decorating hard metal with the designs required by the ceremonial and social role of the weapon concerned. By cutting and ajour-punching the red-hot iron, figures were affixed which frequently had a magic and ceremonial significance. Engraving and incrustation of gold and silver were also known. A special kind of blade decoration is *pamor* work (cf. section on kris in Chapter X).

The smiths excelled in the manufacture and decoration of the kris. In addition to these we may also mention the *mandaus* of the Dayaks, the finely balanced swords decorated with *pamor* work from Palembang, and a kind of dagger known as *röntjong* from Atjeh.

Bronze casting was introduced to Indonesia along with the Dong-Son

Statue of an ancestor on pedestal, wood. (Leti, off the northern tip of Timor). *K.I.T.* (Height 26 ins.)

culture, and reached a peak of artistic excellence in Java in the Hindu-Javanese era. But just as in other parts of Indonesia, so also in Java bronze ceded place almost entirely to brass, a metal so much easier to work. An additional factor was that an alloy, consisting of two parts of copper to one of zinc, was cheaper, and that the yellow colour was also particularly highly esteemed. Javanese braziers were the most highly skilled, but artistically valuable brass objects of high quality were, and still are, frequently manufactured in the Batak districts, the Padang plateau in Sumatra, along the Malayan coastal districts of south-east Borneo, and in the area around Lake Matana in Celebes.

For casting the very old *à-cire-perdue* process is still employed. The brass objects made are mostly articles of everyday use such as vessels, oil lamps, *sirih* receptacles (for the ingredients of *sirih* quid), kettles, etc. The shapes are frequently magnificent. The decorations, where they are in relief, are cast at the same time as the article. But further decorations are probably also made, by means of engraving, chasing and embossing, after the cast has first been polished with pumice stone. It is striking how frequently motifs are to be found which became known in Indonesia through bronzes dating from the Dong-Son era. Spiral lines and geometrical decorative figures are to be found, as well as ancient symbolic signs, such as the tumpal and *bandji* (swastika). But various plant motifs are also popular; they are mostly directly derived from those common in Hindu civilization.

In the Batak districts one comes across objects cast from brass, particularly striking in their ornamentation. These objects are of simple shape, but are most ingeniously embellished with reliefs and/or engraved decorations. The relief is incorporated whilst still in resin form (for in this case a mixture of resin and oil is used instead of wax) and is composed of elements simple in themselves, such as spiral figures, small balls and imitation filigree. Other figures represent animals, and may be interpreted symbolically: lions, *singas* (typical of Batak art), lizards, cats and kerabaus. Bracelets and anklets are also made in this way.

PLATE P. 79

On the Padang plateau a completely different style of decoration is to be found. Hinduism exerted a strong influence not only on the woodcarvings on the Menangkabau houses, but also on the decoration of objects cast from brass. On these, too, we find the familiar motifs of leaves and flowers intertwined with tendrils.

In Bali and Java Hinduism has exerted a persistent influence, but nevertheless on brass objects the tumpal and bandji motifs tenaciously hold their own.

71

Gold- and silversmiths in Indonesia look upon precious metals differently from those in the West. In the West such craftsmen work precious metals in as fine a form as possible, and only select those alloys which are indispensable in order to lend the necessary solidity; moreover, the material value of the object is taken into account as well as its beauty. But in Indonesia the goldsmith or silversmith has a different approach. When he mixes gold with other metals, he does so only in order to obtain various nuances of colour. The way in which he works shows that he is chiefly concerned with aesthetic rather than material values. In this connection it may also be noted that in Atjeh gold is also treated with acid: by a fairly difficult process the gold is given a reddish tone. This craft presumably originates from China. The other striking point is that so few objects are made from solid gold. One reason for this may have been the high cost, but even when the object was designed for religious purposes or to denote wealth or status, and where one would expect to find solid gold used, in fact one generally finds only plate, i.e. an object of wood, brass or silver was coated with a thin layer of gold leaf. This is one of the reasons why articles in gold are hardly ever engraved, as the thin gold leaf cannot be incised deeply.

Precious metals are worked exclusively in those areas where the influence of Hinduism was strongest, that is to say in Java and Bali, southern Celebes, the Malayan coastal districts of Borneo, and in large areas of Sumatra. In these districts the inhabitants engaged in sea-borne trade, and they prospered sufficiently to be able to afford precious metals. Apart from this factor, centres of political power developed in these areas with the passage of time, and there was thus a natural tendency to display wealth and power in an ostentatious manner by making articles of splendid appearance.

Objects in gold and silver were mainly decorated with motifs of leaves, blossoms and tendrils, with figures sometimes being added which were closely connected with Hinduism, such as the *garuda* figure, the *kāla* head, and others. The significance of these motifs will be dealt with in Chapter VI.

Dress-weapons

The best gold and silver work is to be found on weapons kept for great occasions by the Indonesian princes and magnates. Precious and semi-precious stones were often used to give the objects an even more costly and luxurious appearance. But these stones are rarely properly polished. People were generally content to work those surfaces which brought out the colour effect of the stones. It is therefore not to be

Sword of Dayak head-hunter (*mandau*). (Apo Kayan area of central Borneo). *K.I.T.* (Blade 22 ins.)

wondered at that beautifully coloured, if not precious, stones, and even the shiny greenish wing-cases of certain beetles, were decorated with gold.

In the section on wrought-iron objects passing reference was made to incrustation of blades with gold and silver. The application of precious metals to iron evidences a profound reverence for the magic content of this base metal. It also shows excellent taste on the part of the armourers, for abundant use of gold looks particularly fine on gleaming black iron.

In the case of work in gold and silver tradition does not reach back so far as with bronze casting, and with the brass casting which developed from it. Thus decorations on objects made of precious metals dating back to the pre-Hindu era are a rarity. This is the case, however, only when the precious metal is used for decorative purposes and incrustation. A special way of making gold and silver is to be found in Atjeh and on the Padang plateau (Menangkabau). For it is here that all manner of objects are made from gold and silver filigree. The metal is wrought to form long filaments and is drawn through apertures of decreasing width, fixed to an iron draught-plate. Gold filigree is to be found especially frequently in Atjeh: magnificent pieces of jewellery are worn on the chest, for example. Silver filigree is likewise produced in Atjeh, but even more generally on the Padang plateau, where all kinds of objects are made, such as imitation fruit, small boxes, carriages, houses, kerabau, etc. Also the caps of the ornamented bamboo receptacles are decorated with silver filigree.

Finally a particular type of jewellery should be mentioned which is found in Atjeh and the Batak districts. Apparently modelled upon a much more ancient process, already referred to in connection with Batak brass casting, certain objects are decorated by soldering on little silver balls and/or filigree bands. In places other than Sumatra, gold and silver is worked into all manner of filigree jewellery in the village of Kendari in south-eastern Celebes.

The two islands on which gold and silversmiths have produced exceedingly beautiful objects, Java and Bali, will be dealt with later.

1 R. von Heine-Geldern, 'Indonesian Art', New York, 1948.
2 Dr. J. H. Jager Gerlings, 'Sprekende weefsels', 1952.

VI. INDIAN CULTURE
IN ITS COUNTRY OF ORIGIN

Indian civilization is hardly, if at all, differentiated, i.e. its various aspects, such as religion, science, art, and social systems do not exist independently of one another, but form a single entity which cannot be divided into its component parts.

The essence of art in a civilization of this kind can therefore only be comprehended when examined in conjunction with other aspects, and in particular with the religion and general outlook of the people concerned. For it is religion which in the main determines the 'why and wherefore' of artistic creation and activity, and its significance and content can only be understood from this angle.

Relationship of art to religion and view of life

But it is not only that religion and art are closely interwoven with one another; the religious outlook determines the social structure, which finds in it its origin, purpose and sacral confirmation. Consequently art has a strong social flavour.

Before we examine more closely the evolution of Indonesian art, and how it was influenced from India, we have first to take a look at the most important characteristics of Indian culture.

At the beginning of the Christian era, when the first rays of Indian culture started to fall upon Indonesia, India already had a cultural evolution of many centuries behind her. It received a strong impetus when the Aryans came from Iran about 1500 B.C., occupied the fertile Punjab, and in the course of their prolonged migrations traversed and populated the whole of northern India. The oldest written texts which manifest this cultural influence are the *vedas* (*vedi* = knowledge). At first these texts, which were held to be 'revealed', were handed down orally. Written versions evolved as poetry in the form in which we know it chiefly before the 6th century B.C. There are four such works. The Rig-Veda, the oldest book and a magnificent work of literature, contains hymns to deities such as pugnacious Indra, the Sun God, Agni the God of Fire, and many others. These hymns were recited by the priests at sacrificial ceremonies. Later three further *vedas* arose. The first deals with correct recital of sacred hymns, the second contains sacrificial texts, and the third constitutes the canon for the priests. In connection with the *vedas* there appeared the *brāh-*

manas, written in prose, which are commentaries on the customary sacrificial ceremonial, a welcome means for the priests to strengthen their position. For the very esoteric and complex sacrificial ceremony was treated in it with special emphasis; even the deities were made dependent upon correct performance of sacrifices. The period of Brahmanism which followed that of Vedic religion enabled the priests to exercise a decisive social and political influence; even the princes could not vie with them. Only the priests could guarantee happiness, wealth and power through the performance of sacrifices. They were even thought capable of controlling the forces of nature. Sacrifice was thus strictly magic in character.

Small brass receptacle in the shape of a mythical snake, *nāga*. Whereas small vessels made of iron were used in the preparation of colouring matter for blackening the teeth, those in brass were used for preparing *sirih* quid. (Kroë, southern Sumatra). *K.I.T.* (Height 2 ins.)

In addition to this the power of the priests was based on the structure of social classes, the caste system, which has remained characteristic of India's social life. It clearly displays features of a system imposed by a victor upon the vanquished. Thus in theory the population was strictly divided into four groups, each with its own customs, laws, rights and obligations. Only the *āryas* belonged to the first three castes.

The highest caste is that of the Brāhmans, from which the priests were recruited, followed by the Kshatriyas, to which princes and noblemen belonged; inferior to these was the third group, the Vaishyas, which embraced agriculturalists and traders. The fourth group was constituted by the indigenous population, the Sudras. Completely outside this system were the parias, or untouchables — outcasts deprived of all rights.

The religious character of these caste distinctions is evident from the religious ceremonies with which the Indian's caste status was confirmed. But these ceremonies took place only in the case of the first three castes (colours); afterwards, as a visible sign of his social rank, each person wore a sacred thread.

From the 7th century B.C. up to the beginning of the Christian era very significant works, the Upanishads, appeared, written in Sanskrit. They are among the most important literary works of mankind. They contain commentaries on mystical concepts, and reflect the tremendous revolution in orthodox religion which occurred in the 7th and 6th centuries B.C.

The Vedic deities, in most cases personifications of natural phenomena, had to give way to Brahmān, the One, Unchanged, Absolute and Attributeless Being. If this absolute being is regarded as the metaphysical background of all that exists, and of all individual living beings, then it is termed Ātman. From ingenious theological speculations about the relationship between the self — *ātman* — and the divine universe — *brahmān* — whereby the question arises to what extent the soul of the individual has an existence distinct from Brahman, there developed the doctrine of the transmigration of souls, *samsāra*. This forms the nucleus of the Hindu and Buddhist outlook on life and the world in general.

The excessive power of the priests, based upon a barren ritualism, eventually called forth strong forces of reaction. A religious crisis ensued, and many sects sprang up with their own conceptions of doctrine, which *inter alia* contested the meaning of the sacrificial ritual and rejected the authority of the priests. Two of these developed into independent religions: Buddhism and Jainism. Buddhism has become one of the great world religions, and has exerted a strong influence upon Indonesia.

Jainism had no significance so far as Indonesia is concerned, and can therefore be disregarded.

Under the influence of these movements Brahmanism changed, and a third phase in the evolution of Indian culture, Hinduism, followed.

Hinduism Since the old indigenous gods were allotted by the priests a recognized place in the religious system, a veritable pantheon came into existence with entirely new rites and ceremonies. The sacrifice, and above all knowledge of the sacrificial ceremonial, lost its predominant place in the cult as an indispensable prerequisite for the attainment of salvation. The deities were no longer just tools of the priests, but manifestations or creations of a supreme God.

The Hindu theologians failed in their attempt to make Isvara (The Lord), the sublime and mighty counterpart of the Brahman of the Upanishads manifest in the three gods Brahma, Creator of the World, Vishnu, Guardian of the World, and Shiva, Destroyer of the World, and to have him worshipped as the supreme God. Instead of this Trinity, *trimurti*, the product of theological speculation, the faithful generally worshipped Vishnu or Shiva. Accordingly there were two main movements in Hinduism: Shivaism, with its ascetic bias, and Vishnuism, which attached greater value to the service and love of God, in the thought that one is thereby achieving identity of existence with him.

With Shiva there also appears a goddess, *shākti*, who personifies divine power and in a mystical way is regarded as Shiva's wife. She is worshipped fervently in various manifestations, such as Durga, Kali, Parvati, and others. In the Shiva cult other gods also appear which are believed to be manifestations of Shiva himself, or sons from a union between him and Durga. Among these Ganesha, a god in the manifestation of an elephant, is important as the protector of learning. In Shivaism the union of the transcendental with the immanent world is brought about through a sexual union of Shiva and Durga interpreted in a mystical fashion. Hence the Shiva cult has such a strong sexual note, and its emblem is the phallus, *linga*. But those who believe in Vishnu, on the other hand, see their god as personified in many creatures, such as fish or tortoises, and in figures such as Krishna, Rama, and others. Thus it is possible to interpret historical figures, too, as temporal in-

Heavy bracelet, brass, with head of kerabau and lizard (Toba Batak, northern Sumatra). *K.I.T.* (Diameter 4¼ ins.)

carnations of Vishnu, such as we shall come across repeatedly in Java. In plastic art, in Java especially, representations of Shiva and Vishnu and their accompanying *shāktis* are met with very frequently, as well as their mounts: for Shiva a bull, *nandi*; for Vishnu a celestial eagle, *garuda*; and for Brahma a goose, *hamsa*.

The incarnations of Vishnu, as well as of many other gods and demons, play their part in plastic art.

Siddharta Gautama, who later took the name of The Enlightened One, Buddha, was born the son of a minor prince (*rāja*). As a young man he fled his palace, driven by a yearning to find the true path of mysticism, in order to escape from the constraints imposed by the transfiguration of souls, *samsāra*; only then could man be freed from the sorrow inseparable from the life of every individual. Like so many

Buddhism

79

others, he rejected the ritualism of the priests and after much searching and meditation arrived at the discovery of 'the truth'. Seated under a pipal tree (*ficus religione*), later called the Bodhi tree, he gained illumination (*bodhi*).

In the course of long wanderings through north-west India, he preached his doctrine, and by the time of his death in about 480 B.C. had already a large number of adherents.

Buddha rejected the Vedic revelations and extreme ritualism; he followed the doctrines of the Upanishads; he speaks of the relationship between *ātman* and *brahmān*, the transmigration of souls, *samsāra*, and of salvation (from the cycle of birth and re-birth). The belief in *samsāra* is the kernel of Hinduism and Buddhism: each new 'self' is conditioned by the *karma*, the deeds and thoughts of the 'self' in the preceding incarnation. This belief necessarily led to mystical meditations in order to obtain liberation from the demonic cycle of birth and re-birth.

Buddha taught that man himself is able to tread the path towards salvation. For this the indispensable prerequisites are knowledge, morality and meditation. In his famous sermon at Benares, 'turning the wheel of doctrine', he enunciated the fundamentals of his philosophy. Life itself is sorrow, and sorrow is the consequence of desire, which in turn results from ignorance. To achieve salvation, one must attain knowledge, one must attain illumination. With this knowledge desire is eliminated, and the cycle of causation which leads from one life to the next interrupted. For Buddha salvation does not mean assumption in *brahmān*, but attainment of *nirvāna* (the word literally means 'blowing out', extinction).

Social significance of Buddhism
Buddha taught that salvation can be attained by each individual; this doctrine was of importance socially, and greatly assisted the spread of Buddhism.

As Buddhism developed further, Buddha soon began to be regarded as a supernatural being, and two principal tendencies came into existence: Hinayāna and Māhayāna. Indonesia was not affected by the former, but the latter proved to be of the utmost importance there. The so-called 'Lesser Vehicle', *hinayāna*, concentrates upon personal salvation, its ideal being other-worldly monasticism. The 'Greater Vehicle', *māhayāna*, emphasizes the fact that one obtains salvation in order to confer it upon other beings. Those who have attained salvation, *bodhi*, and stand on the threshold of Nirvana, but who renounce it in favour of other creatures are called Bodhisattvas. In this sense every being can become a Bodhisattva here on earth. Mahāyāna sought to be a complement to Hīnayāna; it also permitted the incorporation of elements which had not belonged to it originally.

The historic Buddha was, moreover, thought of as merely *one* in a long series of Buddhas from former aeons — (the process of creation was imagined as being divided into aeons). But these terrestrial Buddhas were regarded merely as reflections of celestial Buddhas, who were seated upon lotus flowers, absorbed in meditation, inactive and in the highest state of tranquillity. These divine motionless Buddhas were called Dhyani Buddhas.

It was assumed that many thousand years had to pass between the appearance of each individual terrestrial Buddha. So as not to leave man during this long period completely deprived of assistance and succour in his endeavour to preserve the pure doctrine, celestial Bodhisattvas were imagined, emanating from rays of light sent to earth by the Dhyani Buddhas. This cult of Bodhisattvas evolved into a new kind of polytheism, which inspired Buddhist art deeply wherever Mahāyāna prevailed.

Once Mahāyānism had evolved into a polytheistic religion, it was only too easy for it to come under the influence of other religions. Popular deities thrust themselves between the celestial Bodhisattvas, and the original doctrine of salvation receded ever further into the background, whilst it was now that Buddhism really began to become widely disseminated.

The ancient magic conceptions, too, merged with Mahāyānism. The terrestrial Bodhisattvas became magicians who could impose their will even upon gods, spirits, and demons with the aid of supernatural powers; they were also thought capable of attaining salvation at any given moment. This 'tantrism' also plays a part in Java, — understandably so, considering that magic was one of the most important primitive Indonesian customs.

Buddhist literature took shape in the last centuries before the Christian era, and is exceptionally rich. Equal to the Upanishads in value is the triad of the three baskets, *tripitāka*: 'basket of the discipline of the order', 'basket of the discourse, sermon', and 'basket of the higher subtleties or of the doctrine'. The *tripitāka* also contains the first large collection of fairy tales, the Jātakas. This work originates from Ceylon, and is not written in Sanskrit, but in the Palava spoken in southern India.

Besides the great works of purely religious content there evolved epics in Sanskrit: the Mahābhārata and the Rāmāyana. The former chiefly deals with the struggle between two families of the Bhārata clan, the Pandāvas and the Kauravas. The work consists of 100,000 couplets; but fragments of sacred Hindu texts and meditations on religion and philosophy are also included.

The author and date of this work are unknown. But it is almost certain that it was already regarded as a venerable collection of traditional verse in the 4th century A.D.

Rāmāyana is generally known and highly esteemed in Indonesia. In 24,000 couplets it tells the story of the hero, Rama. It is attributed to the poet Valmiki, who probably wrote it in the 4th or 3rd centuries B.C.

When dealing with the literature of the Hindu-Javanese period, we shall examine these two epic poems more closely.

VII. THE SPREAD OF INDIAN CULTURE

In the first centuries of the Christian era sea-borne trade began to
develop between the countries of southern and eastern Asia. In many
places Indian commercial settlements sprang up: at first along the
coast of Further India (e.g. Funan and Champa), and later also in the
Malayan peninsula, Borneo, Sumatra and Java. These settlements
presumably generated little in the way of cultural stimulus, and few
significant Indian cultural values will have been transmitted by the
first traders and settlers. But later there developed a number of centres
of political power in these areas, and Indian culture flourished there.
It can no longer be ascertained with certainty whether these centres
were founded and settled by Indian colonists, or whether these married into indigenous families who already held a certain amount of
power (for the immigrants did not bring any womenfolk with them).
Nor is it clear how the change to the new culture took place. It is possible that princes emigrated from India to more easterly regions when
the Gupta Empire, which held sway over a large part of India, expanded greatly between the 3rd and 6th centuries A.D. Brahman and
Buddhist priests may have come with these princes and would naturally have been the most loyal advocates and apostles of the superior
Indian culture. But it is also conceivable that native potentates who
had already attained a certain amount of power came into contact
with Indian culture, and thought it advisable to let themselves be
consecrated by Brahman priests. Thus the ground would have been
prepared for a new centre of culture.

Indian commercial settlements

However this may be, the fact remains that the development of Indian
culture (and here we are concerned only with Indonesia) was bound
up with the changing fortunes of the most powerful indigenous
princely dynasties.

Although the first large Indonesian kingdom (the kingdom of Shrividjaya) came into being in Sumatra towards the end of the 7th century, and a centre of Buddhist learning appeared in Palembang, it is
chiefly Java which deserves our attention. It was here that the most
powerful dynasties arose, and here that the art flourished which came
to be known as 'Hindu-Javanese'.

It is certain that several such centres of power came into being in Java

Bas-relief, *tjandi* Surawana (eastern Java). Influenced by *wayang* style.

as a result of the natural conditions prevailing on the island. Where it is stated below that a certain dynasty could bring 'the whole of Java' under its sway, this does not mean to say that it actually exercised effective dominion over the whole area. Large areas of western Java, for instance, lay so remote, sheltered by volcanoes and dense primeval jungle, that their people can have known and cared little about their nominal prince and ruler. But the dynasty did definitely exercise authority over all those areas which were important for maritime commerce. The same applies to the extension of control over areas outside Java, for sea-borne trade provided the economic basis for the power and glory of the ruling prince.

The kraton These centres of power are usually referred to by a single term, embracing the prince's palace and his whole court: *kraton*. And it may be said that political struggles in Java derived from rivalry for hegemony between the most important kratons.

Whenever a dynasty attains wealth and sovereign power, and peace temporarily prevails, the conditions exist in which great artistic achievements are possible. For this reason any account of Javanese art must be preceded by a brief survey of the history of the Javanese kratons.

It should be borne in mind that a comparatively small number of families are involved of mixed Indian and Javanese stock, for, as already mentioned, the immigrants came without their womenfolk. The children of these mixed marriages will undoubtedly have adopted the religion of their father, and have been brought up in the spirit of the culture which prevailed in their kraton. But it is equally true that the old Indonesian outlook will have influenced their manner of thought and action.

The peasant population had no share in this new culture. They had a firm spiritual basis of their own, upon which rested their sound agrarian culture. In this connection Professor T. P. Galestin remarks: "The village had its own forms of communtiy, as well as its rituals and customs based on agriculture, whose origins go back to the neolithic era, and are thus extremely vigorous." [1] But it may be assumed that a certain assimilation took place, in the course of which specific cultural values from the society of the court (kraton) were adopted, perhaps in a modified form, without this leading to a radical change in the peasants' own spiritual and cultural pattern.

The obligations of the agrarian territorial community, désa, to the kraton will probably have been limited to the provision of dues and labour service, for war and also for other duties.

In Java the oldest Hindu-Javanese works of art made from permanent materials were erected during the rule of the Shivaist dynasty in central Java, which in some way or other maintained contact with the kraton in eastern Java. The last prince of this kingdom, Sandjaya, who lives on in Javanese tradition, is said to have withdrawn to the kraton in eastern Java when the Shailéndra dynasty, who adhered to Mahāyāna Buddhism and ruled between 778 and 864 A.D., established a new centre of power.

Shailéndra dynasty

The Shailéndras were particularly effective in asserting and expanding their political power. Their sphere of influence extended even beyond Further India, and in the 9th century they were able to establish a protectorate over the prosperous kingdom of Shrividjaya on Sumatra, with whose princes they were related.

In approximately 860 A.D. the Shailéndras in Java had to give way to a dynasty from eastern Java, which founded the kingdom of Mataram in central Java and posed as the heirs to the dynasty of Sandjaya. The Shailéndras withdrew to Sumatra, where they took over the government of the Shrividjaya kingdom, which in the 10th century became very powerful under their rule. Presumably under pressure from the Shailéndras of Sumatra, the princes of Mataram withdrew again to eastern Java. After 927 the kratons of central Java disappear from Hindu-Javanese history; dynasties from eastern Java now take over. In view of the great artistic value of the architectural monuments and sculptures which remain, and which can hardly have been created within a century and a half, the cultural life of the kratons in central Java must have reached an impressively high level.

It is therefore regrettable that all the literary works of this era have apparently been lost. Literary history proper does not begin until the reign of Mpu Sindok, the first prince of the house of Mataram to settle in eastern Java. Incidentally, there has been no satisfactory explanation for the complete disappearance of central Java from Hindu-Javanese history. Possibly the silting up of the harbour of Semarang, and perhaps also a violent volcanic eruption (from Merapi?) were contributory causes.

Mataram dynasty

At the end of the 10th century Mataram attacked Shrividjaya, probably to free itself from pressure by the Shailéndras of Sumatra. A counter-attack by this kingdom ensued. The king of Mataram was killed, and as he had no direct successor, the dynasty was threatened with extinction.

But a daughter of the penultimate prince of Mataram was still alive. This princess, Mahéndradatta, was married to Udayana, a prince of Bali. The Brahman priests, as representatives of the kratons of Mataram, approached her son and offered him the crown. He accepted and ruled from 1010 to 1049 as Airlangga, one of the greatest kings of Java.

King Airlangga

During his reign the rivalry with the Shailéndras came to an end, and the whole of Java came under his sway. During his lifetime he partitioned his kingdom between his two sons. The smaller part attained supremacy, and appears in history as the kingdom of Kediri. But the kraton of Djanggala, originally the larger of the two kingdoms, finally brought about the overthrow of this dynasty. At the beginning of the 13th century the regent of Djanggala is killed by a certain Ken Angrok, who takes over the government of this area. He sets himself up as an incarnation of the god Bhatāra Guru, and is also recognized as such by the priests. He expels the prince of Kediri and under the name of Radjasa founds the new dynasty of Singhasāri (1222—1293).

Under Kertanagara (1268—1292) the power of the dynasty attains its climax. Sumatra and Bali are conquered, and on the southern tip of the Malayan peninsula Singapura, the lion city, is founded. The king even allows himself to become engaged in conflict with the mighty Chinese Emperor Kubilai. But before this results in the despatch of a Chinese punitive expedition to Java, the king is dethroned by a revolt of two of his viceroys. The viceroy of Kediri himself is crowned king, but thereby antagonizes the other viceroys. The son-in-law of the dethroned prince, Raden Widjaya, takes advantage of this disunity to uphold the claims to the succession of the dynasty of Singhasāri, and attains his end. He gains a firm footing in the town of Madjapahit, and when the long-awaited attack of the Chinese takes place, acknowledges the Emperor Kubilai as his suzerain. Assisted by the Chinese, he now defeats the king of Kediri; but then suddenly turns against the Chinese and succeeds in driving them out of Java. *Kingdom of* Under the name of Kertaradjasa he founds the kingdom of Madja- *Madjapahit* pahit in 1294.

The greatest figure in this kingdom was the minister Gadjah Mada, who wielded effective power from 1331 to 1364. He extended the authority of the kingdom over other parts of Sumatra, and reconquered Bali, which had become independent during the contest for the succession to the throne. In order to undermine the resistance of the Balinese, he founded a Javanese settlement on Bali which was to prove very significant later on.

The kingdom of Madjapahit attained the summit of its power in the reign of Hayam Wuruk (1350—1389). The Javanese ruled over the whole of Indonesia with the exception of Borneo and northern Celebes, but including a large part of the Malayan peninsula. After the death of Hayam Wuruk the proud kingdom soon collapsed. The supremacy over various islands including Sumatra now passed to the Ming dynasty of China.

Approximately in the year 1450 Islam began to penetrate into Java; *Islam* the viceroys who became Mohammedans made themselves independent, and finally brought about the collapse of Madjapahit. About 1520 this kingdom disappeared completely from history, and soon the end also came of the era in which sea-borne trade formed the basis of the power and authority of the great Javanese kingdoms.

Only the small state of Balambangan managed to retain its independence, and defend its Hindu-Javanese culture for another two and a half centuries.

The only territory to have retained its Hindu-Buddhist character up to the present day is Bali, situated to the east of Java. Its recorded history does not date back beyond the 10th century A.D. It tells the story of a kingdom in which, just as in Java, the religion was a fusion of Shivaism and Buddhism. Bali developed along lines of its own; the language and script, derived like Javanese from the Palava script of southern India, are indigenous.

It was not until about 1000 that contact with Java became frequent. Airlangga, the son of a Balinese prince, as we have seen, united both kingdoms, but after his death there could be no further question of Java exercising any real authority over this island. Not until after its conquest by Gadjah Mada in 1343 did Bali come under such strong Javanese influence that, after the fall of Madjapahit, Hindu-Javanese civilization could survive there. Thenceforth Bali developed independently. Local customs of the most varied kind intermingled with Hindu-Javanese influences to give the civilization of Bali a character that was all its own.

1 Prof. Dr. Th. P. Galestin in 'Indonesië', Part 6, 'Algemene kunstgeschiedenis'. W. de Haan N.V., Utrecht, 1951.

VIII. LITERATURE WITHIN THE AREA OF HINDU-JAVANESE CIVILIZATION

Already before Indonesia was affected by cultural currents from India, it could boast of a notable literature. The term 'literature' is used here in a somewhat broader sense than is customary, for writing was as yet unknown. Sacred myths, prayers, formulas of exorcism, and so forth, were handed down orally, always in verse. Even nowadays we still find many examples of this primitive literary tradition amongst tribes only slightly influenced by Hinduism, Buddhism or Islam.

A written literature could only develop once the art of writing became more familiar in certain areas where Indian cultural influences penetrated. Javanese script, as has already been mentioned, was a development of the Palava script of southern India.

Introduction of writing

The most ancient dated texts were composed in the 5th century A.D., and deal with grants of land, privileges, etc. Documents of this kind are most informative, for they tell us much about social conditions and the socio-economic structure of that era, but they have little or no literary value. One might have expected that the age of the Shailéndras and the first princes of Mataram — an age in which cultural life clearly flourished, as the splendid architectural monuments bear witness — would also have produced valuable works of literature. But there are none. Presumably some such works did exist, but they disappeared with the collapse of the dynasty in central Java.

After 927 even the documents cease. It is only after the collapse of Madjapahit in the 16th century that central Java re-appears on the stage of history.

Literary history proper begins only about 950 A.D., when the first works of some significance were written in eastern Java, during the reign of Mpu Sindok.

Literature, like architecture and sculpture, belongs to kraton culture. Those persons at court who took an interest in artistic and intellectual matters were familiar with the great poems of India, and in this way were stimulated to write works of literature themselves. The earliest known prose work contains, *inter alia*, independent adaptations of parts of that most comprehensive Indian epic, the Mahābhārata. These adaptations are known as parvas, and are followed by other

Parvas and kakawins

Borobudur, general view. Built during the Shailéndra dynasty, approx. 800. (Central Java).

poetic works, kakawins, in the style of the Indian kavyas. Such kavyas were particularly popular in those centuries when Indian influence upon Indonesia was at its strongest. The kakawins, like the kavyas, are ornate poetry; the form had to conform to exceptionally strict criteria, and the actual poetic element fell far short of the technical skill displayed. If there were, however, poets, both in India and Java, who, despite such impeding intellectual requirements, were able to create first-rate works of art, this is a tribute to their great artistic talent.

Ardjunavivaha　One of the finest kakawins is the Ardjunavivāha, composed by Mpu Kanwa in the reign of King Airlangga. It is also the earliest kakawin to which a date can be set.

It describes how Ardjuna repaired to the Himalayas to devote himself to asceticism at the time when the gods were waging war against the demon Nivātakawaca. Shiva tested Ardjuna's mettle by sending celestial nymphs to lead him astray. But Ardjuna resisted these temptations, whereupon Shiva procured for him a weapon with which he could attack the demon. Ardjuna did in fact succeed in killing Nivā-takawaca, and as a reward for his spiritual superiority and unsur-passed valour was now permitted to spend seven days in heaven in the company of the celestial nymphs.

In the Javanese conception this romance portrays symbolically the struggle of the perfect man against the perpetual threat of evil. Thus for centuries the Javanese regarded Ardjuna as their ethical ideal.

Another masterpiece is the kakawin 'Bhāratayuddha'. This poem con-sists of 52 cantos, and its subject-matter, though drawn from the Mahābhārata, deals only with the struggle of the five Pandāvas with their cousins, the Kauravas. It was begun by the poet Mpu Sedah in 1157 under the Kediri dynasty, and completed by Mpu Panuluh. Although the principal motif was borrowed from the Mahābhārata, it differs greatly from the original in its details, probably as a result of local environmental influences. *Bhāratayuddha*

The poem begins with the despatch of an emissary from the Pandāvas to Hastinapura, a town of the Kauravas. The main content is the description of the tremendous 18-day battle, and the chivalrous and heroic deeds performed on this occasion.

Amongst the Pandāvas, who became familiar figures in Java, Ardjuna stands out as the most chivalrous hero.

The other great Sanskrit poem, Rāmāyana, composed by the Indian poet Valmiki, provided the subject-matter for a magnificent Javanese kakawin of the same title, which attained immense popularity. The author cannot be ascertained with certainty, but the work can prob-ably be dated to the beginning of the eastern Javanese period. *Rāmāyana*

There is no other tale that can boast of such widespread circulation. Its elevated moral note is unmistakable, the dramatic action convinc-ingly moving. Thus it is not surprising that this work has greatly stimulated plastic art. Both on bas-reliefs as well as in wayang plays the Rāmāyana occupies a worthy place.

It tells the story of the noble prince Rama, who forfeits his rights to the throne on moral grounds and, accompanied by his wife Sita, retires to the wilderness. Sita is abducted by Ravāna, king of the Raksasas, and is held captive in his palace at Langka, in Ceylon. But Rama, aided by Hanuman and his monkey hosts, manages to set her free. In defiance of Ravāna's wiles and threats, Sita remained true to her husband. But when Rama succeeds to the throne on his father's death, and notices that the people are sceptical of Sita's chastity, he puts her away, because he believes that his own immaculate honour would be impaired if he seemed to pardon his wife's infidelity, even if this were only imputed, and not proved.

Later Rama was interpreted as an incarnation of Vishnu; thus this work acquired a strong religious flavour, as already mentioned.

Nāgarakertāgama   As the last kakawin one may mention 'Nagarakertāgama', 'The History of the Growth and Flourishing of the Empire'. It was composed by Mpu Prapanca in 1365 in the reign of Hayam Wuruk. Madjapahit stood then at the summit of its power.

This poem is typical courtly literature. It is not modelled on an Indian prototype, but gives a contemporary account of Madjapahit, the government and the personality of the prince. As it is devoid of any objectivity, it is of little historical value: the poet was anxious merely to glorify the prince. He does not limit himself to Hayam Wuruk's reign, but begins with the partition of the kingdom under King Airlangga in 1049. The dynastic details also serve the purpose of allowing Hayam Wuruk to emerge with all the honour.

Kidungs   At the same time as the kakawins, but chiefly after them, there appeared other works of poetry, the kidungs. They differ from the kakawins in so far as the form of the verse was not taken from an Indian model, but was indigenous. In addition to this, these poetical compositions manifest much greater Javanese influence.

One group of these kidungs draws it subject-matter from the Pandji romances which are usually grouped around a prince of Koripan. All imaginable complications keep him apart from his bride, a princess of Kediri, and it is only after innumerable adventures that he can gain her. A characteristic feature of these kidungs is that the principal motif can frequently hardly be recognized amongst the subsidiary motifs originating from primitive myths. In this case heroic deeds of mythical ancestors are ascribed to the prince.

A second group is composed of historical romances. These relate the history of Singhasāri and Madjapahit until about 1360, as well as of the Javanese colony in Bali until 1651.

The description is often very lively. Unhampered by the metre of the kakawins, which was unnatural in Javanese, the poet could express himself more freely and vigorously. We have selected for illustration a small fragment of a historical romance describing the love of Hayam

Kidung Sunda   Wuruk for the princess of Sunda, 'Kidung Sunda'.

The king is depicted as follows:

"He wore splendid armlets with bantalas, pearl ear-pendants, his

Lara Djonggrang, central temple of the Prambanan complex, dedicated to Shiva, built approx. 915. (Central Java).

top-knot adorned with areca blossoms, his crown of gold with a fiery blazing ornament of most precious stones, and flanked by kalpicas of jewels and beryl. Bedecked with angrek bulan orchids, he looked the very picture of a king. His skin gleamed fresh and tender, the complexion lightish brown. And to enrapture the hearts of men yet more, the charm with which he raised his eyes was as if they were of melting honey." 1

Tantris The tantris, comparable to the kidungs in form, contain adaptations of Indian fables. The framework in which they are encompassed is reminiscent of the tales of the 'Thousand and One Nights'.

Popularizations of kakawins, as of the Rāmāyana, for example, were also adapted in the form of kidungs.

Pararaton In conclusion one must mention a great work in prose, the Pararaton. It contains a collection of various tales relating to the history of the Singhasāri and Madjapahit dynasties. As well as tales in which Ken Angrok, Raden Widjaya and Gadjah Mada figure as the main characters, the work also contains chronicles and accounts of the princes of Singhasāri and Madjapahit. There is no reliable information as to when and where this work appeared. The Pararaton, too, is not an objective historical account: there are many descriptions of supernatural events, such as the birth of Ken Angrok as the son of Brahma, or the shimmer of light radiating from him as a child, or his later escape from the enemies which encompass him, and so on. The author by no means denies or suppresses his less positive deeds, but proceeds from the fact, which for him is incontrovertible, that an incarnate deity must be judged by other criteria than an ordinary mortal. The whole historical account has something typically static about it. The princes portrayed are equated with figures from the remote past. Javanese literature appears to the Westerner as very alien. A world in which men, gods and demons often play out a grotesque game must seem strange to modern man, with his rational outlook and his specialization — unless he should be something of a '*homo ludens*', with understanding for the 'game of life', in which man acts out his fears, joys and desires in the presence of his Creator.

LITERATURE With the collapse of the Madjapahit kingdom the literature of east-
ON BALI ern Java comes to an end in Java itself, but it is pursued further in Bali. In the eastern Javanese poetry which continued to exist on Bali, kidungs gradually replaced kakawins. This is perhaps due to the fact that at the time of Javanese colonization on Bali, kakawins no longer played such an important part.

94

The kidungs mentioned, like the Pararaton, are offshoots of the Javanese literature which prevailed on Bali. On this island, affected only by minor local incidents, many a work was added to Hindu-Javanese literature, and later to Hindu-Javanese-Balinese and later still to Hindu-Balinese literature.

But Javanese could not survive permanently on Bali. At first the spoken language disappeared, and towards 1700 it also fell into disuse as a literary language. Nevertheless the influence of Javanese upon Balinese is unmistakable, particularly in the language spoken at court. Although Javanese has become a dead language for the people of Bali, their predilection for ancient literature has not on that account become extinct. And for this reason great store was set upon the preservation of the literary riches inherited from eastern Java, which undoubtedly would otherwise have perished with the downfall of Madjapahit.

1 C. C. Berg, Inleiding tot de studie van het oud-javaans.

So-called Prambanan motif (bas-relief), frequent on the base of Lara Djonggrang (cf. Plate on p. 93).

KEY TO SKETCH-MAP ON PAGE 97 ▶

1. *Dieng Temple*
2. Pringapus
3. Gedongsanga
4. Selagriya
5. *Borobudur*
6. *Pawon*
7. *Mendut*
8. Sari
9. *Kalasan*
10. *Sewu* (Plaosan)
11. *Prambanan*
    (Lara Djonggrang)
12. Ratubaka
13. Medangkamulan
14. Sukuh and Tjeta
15. Wengker
16. Ngetos
17. Selamangleng
18. Bayalangu
19. Dadi
20. Selamangleng
21. Sumberdjati
22. Bara

23. Sawentar
24. *Panataran*
25. Sumbernanus
26. Tigawangi
27. *Surawana*
28. Ngrimbi
29. Madjapahit
30. Canggu
31. Djedong
32. Belahan
33. Djalatunda
34. Djawi
35. Pari
36. Gununggangsir
37. Sanggariti
38. *Singhasari*
39. Badud
40. Karangkates
41. *Kidal*
42. *Djago*
43. Payarakan
44. Kedaton
45. Djabung

Monuments in italics are mentioned in the text

IX. INFLUENCE OF BUDDHISM AND HINDUISM UPON ARCHITECTURE, SCULPTURE AND THE WAYANG PLAYS

Hindu-Indonesian works of art made from permanent materials are to be found on various islands, but predominantly in Java. They are also present on Bali, with the significant difference that Hinduism has survived on Bali up to the present day. In Sumatra fragments have been found apparently dating from the period between the 8th and 15th centuries, but they are for the most part in such a state of ruin that they will not be examined in this volume.

It may be noted that in various places, and partly in the areas marginally affected by cultural movements from India, statues of Buddha

ARCHITECTURE AND SCULPTURE

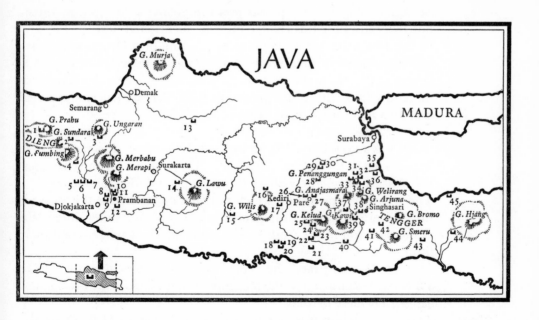

Sketch-map of the most important antiquities in central Java (Kingdoms of King Sandjaya, the Shailéndras, and Mataram) and in eastern Java (Kingdoms of Kediri, Singhasári, and Madjapahit).

have been found in the Amaravatī style — a style which flourished in India between the second and fifth centuries A.D. It is conceivable that these bronze figures were brought from India. A large stone figure of Buddha, about 10 feet high and executed in the same style, has been discovered in the district of Palembang. In this case, too, the place of origin cannot be ascertained for certain.

JAVA Monuments which were erected on this island under the dynasties of the Buddhist-Hindu period have for the greater part fallen into ruin with the passage of time. It was not until the twentieth century that restoration work was begun on some monuments that have been preserved, which fortunately include several sanctuaries of particular value, such as Borobudur in central Java and the great temple complex of Prambanan.

MAP. P. 96 As can be seen from the short survey given of Javanese history, the central Javanese period which lasted until 927 was followed by the eastern Javanese period, which came to a close with the collapse of the last Hindu-Javanese kingdom of Madjapahit. Both architecture and sculpture display considerable modifications in style, and consequently the art of the later period differs markedly from that of the earlier. We shall return to this point in greater detail in due course, but two causes for this change must be mentioned here.

In the first place we must point to the Buddhist-Hindu syncretism which appeared in Java, reaching its climax in the reign of King Airlangga of the Mataram dynasty. This prince became a monk towards the end of his life, which points to Buddhist influence, and styled himself a re-incarnation of Vishnu (1042 A.D.).

The Javanese finds it easy to fuse various religious conceptions. Mysticism was a necessity of life for him, whilst he rarely attached decisive importance to theological problems. This accounts for the characteristic feature of religious life in Java, an open-minded tolerance.

The second characteristic which must be mentioned is the ancestor worship originating in the neolithic age, which resulted in certain changes on and in the temples, affecting both their purpose and their form.

In order to understand the exposition that follows, one must make a formal classification of the monuments dating from the central and eastern Javanese periods.

Tjandis Tjandis are monuments existing in great numbers, all built on the same principles. Their appearance coincides with the influx of Indian

PLATES PP. 102, 106 culture, and thus it has been assumed that the plans of construction

98

must also have originated from India. But it cannot be established how these plans were transmitted to Java, since reliable historical references are not available. It is also striking that no monuments exist in India comparable to the tjandis in Java.

But even if such plans were transmitted, they can hardly have been so strictly enforced as in their country of origin, where any divergence from the plan would have led to certain precisely-defined fatal consequences. An attempt to adhere to plans drawn up in a remote area would almost certainly have resulted in complete rigidity. The genius of Indonesian artists clearly refused to be confined within limitations that were too narrow. They developed their individual interpretations even in such areas where this would have been quite impossible in India. However this may be, Javanese architects created works of art surpassing some of those in India.

Bull (*nandi*), mythical mount of Shiva. The surrounding *tjandi* has been destroyed. Prambanan complex.

A tjandi, or sepulchral monument, consists in its simplest form of three parts: the base which bears the temple proper is cubic, the plan and top surface are square. The temple forms a cube, and is smaller than the base, leaving a terrace for perambulation around the temple; the third part of the whole structure is the temple roof, gradually receding in steps towards the top on the exterior, whilst in the interior it forms the rising ceiling of the shrine. It culminates on top in a crowning, usually in the shape of a *linga* or *stūpa*. Under the shrine a small space is left open in the base, in which the ashes of a deceased prince may be preserved. We shall come back to this point later. Over it stands a statue of a god or the *linga* of the Shiva cult. A stairway, generally on the eastern side, leads up to the terrace, ascending alongside the base and terminating opposite the entrance to the shrine.

PLATE P. 93

This is the most simple form, but there are innumerable variations, retaining this same basic form. A projection may be added to every side of the three parts of the building. The plan has thus twenty corners instead of four, but is still square. In the case of the larger tjandis, this is the most common form.

There are many divergencies in points of detail: for instance, niches on the outer side of the three walls of the temple other than that in which the door is cut. Such niches, although not so deep, can be found on the sides of the step-like parts of the temple roof. In these niches sculptures are rare. The entrance to the shrine is often built out towards the stairway, thus forming a kind of porch. And finally the construction of the whole monument in the form of terraces or storeys permits many variations in the degree to which these terraces recede. The decorations of the tjandis vary greatly both in content and in shape, but several common features occur. The *kālamakāra* ornament, decorating the frame of the doors and niches, is very widespread. Above the door or recesses one finds the stylized head of a lion, *kāla*, linked by bands with two heads of animals from Indian mythology, *makāra*.

Makāra gargoyle,
Borobudur (Java)

In the tjandis in eastern Java we do find the *kāla* head, but the *makāra* figures are replaced by snakes, *nāga*. In both cases they serve the purpose of warding off demonic influences.

It must always be borne in mind that monuments of this type were originally intended to represent the celestial mountain, *meru*, the abode of the gods; this idea is also reflected in the ornamentation. For this reason the lotus flower is generally found as a motif: according to Indian mythology, gods are born out of lotus flowers, upon which they are seated.

In conclusion it may be noted that there are both Buddhist as well as Hindu tjandis, whilst the ornamentation of certain temples was influenced by the fusion of *Weltanschauungen* mentioned above.

Stūpas

Originally, at the time of the Maurya dynasty, which ruled in northern India from the end of the fourth century to the second century B.C., the stūpa was quite a simple structure: a hemispherical burial mound over the ashes or a relic of Buddha crowned by an umbrella, symbolic of his high status. This umbrella was enclosed by stone railings, and at the foot of the whole structure there was a processional path, secured from the outside by railings with entrance-gates, *torana*. Later on such stupas were also erected both at places where according to tradition Buddha was supposed to have preached, as well as on top of the ashes of Buddhist saints.

In the course of time the hemisphere evolved into a bell shape, in which we can perhaps see an upturned begging-bowl such as is carried by Buddhist monks. And this shape is also to be found in Java.

No doubt many smaller stupas were erected in this island. In many places we still can see ruins, for example in southern Kediri, in eastern Java; but only the base remains. The most magnificent example of stūpa architecture has been preserved in an edifice, the Borobudur, undoubtedly one of the most imposing creations of mankind.

PLATE P. 90

In Borobudur the main stūpa which crowns the whole structure forms the centre and climax of a grandiose conception of Mahāyāna Buddhism. This monument, incidentally, does not contain a space, but is built around a natural mound of earth.

Monasteries and hermitages

Monasteries must undoubtedly have existed, but since they were wooden buildings, only very few have remained. They are only mentioned here because of their significance in the religious life of the past. Hermitages have also disappeared, since the building materials used were impermanent. But as some hermits lived in caves and grottoes and covered their walls with reliefs, we can draw conclusions regarding their spiritual life. In Java there are two such grottoes, both in the east of the country. In one of them, near the village of Tulung Agung, scenes from Ardjuna's life, Ardjunavivāha, are to be found. There is a kāla head over the entrance to this grotto similar to those found over the doors in the tjandis.

Bathing-places

On Bali, where Hinduism survived, there are many bathing-places to be found. Since this island was strongly influenced by the Hindu-

Javanese culture of the eastern Javanese period, it can be concluded that many such bathing-places existed in Java, too — a surmise which is confirmed by the few, but nevertheless instructive, ruins that still exist. These baths are above all significant in that they were erected at the burial of a prince.

Thus on the northern slope of Mount Penanggungan we find a sepulchral bathing-place, in which the ashes of King Airlangga were interred beneath the actual basin. In two adjacent recesses there stand next to one another figures of Shri and Lakshmi, the two incarnations of Vishnu's *shākti*. A statue of the king himself originally stood above the two female figures. Behind the tjandi of Panataran in eastern Java there is a bathing-place with reliefs, connected with the *tantri* tales, Indian fables in the form of kidungs.

Tjandi Singhasāri, uncompleted. Approx. 1280.

The word *tjandi* means a sepulchral monument. For a long time this popular name was considered inappropriate. But subsequent research has shown that the majority of buildings are more accurately designated in this way than by the word 'temple'.

Originally the role of Indian culture was probably somewhat exaggerated, and from certain stylistic resemblances is was concluded that these monuments served the same purpose as those in India, with its more ancient culture. In other words: on the basis of a certain affinity of architectural style it was assumed that the buildings fulfilled the same function, overlooking the fact that in every religion the appeal to the emotions is greatly influenced by the national characteristics of the population adhering to it. And the 'motivation' of these monuments is closely connected with religious experience.

An additional factor is that Hindu and Buddhist dogma was not interpreted in a particularly strict fashion in Java. In their religious experience the people there found mystical meditation more to their liking, and more convenient, than adherence to dogmatic principles. For this reason there occurred in Java within a short space of time an unmistakable fusion, a syncretism, of systems. It was inevitable that indigenous religious conceptions and memories which had temporarily faded when confronted by the splendour of the impressive new system of doctrine should come back into their own and merge with Hinduism and Buddhism. Much of the primitive religious outlook survived to influence the princes in their way of thinking and acting even when the strong direct Indian influence abated. But to the population at large, familiar with belief in ancestor worship, the erection of monuments must have seemed something self-evident. A deceased prince was regarded as an ancestor in the most reverent sense of the word. Whether he was a Buddhist, Shivaist, or Vishnuist did not really matter to them. The people were familiar with death rites and funeral sacrifices; and when the priests performed some complex unintelligible ceremony, it was accepted as a matter of course, as something well becoming a prince, as a particularly illustrious ancestor of the people. Also the images of deities and demons to be found on the monuments were incorporated in this way into the popular ideology. Like the gods themselves, a deceased prince was deemed to have his relatives, servants, wealth and celestial power in the next world. And so in these temple sculptures the deceased was represented as provided with everything to which he was entitled.

Also in the court circles of the kratons ancestor worship was an important stimulus to the erection of tjandis. This is demonstrated by the changes made in the course of centuries in the form of the images and decorations. Borobudur, incidentally, should not be regarded as as tjandi; it symbolizes rather the totality of the cosmos according to the doctine of Mahāyāna Buddhism.

Several important differences apart, the tjandis of the central Javanese period more or less constitute a group, at least when they are compared with monuments of the east Javanese period. There are both Buddhist and Shivaist monuments; the Shivaist tjandis in particular were apparently connected with the ancestor cult from their very origin, for the ashes of a deceased prince were interred in these monuments, generally in the shaft of a well in the centre of the base. This determines the essential 'motivation' of the monument. The ashes of a deceased ancestor must have been regarded as a 'magic centre of power'; it is here that the authority of the living prince continued to be exerted. "Like the skulls venerated in earlier days, the ancestor was considered as providing the essence of princely power; the mausoleum in which ancestors were buried became a place radiating power, now guarded and cherished in a new way by the priests." [1] Thus a tjandi becomes the outward symbol of the relationship deemed to exist between the living and the dead.

In eastern Java, too, the external form of the tjandis was continually modified, and characteristic Javanese conceptions concerning the form and hierarchical arrangement of the individual parts came to the fore. Thus images of deities such as were to be found in the central Javanese tjandis were ousted by images of princes exalted to the rank of gods. But this can be regarded as an attempt — a successful one, incidentally — to attain a synthesis of ancestor cult and Hinduism: the prince becomes an incarnation of the divinity.

Synthesis of ancestor cult and Hinduism

The temple proper is moved from its central position in the base further towards the rear. The strictly geometrical arrangement of the various tjandis in a temple complex, as found in central Java, disappears. Without any regard for symmetry, monuments of very different types, such as tjandis, assembly halls, places for ritual sacrifices, etc., are erected together, all in the adaptable manner found elsewhere in Indonesia in ancient places of religious worship.

The style of the bas-reliefs is no longer Indian in character, but evolves into one akin to that of the indigenous wayang plays.

A change is also apparent in the way in which the bas-reliefs are worked. Bas-reliefs of the central Javanese period are hollowed out deeper;

So-called 'date of the year temple' (*shaka* 1291 = 1369 **A.D.**) of the Panataran complex. A fine example of eastern Javanese *tjandi* architecture.

those of the east Javanese tjandis, on the other hand, are much shallower. Whereas the sculptural decorations of the tjandis in central PLATES PP. 3, 84 Java are completely subordinate to the conception of the building as a whole, these now become more and more works of art in their own right. Thus decoration and ornamentation become more lavish, but at the same time less closely connected in their inner significance with the building as a whole.

The eastern Javanese tjandis are generally more slender, as the temple roof is constructed rather in the shape of a pyramid. Also wooden roof structures existed.

With free-standing statues a very similar development may be observed. When statues were erected on tombs in eastern Java, they followed the traditional style of representing the dead. The typical statues on the Indian model are superseded by a style which conforms to that of the ancestor images of the pre-Hindu era.

There has been a tendency to interpret eastern Javanese art as in decline, i.e. to confuse it with the art of central Java. In my opinion this disparagement is unjustified. We are dealing here in eastern Java with pre-Hindu conceptions which determine the 'why' of the work, subordinating it to the 'wherefore'.

The modifications made in the images of deities during the course of the Hindu-Javanese period display this process clearly. Three main tendencies may be discerned:

1. In the central Javanese period sculpture displays the style, introduced from India, which is characteristic of so-called Gupta art. The latter flourished in India in the fifth and sixth centuries A.D., which can probably be called the classical era of Indian art.

2. In the eastern Javanese period the images of deities become representations of a deified prince, usually as an incarnation of Vishnu.

3. At the end of the eastern Javanese era the style again evolves in a different direction, preference being given to the frontal-type statue, with a more or less archaic effect.

If one concentrates upon the change of external form, one may of course easily be led to the erroneous conclusion that in this case we are dealing with a degeneration of plastic art in the central Javanese era. But this question cannot be treated as simply as all that. In examining the visible change of form it must be borne in mind that we are dealing here with religious art, the essence of which can only be understood in conjunction with the culture in which it exercised its definite function. In this light the problem we are confronted with can be outlined clearly. For in Java it is not a question of one single uniform culture, but only of two interacting cultural movements. The most important of these is the ancient indigenous culture of the Javanese people, a peasant culture, which has spiritually much in common with the neolithic from which it sprang. Ancestor worship, a *Weltanschauung* based on myths, strong close communal bonds, and an almost unshakable traditionalism, — all these are characteristic features of this indigenous culture. Into this culture came an influx of new ideas from India. Indian civilization already had a centuries-old history behind it, and reached Indonesia as something firmly established and alien. But the bearers of this culture exercised no influence whatsoever upon the masses of the population. Only the kratons were open to the manifold attractions and values the new civilization had to offer. It was here that writing developed, as well as a literature stimulated by Indian masterpieces; it was here, in the powerful and wealthy kratons, that the material basis existed on which architecture could develop.

In the earliest centuries of the Hindu-Javanese period, when the direct contact with India was vigorous, kraton art was predominantly modelled on Indian prototypes. But already in this very early period there are examples of the influence of the ancient indigenous culture: thus in many cases, as a consequence of ancestor worship, temples became sepulchral monuments.

In the eastern Javanese period the direct connection with India lost some of its importance, and the works of art which now appeared were to an ever increasing extent determined by ancient Javanese culture. It is surely not accidental that Ken Angrok, the founder of the kingdom of Singhasari, was a child of his people, born of parents of humble rank (1222 A.D.). Tjandis and images of deities now change their external form and again approach traditional Javanese conceptions.

On the Dieng plateau, to the south-west of present-day Semarang, there are several tjandis, amongst the most ancient in Java, presumably erected in the eighth or ninth centuries A.D. It is not improbable that some of them at least were erected during the dynasty preceding that of the Shailéndras; this is also indicated by the fact that these tjandis are all Shivaist.

MOST IMPORTANT MONUMENTS IN JAVA

They are not large monuments: on the average they are not more than about 50 feet high. As far as any general impression can be formed from the ruins, these monuments were fairly compact, with sparse ornamentation. The *kālamakāra* motif is to be found over the entrance-gate and sometimes over the recesses in the temple itself.

On one of these sites (Tjandi Bima) there are also recesses on the top of the temple with sculptured heads of human beings in them.

Because of its many sulphur springs the Dieng plateau is not a particularly attractive district, and it is therefore at first sight striking that there should be so many tjandis there. But an area where the mysterious forces of nature manifested themselves in such a remarkable way was probably regarded as particularly appropriate for seeking to establish contact with one's ancestors.

Tjandi Kalasan   Kalasan is the oldest tjandi to which a date can be set, namely 778 A.D. This monument is situated south of the volcano Merapi on the left bank of the river Opak, and was erected by the first prince of the Shai-

MAP P. 97   léndra dynasty; it is therefore Buddhist. It was dedicated to the Buddhist goddess Tara, and was apparently designed as a sepulchre for the prince's consort. The *kālamakāra* motif is to be found both above the entrance as well as above the recesses, and its ornamentation is magnificent.

In the interior there must have stood large bronze statues, amongst them a huge one of the goddess. But they are no longer extant, having disappeared along with so many other treasures of the Hindu-Javanese era when the Madjapahit kingdom collapsed and Java became the battleground in a violent struggle for hegemony.

Tjandi Sewu   Tjandi Sewu, a Buddhist shrine to the north-east of Kalasan, situated on the right bank of the river Opak, is also largely in ruins. Originally this complex consisted of a central temple surrounded by two double series of side chapels, 250 in all. In this central temple, too, there must have been a bronze Buddha about thirteen feet high. In each of the side chapels a deity was represented, or at least suggested. The whole construction, symbolizing the cosmos, *mandala*, was intended to assist the hermit in his meditations.

Borobudur   Borobudur, the most impressive monument which remains from the time of the Shailéndra dynasty, is not a tjandi, but a natural mound of earth enclosed within a building. It is a portrait in stone of the Ma-

PLATE P. 90   hāyāna Buddhist cosmic system. The structure rests upon a stone foundation, two layers, square in plan with regular redan-shaped projections making 36 corners in all. First of all there are four galleries in ascending order, each gallery receding proportionately farther than the one below, on the same plan as the base. On the top gallery there is a flat surface, upon which are three more terraces, piled concentrically one upon the other. The highest point, and at the same time the symbolical centre of the edifice, is formed by a large closed-in main stūpa. In the middle of each side a stairway leads upwards, ending with a door to each gallery. Above these doors and the recesses (to be discussed below) the kālamakāra ornament is again to be found.

The inside walls of the four galleries are embellished with bas-reliefs in stone, of a total length of over one kilometre. Above these bas-reliefs niches have been hollowed out at regular intervals.

PLATE P. 3

On the three circular terraces there are open stūpas, viz. 32 on the first terrace, 24 on the second, and 16 on the third. This part of the terraces is devoid of sculptural decoration. The base of the whole monument is likewise furnished with bas-reliefs. These are no longer visible, since when the building was restored (1907—11) a broad protective wall had to be built against the base.

The plan of the entire monument, as of the bas-reliefs, sculptures and stūpas, has a symbolic meaning. The gradation from base to main stūpa represents the individual stages towards perfection, and also the celestial spheres.

The bas-reliefs at the foot depict everyday events and the punishments of hell; they thus refer to the stage of development when man is still bound — bound to his desires. The bas-reliefs of the four galleries represent, successively, the most important incidents in the life of Buddha (First Gallery) and in the lives of the various Bodhisattvas (the following galleries). This is thus a representation of the successive phases through which spiritual enlightenment can be attained.

The circular terraces with the stūpas symbolize salvation attained: man is no longer doomed to re-birth. In the niches above the four galleries there are statues of *dhyani* Buddhas, each pointing in the direction of a different point of the compass with a certain symbolical gesture, *mudrā*.

In the open stūpas on the terraces there are likewise statues of *dhyani* Buddhas, and in the main stupa an uncompleted statue of Buddha himself.

This entire colossal monument served the purpose of veneration, worship and meditation; in the perambulation gallery for meditation, the worshipper always had bas-reliefs on his right-hand side. During the course of centuries Borobudur fell into a state of almost complete ruin, but in 1907—11 it was restored by the distinguised archaeologist and architect Dr. T. v. Erp, and thus the world once again obtained a monument which, next to the Hindu temple Angkor Vat in Cambodia, built in the 12th century, represents the most imposing and beautiful achievement of architecture and sculpture inspired by Hinduism and Buddhism.

Tjandi Mendut   To the Borobudur complex most probably belong two tjandis, which are naturally both Buddhist: the smaller Pawon and the larger Mendut. These two edifices are situated exactly on the West-East axis, and have been restored so far as it was possible to do so.

Tjandi Mendut is particularly valuable, as the sculptures in the temple interior have been preserved. They are of stone, and the most important of them represents Buddha, seated and relaxed. His feet rest upon a stylized lotus flower, symbolic of his divine sublimity. He holds his hand with the gesture of a preacher (*mudrā: dharmachākra*). The back support is flanked by an elephant, a lion, and the *makāra*. To the left and right of this main statue are two statues of Bodhisattvas.

The inner part of the temple is filled with a quite unique serenity and tranquillity, and it is thus understandable that the Javanese, so susceptible to everything mystic, still render sacrifice of flowers and incense here.

Mendut must be regarded as a genuine Buddhist 'temple', not as a sepulchral monument.

Prambanan   To the south of Tjandi Sewu there stands the great complex of Prambanan. The central tjandi, the Lara Djonggrang, is supposed to have been erected by King Daksha, of the Shivaist dynasty of Mataram, in about 915.

The most important part is a square terrace, raised above the surrounding parts and enclosed by a wall. Upon it eight tjandis tower up in hierarchical order. Lara Djonggrang, the largest and most important tjandi, is dedicated to Shiva. South of it (to the left, from the viewpoint of the observer standing in front of it) lies the tjandi of Brahma, and north of it that of Vishnu. Opposite are the tjandis of the mounts of the three gods of the *trimurti*. This whole group is flanked by two smaller tjandis, which perhaps served as treasuries. The main terrace is surrounded by a lower one, also square, with very many smaller tjandis; these are set around the central part of the whole complex in two double series rising towards the centre. Until recently this monument was a pitiful ruin. Even in the last century stones from it were taken for use in paving roads and building sugar works. In the twentieth century restoration work was begun, but, as may easily be imagined, it met with great difficulties. A considerable

PLATE P. 93   part could not be rebuilt, but Lara Djonggrang, restored according

Statue of Buddha, bronze (*à-cire-perdue* process). Gesture, *mudrā,* of a reciter of doctrine. Mudra: *witarka.*
The style is characteristic of the central Javanese era (8th and 9th centuries A.D.) *Collection of Prof.
S. Eilenberg.* (Height 7½ ins.)

to the original plan, now again rises its full height of approximately 130 feet.

PLATE P. 95 At the base, with its twenty corners and lavish decorations (including the so-called Prambanan motif, a frontal-type lion flanked by celestial trees), four broad stairways lead up to the perambulation gallery around the temple proper. These stairways are situated in the centre of the four sides, which face the four points of the compass; they have arched balustrades with *makāra* heads at the foot. Each stairway ends, slightly higher than the perambulation gallery, in a gateway, the superstructure of which forms another tjandi. From that point a stone path leads on to the four cellas of the temple, whilst smaller flights of steps ascend to right and left up to the gallery.

The stairway on the east side leads to the actual centre of the tjandi, i.e. a cella situated in the centre of the temple, in which stands a statue of Shiva incarnate as Mahā-Déva, the Supreme God. To the left and right, beside the eastern entrance-gates, are figures of Mahā-Kāla and Nandisvāra, both other incarnations of Shiva.

The stairway on the south side leads to one of the smaller cellas of the temple, in which stands a statue of Shiva incarnate as Mahā-Guru, the supreme teacher. In a similar cella on the west side we find a statue of Ganesha, the God of Wisdom, son of Shiva and his consort Durga; a statue of the latter is to be found in the northern cella.

The gallery is enclosed along its outer perimeter by a wall upon which countless stupas rise up, perhaps denoting a trace of Buddhism in this Shivaist monument. On the inner side of this wall there are 42 bas-reliefs representing part of the Rāmāyana: from the beginning to the march across the bridge to Ceylon, the land of the demon Ravāna. In order to follow the unfolding of the tale, one must ascend the east stairway, descend again to the left after the gallery, and then walk around the temple proper.

All the gate arches and entrances abound in ornamentation, with the kala head in the centre. Kālamakāra ornaments are also to be found on the gargoyles on the corners of the tjandi.

With the whole monument being constructed on such a hierarchical pattern, one would assume that the central temple would be situated at the point of intersection of the diagonals of the central temple court. This is, however, not the case. On the contrary, the point of inter-PLAN P. 113 section lies exactly in the left-hand corner, which is formed by the eastern approach stairway and the base. This asymmetry would seem illogical, except on the assumption that the actual centre of the whole structure is not formed by the large statue of Shiva, but by something far more important, but something which is of course not directly apparent from the exterior of the buildings. And this is indeed the case. When the restoration work was in progress a bronze urn filled with ashes was discovered at the precise spot where the diagonals intersect. This was evidently the real centre of the whole edifice, and it is in this subtle way that the builder indicated its real character: a sepulchral monument for a prince enrolled amongst the gods, whose ashes have been interred here.

Brahmā tjandi, situated south of the central temple, has likewise a base with twenty corners, but is smaller and has only a single cella; the continuation of the tale of Rama is represented in 30 bas-reliefs. Also in this case these reliefs are placed along the inner side of the wall of the gallery. This tjandi has been badly damaged, as has been the Vishnu tjandi north of Lara Djonggrang. In its structure this tjandi corresponds to the Brahmā tjandi, but part of the bas-reliefs on this tjandi have been lost.

In the shrine of the small square tjandi opposite the main eastern entrance to the temple of Shiva, there lies, upon a stone pedestal, almost undamaged, Shiva's bull, *nandi*. It is the only free-standing stone sculpture of an animal in Indonesia, and in its austerity an example of the way in which a great work of art could be created by artists content to employ a naturalistic style on the simplest base-lines. On the PLATE P. 99 rear wall of the tjandi are images of two primitive Hindu deities, Surya, the Sun God, and Chandra, the Moon God.

The two similar tjandis opposite the Brahmā and Vishnu tjandis, in

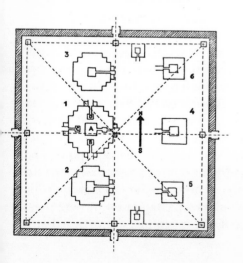

Prambanan complex. Plan of central temple area.

1. Lara Djonggrang.
   A. Central cella with statue: Shiva as Mahā-Déva.
   B. Cella with statue: Shiva as Mahā-Guru.
   C. Cella with statue: Ganesha.
   D. Cella with statue: Durga.
2. Brahmā tjandi.
3. Vishnu tjandi.
4, 5, 6. Tjandis of mythical mounts of Gods of the Trimurti.

On 4: statue of Shiva's *nandi*.

addition to the side-chapels and the eight very small tjandis on the border of the central terrace, have partly been badly damaged, and partly are of little importance.

A great deal of the whole temple complex has been lost. But the restoration work has been undertaken with infinite patience and the greatest expertise by the archaeologists and their colleagues, and thus we can once again enjoy this most impressive testimony to the superb artistry and talented craftsmanship of the ancient architects and sculptors.

Already shortly after the erection of Prambanan the princes of Mataram withdrew to eastern Java. This marked the end of central Javanese art. Few tjandis have been preserved from the subsequent three centuries from 927 to the rise of the dynasty of Singhasāri in 1222. Perhaps this almost total absence of tjandis is due to the fact that only bricks of inferior quality were used.

The 'temples' built later diverge considerably in many ways from those in central Java.

Tjandi Kidal   The tjandi Kidal in the vicinity of present-day Malang in eastern Java is another sepulchral monument, erected for the second prince of the Singhasāri dynasty, King Anusapati, who died in 1240. The general effect of the building is more slender, since the base towers up high, and the temple tapers off at the top in the form of a pyramid. Over the door to the shrine there is a comparatively very large and particularly beautifully worked kāla head, supporting, so to speak, the crowning of the temple. Kāla heads of the same kind are also found over the recesses. Ornamentation is exceedingly lavish, applied without thought for the effect upon the building as a whole. On the almost cubic terminal stones over the recesses there is to be found the very ancient tumpal motif to which we have already referred.

Tjandi Djago   The tjandi Djago, built in 1268 and also situated in the vicinity of Malang, manifests even more clearly the characteristics of eastern Javanese style and ornamental decoration. There the temple proper is displaced to the rear, and the very high base is brought into prominence. Thus the impression given is completely different from the last tjandi mentioned. The bas-reliefs are both Buddhistic and Shivaistic PLATE P. 84   inspired; in style they are akin to that of the wayang. Furthermore flames and rays of light are intended to suggest the magic powers possessed by certain men, undoubtedly influenced by tantrism (cf. chapter on Buddhism). Equally worthy of note are the *panakawan*, which FIG. P. 131   play a special part in the wayang plays (cf. chapter on wayang plays), and originate from Java. The roof of the temple, the so-called *meru* roof, bears a turreted structure, towering up to a great height, consisting of an uneven number of roofs, each receding further than the one below. Towers of this kind were built of wood.

Tjandi Djago was erected as a burial place for the ashes of Vishnuvardhana, the father of Kertanagara, the most important prince of the Singhasāri dynasty. The deceased prince was represented as a Bodhisattva.

As the last monument of the Singhasāri period, the tjandi may be mentioned which bears the name of the dynasty itself. The tjandi Singhasāri is so remarkable because ornamentation can be seen *in statu nascendi,* so to speak. The working of the details apparently took place from the top downwards. *Tjandi Singhasāri*

PLATE P. 102

A considerable number of tjandis have been preserved from the Madjapahit era, several of which have been restored, although the majority of them are in ruins.

The largest and undoubtedly most important monument of the eastern Javanese period is the temple complex of Panataran. Although work on this edifice must have begun already during the rule of the Singhasāri dynasty, the most important parts were, however, erected at the time of the Madjapahit kingdom. *Panataran*

With Panataran there is no question of a geometrical arrangement of the individual buildings, as was the case with the Prambanan complex. Three temple courts, originally divided from one another by the temple walls, are situated one behind the other. Gateways permitted entrance into the temple courts. As far as can be ascertained from the walls of the foundations, which are all that are left, in the first court there were two buildings, which served as a place of assembly. The buildings themselves were of wood, and have not survived. The vertical external walls of one terrace are completely covered with bas-reliefs relating the tales of the kidungs.

In this court there is also a small tjandi dating from the Shaka year 1291, or 1369 according to our calendar. Carefully restored, it is a fine example of eastern Javanese tjandi architecture. Its general appearance, the kāla heads, and the tumpal motif — in this case on the terminal stone of the crowning of the temple — bear a strong resemblance to tjandi Kidal. PLATE P. 106

In the second court there is a small temple, quite unique in point of sculptural decoration. The wooden superstructure is no more; only the base and the shell of the temple still stand. On the upper edge of the latter a colossal snake, *nāga,* is coiled round, borne by priestly

Prince's golden ornament, worn on head or chest. Three sun-wheels constitute the chief motif. At the top is a *kāla* head (mythical figure); the sides are formed by two snakes, *nāgas*. The foliage has probably been added later. (Madjapahit dynasty, eastern Java). *K.I.T.* (2½ × 5¼ ins.)

figures. The kāla head above the door is missing. On the front of the two flights of steps tumpal motifs are once again to be found.

In the third court stands the main tjandi. It, too, once had a *meru* roof, but of impermanent material. The base and the shell of the temple are lavishly decorated with bas-reliefs, which represent, *inter alia*, the tale of Rama, and again conform to the wayang style.

There is much about this structure which resembles the temples on Bali. There, too, one comes across courts situated one behind the other, the asymmetrical arrangement of the various buildings, the place of assembly in the first court, the *meru* roofs, and the temple walls and gates.

Among numerous other tjandis of the eastern Javanese period several deserve closer examination, though apart from the base little of them has survived. But even so the bas-reliefs still testify to the artistry and craftsmanship of their architects, who found in literature a boundless store of inspiration in their representation of religious themes. Thus the bas-reliefs on the Surawana tjandi (ruin, 14th century) near Pare (Kediri) have borrowed their subject-matter from the Ardjunavivāha. Stylistically these bas-reliefs conform most exactly to the wayang style.

PLATE P. 84

STATUES AND OTHER SCULPTURE

In the previous section we already mentioned statues which formed part of various monuments. They were mostly hewn from stone. Undoubtedly there must also have existed several large bronze statues, but these were mostly re-cast later and the metal used again for other purposes. Reference has also been made to the fact that the figures in the tjandis of eastern Java served a different purpose from those in central Java. The former were intended to assist in meditation; the latter, on the other hand, represented incarnate as a deity the prince whose ashes were interred there. These incarnations are mostly of Vishnu, as shown by the accompanying attributes: shell, flashing wheel, and celestial eagle, *garuda*, as a mount. Only once does the prince appear as an incarnation of Shiva riding upon a bull, *nandi*, whilst the four-armed Shiva carries in his rear hands a rosary and a fan. This custom of giving Hindu deities more than one pair of arms developed in India already at a very early stage. For these symbolical representations we are chiefly indebted to sculptors of the Mathura school. Mathura is situated in the centre of northern India, on the important river Jumna, and the distinguished school for sculptors, which flourished there after the second century B.C., had a strong influence upon sculpture for seven and a half centuries.

Influence of Mathura school

117

Princesses were usually represented as Parvati, the wife (*shākti*) of Shiva; also this goddess carries the rosary and the fan.

Amongst the statues one very frequently finds Ganesha, the Elephant God, son of Shiva and Durga; consequently he was particularly venerated. In Shivaist tjandis his image is always placed on the rear wall of the temple. If the main entrance is on the east side, then the figure stands in a recess on the west side.

Images of Ganesha are also to be found in places other than tjandis, mostly where danger threatens. They were probably intended to protect people from certain dangers, and thus the veneration of these figures was of a characteristically magic quality.

The so-called Raksaka figures — giants, usually armed with clubs — must also be interpreted symbolically. They were generally erected on either side of the entrance-gates to a temple complex.

Besides these large sculptures numerous small bronze figures have also been found, all of them no more than four to six inches high. From these small figures we can form an idea of the perfection to which the artists of the Hindu-Javanese era mastered the art of bronze casting. Undoubtedly works were produced here that were amongst the finest ever to have been made anywhere.

PLATE P. 111 These bronze figures presumably served monks and hermits as images for meditation. For this reason they are probably also mainly figures taken from the Buddhist pantheon; for only Buddhism had monastic orders. For some reason the style of these figures remained free of the influence of ancient Javanese conceptions. It was of course a simple matter for the Buddhist tradition to be preserved in pure form in the monastic orders.

These small figures, too, were produced by the *à-cire-perdue* process described earlier; the figure was moulded from wax over a core of clay, and then carefully covered over with a layer of clay in which the necessary funnels were left open.

Yet one wonders whether such a simple process could really suffice to produce such fine bronze statuettes, often elaborately worked down to the minutest detail, and often also bearing various decorations. If the small figures were not to suffer too much damage, the number of funnels had to be limited. For at the mouth of such a funnel no details are possible. Moreover, the whole mould was often so small that, when the cast was poured on, the hot air could not escape, or could do so only in insufficient quantities. The mould would then crack, or — particularly in the finer parts — the air remained inside and thus the cast could not penetrate. It is as good as certain that a supplementary process was evolved similar to that in use in another district where the art of bronze casting was highly developed, namely in Benin, on the lower reaches of the Niger in West Africa. There the outer layer of clay was mixed with finely chopped goats' hair; after heat was applied these hairs became charred, and microscopically small channels remained in the clay, through which the air escaped when the cast was poured in. Only in this way was it possible to reproduce exactly in bronze the small figure modelled in wax.

Various objects used for religious purposes were also naturally cast in bronze, such as censers for incense, lamps, bells, sacrificial dishes, vessels for holy water, and so on. Often these bronze objects are decorated, especially by engraving, with all manner of figurative representations. Some of these objects are real masterpieces of metalworking.

Figures of silver and gold have also been preserved, although very many objects made of these costly metals must have been melted down again in later centuries. The high level of artistry attained in gold and silver casting is shown by the many pieces of jewellery and ornaments excavated: necklaces, bracelets, ear- and finger-rings, chains and groin-shields all testify to consummate workmanship and a highly-developed sense of beauty. The ornamental decorations are generally embossed.

PLATE P. 116

Finally, mention must be made of some works of art of a special kind: terracottas. This art reached its climax towards the end of the Hindu-Javanese era. The material is of course extremely delicate, and since most of the objects discovered have been buried in the soil for centuries, little that we have is undamaged. But even these few objects testify to the fact that this was an art of particular charm and great beauty. It is quite possible that these terracottas ought to be considered together with the bronze figures. Moulding in wax and clay are too closely related for these two methods not to have influenced one another. But here we are faced with a completely different problem. The small terracotta heads found are not at all Javanese in style, but exhibit so many Greek characteristics that one may presume that the influence of Greece was felt in Java during the Madjapahit dynasty. But we cannot as yet say with certainty how such influences came about.

PLATE P. 121

Nowhere in the world has an art been fostered which was so closely interwoven with the life of a whole nation for so long as is the case

WAYANG
PUPPET-SHOWS

119

with the Javanese wayang puppet-shows, *wayang kulit (wayang* =
shadow, ghost; *kulit* = leather), performed with flat leather puppets.
Although the origin of this type of wayang show is still a matter of
dispute, it is certain that is was already both popular and generally
known by the year 1000 A.D. In subsequent centuries the culture
introduced from India exerted a strong influence upon it. It survived
the collapse of the Madjapahit kingdom, held its own when Islam
became the predominant religion, and has remained popular up to
the present day.

The Javanese must have been fascinated by these puppet performances, in which the puppets themselves and their shadows each had a
role to play. The wayang show must have satisfied a deep emotional
need, providing the Javanese with a stimulus to, and a medium for,
mystical meditation. For him the wayang-kulit is not just a show; but
represents an abstract world in which ideas become figures and imagination becomes reality. The performance is actually a mystical
event in which the invisible becomes visible, and something that cannot be adequately expressed in words becomes comprehensible. Despite all the changes that took place in religion and culture during
the course of several centuries, the wayang was able to maintain itself
as a unique medium for conveying the eternal, a medium through
which the interplay between man and the metaphysical world could
be expressed.

This has been put most impressively in the following poem written
in the 1920s by the Javanese poet Noto Suroto, in which he considers
the wayang show against the background of religious thought:

Wayang

O Lord, let me be a wayang in Thy hands.

Whether I be hero or demon, king or commoner, animal, plant or
tree, let me be still a wayang in Thy hands. Then shall I speak
your tongue, whether I be valiant in the turmoil of battle or small
as a child at play amongst the waringins.

This life of mine on earth is filled with toil and strife, and my
enemies, who are many, mock me. Their ridicule flies to its target
swifter than plumed arrows; their words strike deeper than krisses.

My struggle is not yet at an end. And soon Thou wilst take me, and
I shall lie amongst the others whose plays are over. I shall be
amongst the thousands in darkness. And my struggle was not yet
at an end: still my enemies dance.

Small head, terracotta (Madjapahit, eastern Java). *Collection of the author.* (Height 1½ ins.)

Lord, let me be a wayang in Thy hands.
Then after a hundred or a thousand years Thy hand will bestow
upon me life and movement once more.
    Then, one day when my time has come for Thy eternity, Thou
wilst call me to Thee again, and I shall speak and contend anew.
And one day my enemies will be silenced, and the demon will lie
prostrate on the ground.
O Lord, let me be a wayang in Thy hands.

(From *Wayang liederen*).

Without going any further into the various theories about the evolution of the wayang show, we may take it as certain that it had a
religious significance from the very first. The puppets, and undoubtedly also the moving silhouettes, suggested ancestors; the interpreter
of this mysterious event was regarded as the priest who established
contact between the living and the dead. Thus this show acquired an
important place in the entire magic ceremonial. The wayang-kulit
has always retained its magic character; thus up to the present day it
has been performed, for example, in order to avert some threatening
calamity.

Technical The technical apparatus employed is basically simple: a transparent
apparatus white canvas is stretched out on a vertical wooden frame. The puppets
are moved by the performer, the *dalang*. Over the dalang hangs a
lamp, the light from which falls upon the tautly-stretched canvas, thus
throwing the shadows plainly into view.

To the left of the dalang stands an oblong chest with its longer side
at right angles to the screen, in which are kept the puppets and other
properties, such as weapons, horses, chariots, etc. From this chest
several small metal or wooden discs are suspended, by means of
which the dalang can imitate noises at appropriate moments. If he
has to use both hands at once to operate the puppets, he moves the
discs with his foot.

To his right the dalang has the lid of the chest, on which he can place
his properties.

The puppets appearing in the performance — and there are usually a
great number of them, since each character is represented by a special
puppet — have a rod made of horn; thus they can be slid into two
pisang stalks (pseudo-stem of the banana), one of which is set slightly
higher than the other and reserved for the most important characters.
Behind the dalang there is room for the orchestra which illustrates

the action with music. The dalang gives the players their cues by tapping on the chest with a small hammer of horn or hardwood.

The dalang is without doubt the most important person in the performance. He not only moves the puppets, but also speaks the various parts, and in between gives descriptions, directions, etc. He has a most varied and exceedingly difficult task. Only some points can be singled out here. *The dalang*

He has to ensure that the wayang performance lasts from half past seven in the evening until six o'clock the next morning. During the performance he must not move from the screen, and is not allowed to say anything apart from the text. He must characterize the figures which appear by modulating his voice to suit each of the *dramatis personae*, and in addition to this must be well acquainted with the form of speech used by the various characters. It goes without saying that he must have a complete command of the action in the play performed, and must know exactly with which puppet one character or another can be represented. That this task is anything but simple is obvious from the fact that in one play alone, that dealing with the Pandāvas and the Kauravas (from the Bhāratayuddha) 37 main characters appear, not counting the constantly changing parts played by these characters in the various situations in which they appear.

From this it is also clear that every dalang must at first undergo arduous training for several years in order to satisfy the demands made upon him.

Although the leather-workers of Indonesia have not much of note to their credit, on Java, Bali and several islands in the east of the Archipelago they did learn how to make good parchment. This is partly transparent and coloured an ivory shade. *Wayang puppets*

In making wayang puppets the material is first cut out in outline; then the stencil is fastened to it with a sharp pin, and the details cut out by means of small chisels of various shapes and sizes; finally the whole figure is coated with white clear-cole, upon which the colours desired are then painted. Gold foil, too, is almost always used. These Javanese wayang puppets are invariably highly stylized, both as regards the reproduction of the human figure — the faces being particularly characteristic in this respect — and the hair-dress, clothes and jewellery. The figures made in this way have, so to speak, become symbols. The colours, too, need not necessarily be natural. The skin is mostly gilded or black, whilst the face may be painted in various colours: gold, white or black, red, light red or pink, reddish-brown or blue.

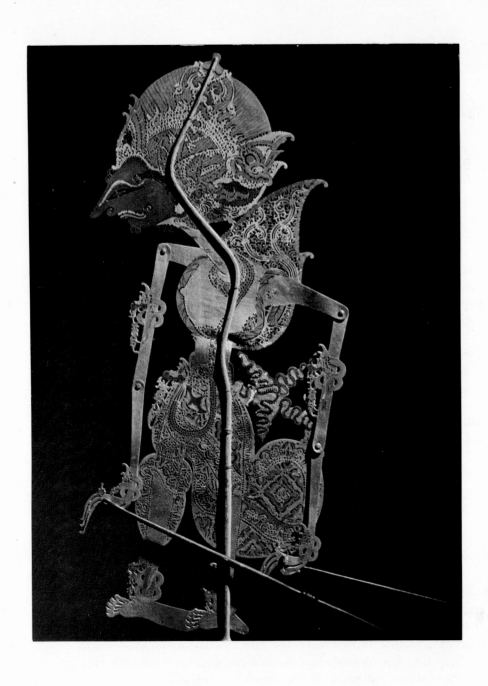

Wayang-purwa figure representing Bupati Karma, Prince of Wangga, half-brother of Ardjuna. (Java). *K.I.T.* (Height of figure 18½ ins.)

The ornamental hair-dress, clothes and jewellery are often especially elaborate, testifying to the Javanese artists' love of carefully-worked detail.

PLATE P. 124

A special feature of the wayang puppets is the conspicuous prolongation of the shoulder line, so that the arms are joined on far beyond the actual shoulder-joints. They are rotatable at the shoulder- and elbow-joints, and the dalang can move them by means of thin rods attached to the hands of the puppets. This resulted in the angular movements, which were regarded as so unique that such arm movements were adopted in Javanese dances.

The face always appears in profile; the body is turned partly to the front, whilst the feet mostly point to *one* side, as with representations in profile.

The legs are held in one of two main postures, either wide apart or close together. The posture with legs held wide apart is to be found with warriors and rough characters, whilst female figures are always shown in the posture with legs close together.

FIG. P. 127

From the above it is sufficiently clear that many modifications are possible in the shape of the head, facial expression, leg posture, and colour of the decorations, and that each figure can be shaped individually; the size, too, can be varied to suggest the character portrayed. As an example one may examine in more detail here the figures of several main characters of the Bhāratayuddha. As already outlined, the Bhāratayuddha is a free version of the heroic struggle between the Pandāvas and Kauravas, as described in the Indian epic poem, the Mahābhārata.

We shall come back to this point later when considering the *lakons*. Of the five Pandāvas, the main characters in this heroic poem, the three elder brothers stand out: the sons of Pandu and Kunti, Judistira, Bima and Ardjuna. Their characters are perceptibly different, and this is also well brought out in the relevant wayang figures.

"Judistira is the most virtuous of the brothers, but his piety does not allow him to achieve great and noble deeds, though he is not inferior to the others in valour. Charity, magnanimity, and meekness are his characteristic qualities. He pursues his course with more deliberation than his brothers, but does not shrink from duping his adversaries by making false statements.

Bima is the valiant knight *sans peur et sans reproche*, a man of a certain rough surliness, who does not fear to speak his mind freely, maintaining his point of view emphatically against all comers, if one of them, in his opinion, is mistaken. Honest and courageous, of firm resolution and staunch character, he is ever ready to stake his life to defend a person or a noble cause.

Loyal and helpful to anyone who treats him well, but relentless towards his enemies, he is a wild bear whose incredible bodily strength alone gives his brothers the advantage over the hundred Kauravas. In the Bhāratayuddha he mocks mercilessly Judistira's scruples and Ardjuna's considerate manner. The club he wields fills his enemies with the utmost terror, but hardly any less fearsome are his nails, which, when wrestling, claw his adversary's body and tear into it, however much resistance they meet with. Where others appear on horseback, riding elephants, or in chariots, he invariably goes on foot. Only PLATE P. 129 once in the whole of the Bhāratayuddha do we see him entering a carriage, and then only after all the others have alighted to seek cover from the guns of the enemy.

Ardjuna is a chivalrous hero and in some respects stands midway between his elder brothers. In the *lakon* he appears as the darling of the fair sex, rather than as their suitor; women thrust their favours upon him without him seeking them. In a whole series of *lakons* many unknown sons and daughters come and see him from unknown districts where he had passed by, and loved in passing." [2]

The noble characters mostly have the same shape of face as Ardjuna (cf. Plate on p. 139): forehead and nose form one straight line; the nose is delicately shaped; the eyes are slit. Demonic types have eyes as round as balls and large, often crudely-shaped noses, set at an angle to the line of the forehead, and a threatening expression. The figure of Ardjuna is an exception: intrinsically he belongs to the noble Pandāvas, but in his external appearance he displays greater affinity with the demons, which explains why we often find him appearing in the guise of a spy.

The style of these wayang figures has changed along certain lines during the course of centuries, and as a result of a fortunate turn of events we can follow the course of these changes. As has already been mentioned in the section on architecture and sculpture, bas-reliefs appeared on the tjandis of eastern Java in a style differing appreciably from those on the temples of central Java. The figures placed there bear a definite resemblance to wayang figures, but have not yet acquired the far-reaching stylization of the later figures. One can find examples of this on the bas-reliefs of tjandi Panataran which depict incidents from the Rāmāyana.

When one remembers that under the rule of Gadjah Mada — and it was at this time that these bas-reliefs were carved—a Javanese colony was founded on Bali, one may assume that these Javanese brought their wayang shows to Bali with them. And thus it is worth noting that the style of the wayang figures still in general use on Bali corresponds exactly to the figures on the bas-reliefs mentioned. The style has therefore evidently not changed to any marked degree on Bali, whilst the figures in Java diverged ever further from the styles that had once been customary. It is by no means excluded that Islam exercised a contributory influence on this process of evolution. Orthodox Mohammedanism does not permit the representation of living beings, and even though this ban was probably not strictly applied, nevertheless there may well have been a certain tendency to diverge from purely naturalistic forms.

Incidentally, the variations in size of individual wayang figures also have a symbolic meaning: thus demons (giants), gods, human beings, and so on, each have a specified size.

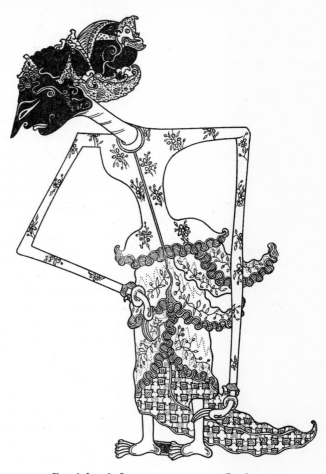

Kunti, female figure, wayang-purwa. (Java).

The screen-like 'mountain' (*gunungan*) or 'tree' (*kekayon*) is a curious stage-property which is found at every wayang-kulit performance. This, too, is made of parchment, worked in the same way as the wayang puppets themselves; the back, however, is coloured red, i.e. is not polychrome.

Before the beginning of the performance, and also during the intervals, the dalang places the gunungan in front of the screen, in the centre. The end of the play, too, is marked by the gunungan, but it is then usually turned back to front, with the back showing, and is stuck into the *pisang* stalk.

The gunungan

127

In its general shape, as well as in several points of detail, the Javanese gunungan differs markedly from that on Bali. The Javanese one is leaf-shaped, and is painted on top. The Balinese one has rather the shape of an umbrella with a gently-curved upper edge. Both of them have a stylized tree in the middle, generally also decorated with flowers, birds, and other ornamentation. All over the world the tree is commonly regarded as a magic or mystic symbol — as the 'tree of heaven', for instance, or the 'tree of life'. This symbol is not only to

PLATE P. 16 be found in this form in Indian literature and sculpture, but the tree of life is often also used, especially on textiles, by several of the Indonesian tribes that remained unaffected by external cultural influences.

PLATE P. 132 The Javanese gunungan has on its lower portion the representation of a gateway, the roof of which is flanked by stylized wing motifs. To its left and right there are often the so-called temple guards, giants (*butas*), figures designed to instil fear, armed with clubs to ward off demonic influences. This is probably a 'gate of heaven', the entrance to a wonderful garden where the tree of heaven grows.

In a Javanese work, 'Ardjuna Sasra Bau', compiled from ancient manuscripts by M. Ng. Sindusastra in 1829, there is to be found a fragment which unmistakably refers to the picture on the Javanese gunungan. Some sentences from it are given here in a translation by Palmer van de Broek:

> "The great gate was made of gold, shaped like an eagle hovering in the air.
>
> The walls to the left and right of the gate were as wings, the pinions azure with other colours interspersed, partly red and blue, embellished with gold of many hues. Flanking the gate there were two stone sculptures resembling butas. They guarded the side-posts of the gate; they appeared to be throwing clubs into the air, and carried a shield in their left hands, as though about to strike anyone who dared to enter."

PLATE P. 134 There is no such gate on the Balinese gunungan. On these the background is usually formed by snakes (*nāgas*) coiled around one another. Both in Java and on Bali we find, at the foot of the tree above the gate, two animal figures, such as a lion and a bull, set opposite each other.

Lakons The wayang repertoire and its evolution reflect the way in which the Javanese have modified the various external cultural influences which have reached them, and how their primitive ideas repeatedly came to the fore in an art form such as this, which was entirely indigenous.

Wayang-purwa figure: Bima, one of the Pandāvas. (Java). *K.I.T.* (Height of figure 24 ins.)

The most ancient wayang plays may perhaps have portrayed the exploits of heroic ancestors from mythical antiquity.

But as Indian cultural influences gradually became stronger, and as old Javanese adaptations of Indian myths and sagas appeared, these tales had an enduring retroactive effect on the content of the wayang plays. This does not mean that religious worship of ancestors was now displaced. It was rather the case of a gradual approximation than of an actual reception of Indian works in ready-made form. And indeed, it could hardly have been otherwise: the religious and cultural climate in which the Indian works had developed was completely unfamiliar to the people of Java. In the same way Indian names of many gods, goddesses, demi-gods, heroes and demons were undoubtedly only adopted very gradually. And even when this process became more and more widespread, and had a more enduring effect, this did not by any means signify that Indian tales were simply translated without any change being made in their content and spirit. On the contrary, the Javanese transplanted the events described there into their own environment, and the background was supplied by their own traditional pattern of ideas.

Thus in the long run a curious mixture of native and alien elements was brought about. The old sacred myths and the new tales were combined in motley form; deified ancestors were identified with Indian gods and heroes, or were allotted their place in the *lakon* in a new form that was hardly any longer recognizable.

Panakavans

Three figures must now be mentioned which were to be found in every single wayang performance, Semar and his two sons, Petruk and Nalagareng, the so-called Panakavans, (scholars, disciples). They introduce a note of rustic humour, but Semar has been allotted another special role. He is the servant of the hero of the moment, and as such often his counsellor, whose perception turns out to be keener than that of his master in awkward situations. He even thrusts his way forward up to the very seat of the gods; at times he disposes of magic forces, and can encompass the ruin of mighty demons. He also appears sometimes as the incarnation of a deity.

The form of the Panakavans differs considerably from that of the other wayang puppets. Their names, too, have not been borrowed from Indian literature, but are old Javanese. Everything points to the

Fig. p. 131 fact that we have here a survival of the ancient ancestor cult.

It may also be mentioned here that in addition to the term wayang-kulit (*kulit* = leather) the designation wayang-purwa is very frequently used. Probably the word *purwa*, meaning 'first', is derived indirectly from '*parwa*', the name given to the oldest known Javanese literature in prose. 'Wayang-purwa' thus means 'first (oldest) wayang'. Whilst the *lakons* were influenced by old Javanese literature, the wayang shows in turn exercised an influence upon sculpture. It is presumably for this reason that the figures on the bas-reliefs were similar to those of the wayang puppets common at the time — especially since old Javanese literature, the lakons, and the bas-reliefs all portrayed the same persons and events.

After the death of Hayam Wuruk (1389) the decline of the Madja-pahit kingdom set in. Already at that time, but especially after the

Wayang-purwa: group of Panakavans (Java).

Gunungan, wayang-purwa. (Java). *K.I.T.* (Height 2 ft. 5½ ins.)

fall of Madjapahit, when Java gradually became Mohammedanized, and Muslim princes were struggling for hegemony, the connection between poetry and the lakons grew weaker and weaker, until it finally ceased altogether.

As has already been mentioned, a considerable part of the old Javanese literary works has been lost, at least in Java. Moreover, as time went on, the influence of the new religion caused interest in Hindu-Javanese literature to subside. It was only much later that there was a revival of interest in early Javanese poetry, but by this time the lakons had gone a long way towards becoming independent works. So many other local pressures had come into play that a resumption of the old connection between the two was no longer possible.

A few exceptions apart, the lakon texts have not been written down *in toto*. The dalang does indeed have a brief summary of the contents, a sort of outline, upon which he can construct his improvisations, but here again he is not allowed much scope, but is limited in more ways than one by very strictly defined directions. Thus the performance must follow a fixed pattern. The gamelan orchestra (cf. following section) opens the performance with a long introduction, after which the dalang describes the kraton in which the action takes place and the *dramatis personae*. Then at nine o'clock in the evening commences the performance proper, which falls into three parts: the first part, the introduction, lasts from nine o'clock until midnight; the second part, from midnight until three o'clock, deals with the actual plot, whilst the third, till six o'clock, presents the dénouement, with the triumph of good over evil.

But no one performance is like another, even when the subject-matter is identical.

It would be impossible to give even the barest survey here of the lakons which exist. We shall limit ourselves to dividing them into four main groups, and sketching in outline the contents of each group.

The main groups are: (i) the early history, or introductory history; (ii) the Ardjuna Sasra Bau cycle; (iii) the Rama cycle; (iv) the Pandāva cycle.

In these lakons three groups of characters are presented which are   *Early history*
to be found in all the other lakons: gods, demons (giants), and men. It is the eternal struggle between gods and demons that is here portrayed, a contest in which man himself is able to take sides. Thus the content of this lakon becomes a symbol of the struggle between good

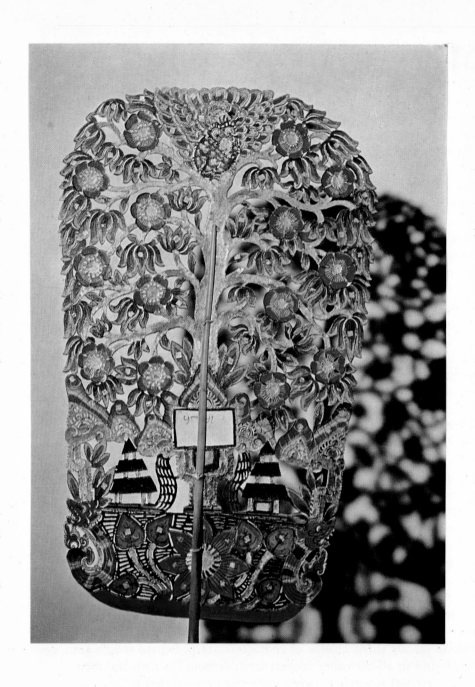

Gunungan, wayang-kulit. (Bali). *K.I.T.* (Height 21 ins.)

and evil, in which man either shares in the victory or goes to his ruin. Curiously enough, the gods in the lakons are often in no position to ward off the demons' attacks. Then it is invariably a man, endowed with extraordinary magic powers and excellent valour, who comes to their assistance, and succeeds in turning the scales in their favour.

Man receives from the gods precious gifts, such as the principal products of the fields, which are of divine origin. It was from the gods, too, that man learnt how to make use of the buffalo for cultivation, and how to practise the armourer's craft.

The threat of evil with which man is confronted is personified in the figure of Batāra Kāla, the consort of Devi Durga. This name shows Shivaist influence, for Durga is the *shakti* of Shiva.

In the centre of this cycle stands the mighty demon Dasamuka. With his marauding expeditions and acts of violence he spreads terror amongst gods as well as men. Then Vishnu decides to intervene. Incarnate as Ardjuna Sasra Bau, he defeats Dasamuka, but does not destroy him completely; for when Dasamuka vows obedience Ardjuna spares his life. After Ardjuna's death — for even a god must die when incarnate in human form — the demon resumes his destructive existence and once again threatens gods and men. *Ardjuna Sasra Bau cycle*

These lakons are the sequel to the foregoing ones. In order to put an end to fresh outbursts of rage on the part of Dasamuka, who now appears under the name of Rawāna, Vishnu returns to earth once again as man, this time in the form of the hero, Rama. The story of the battle between Rama and Rawāna, the contents of which have already been briefly related above, gives an account of the demon's destruction and the rescue of Sita. The lakon tale, on the other hand, ends with Rama's death by fire, Sita and Rama's loyal brother, Lesmana, perishing voluntarily with him in the flames. *Rama cycle*

In this cycle several other lakons have been incorporated, linking it with the Pandāva cycle. Here Rama and his men appear as contemporaries of the heroes of the next main group of lakons. *Pandāva cycle*

In these the centre of emphasis shifts from gods and demons to men. The struggle between good and evil is fought out here by the noble Pandāvas and their nephews, the wicked Kauravas. Gods and giants also play their part in the countless adventures described in these lakons. No other epic has yielded such a wealth of material for the wayang plays as the Mahābhārata cycle, but the setting of these lakons is not ancient India, but here in Java, and it is the Javanese themselves who finally live to experience the triumph of good over evil. According to the sacred prescriptive right, the *adat*, at a wayang performance the men sit next to the dalang, whilst the women sit behind the screen, and thus see the shadows of the figures. This is feasible owing to the primitive design of the Javanese house, which has in front an open vestibule with a low overhanging roof; this is supported by several rows of posts, placed in lavishly decorated stone pedestals. The ceiling is richly adorned in the centre with wood-carvings, as are the main posts. The rear of this open vestibule, *pendapa*, is connected by a covered passage to an open gallery, *pringgitan* (place for the *ringgit*, i.e. wayang puppet).

And it is in this locale that the wayang play is performed. The frame with the canvas stretched out on it is erected in the passage, so that the women are in the living room, which is situated behind it.

On Bali the wayang shows are usually performed in the open air, and the women and men are not so strictly separated from each other; nor is separation laid down by the *adat*.

Several other kinds of wayang shows are known in Java, but none of them play such an important part in the life of the people as wayang-purwa. These developed later, and draw partly or wholly upon other sources for their material. There is one exception: a kind of play in which human performers appear, wayang-wong (*wong* = man); but the epic subject-matter on which it is based is the same as in wayang-purwa. We shall come back to this later in the section on Javanese art after the Hindu-Javanese period.

Wayang-gedog   Wayang-gedog is a variation of the wayang-purwa in which leather puppets are also used. The subject-matter is drawn from the history of the last century of the Hindu-Javanese period under the dynasties of Kediri, Djanggala, Singhasāri and Madjapahit. The origin of the wayang-gedog is connected with Prabu Sadmata, a champion of Islam in Java, who is venerated as a saint under the name of Sunan Giri (cf. section on Islam).

Wayang-krutjil or   In the wayang-krutjil or wayang-klitik flat polychrome wooden pup-
wayang-klitik   pets with movable leather arms are used. Performances are given in the daytime as well as at night. The subject-matter is drawn from the struggles between the kingdoms of Madjapahit and Balambangan in
PLATE P. 137   eastern Java, in which Damar Wulan, a youth of humble origin, wins honour and dignity. This kind of wayang may be seen as a prelude to the wayang-golèk.

In the *wayang-golèk* the puppets used are three-dimensional and are

136

Coloured wayang-klitik figure, wood. (Java). *K.I.T.* (Height 14¼ ins.)

of wood (*golèk* = round). The head is supported by a wooden spindle which runs through the body and is rotatable. The arms, too, can be rotated at the shoulder- and elbow-joints, and can be moved by thin rods attached to the hands. The dalang is exceedingly skilled in operating this rotatable spindle and the two rods, so that the puppet really gives the impression of a living human being.

PLATE P. 139

This play is performed both by day and by night. As in all types of wayang show, the action revolves around certain persons, and is closely connected with the penetration of Islam into Java. Thus a play is performed about one Prince Menak, who by his military campaigns and victories prepares the world, so to speak, for the coming of the prophet Mohammed, and is thus a sort of forerunner, as John the Baptist was for Christ, but in the world of chivalrous romance.

The style of the puppets used in the various kinds of wayang show is more or less closely related to that of the puppets in wayang-purwa. The designer, however, is not so restricted by rigidly prescribed details. The greater freedom in design leads to considerable differences in artistic value, particularly in the case of the wayang-golèk puppets. But the best examples display, often in a surprising way, designs with very human features.

Wayang-bèbèr

In the wayang-bèbèr no puppets are needed at all. Whilst the dalang recites the narrative, some appropriate pictures painted on a long strip of canvas or paper are drawn across from one vertical roll on to another. This play is now no longer performed at all, and is only mentioned here because these paintings are, so to speak, the last 'stragglers' of Hindu-Javanese painting which has otherwise, in so far as it was painted in the style customary at that time, been lost.

1 Prof. Dr. Th. P. Galestin, 'Indonesië', Algemene Kunstgeschiedenis, Pt. VI, Utrecht, 1951.
2 Abridged from J. Kats, 'Het javaanse toneel', 1, Wajang Poerwa.

Wayang-golèk figures: Ardjuna and Prabu Gilling Wesi. (Java). *K.I.T.* (Height of figure of Ardjuna 20½ ins.)

X. CULTURAL PROGRESS DURING THE
ISLAMIC PERIOD TO THE
BEGINNING OF THE 19TH CENTURY

Indonesia is one of the few Mohammedan countries where Islam did not supplant the existing religions by conquest or external force. On the contrary, the new faith came to Indonesia much in the same way as Indian culture had done. The protagonists of Islam originated mainly from the same district, Gujarat in north-western India, with which links had been established centuries before. Islam spread, not by systematic missionary activity, but by personal contacts on an individual basis which were chiefly established in the course of trade. Later, when Islamic kingdoms came into being in Indonesia, in some areas the faith was indeed spread by means of the sword, but here it was political considerations that were the decisive factor.

The most important route along which sea-borne trade was carried between the West and the Indonesian Archipelago was through the straits now known as the Straits of Malacca. Thus it was the princes of the two coastal states in this area, North Sumatra and the Malayan peninsula, who were the first to establish contact with Mohammedan merchants, Muslims from Arabia and India who sailed these waters. From historical data it is clear that economic and political reasons caused these princes to accept the new religion. Hand in hand with this went an intellectual revolution, but not a very profound one. When Islam spread from Madinat an-Nabi in Arabia via the Middle East to Further India, it was already thoroughly imbued with Oriental mysticism and had thus lost much of its original rigid orthodoxy. The Indonesians, so susceptible to mysticism, found many points of spiritual contact with the new religion in the form in which it was introduced by the Gujaratis, once it had undergone this modification in the direction of mysticism. Thus reception of the new religion was appreciably facilitated, but at the same time this allowed alien elements to creep in unobserved.

MAP P. 141 On Sumatra small Islamic states developed, of which Samudra on the north-east coast already exercised appreciable influence by the year 1300. Under the pressure of these small states the kingdom of Malayu, which still adhered to its Indian culture, withdrew to the district of Menangkabau in the interior of central Sumatra. The close contact with Gujarat is evident from the fact that the grave-stone on the tomb of the founder of the kingdom of Samudra came from Cambay, the capital of Gujarat. In the latter half of the 14th century the Mohammedan principality of Pasei, also situated on the north-eastern coast of Sumatra, exercised hegemony in the area, but already by the beginning of the 15th century authority passed to the kingdom of Malacca, another Mohammedan state, which extended its control over almost the whole of Sumatra.

As a result of its extremely favourable location, and the swift collapse of the Javanese kingdom of Madjapahit in the 15th century, Malacca now became the most important commercial state in Indonesia.

But already at the beginning of the 16th century the power of this kingdom was checked, and a new era in the history of Indonesia began: its fate was now no longer determined by internal struggles for supremacy, but by Europe, with its superior might and influence. In 1498 the Portuguese explorer Vasco da Gama discovered the sea-route to India, and already by 1509 the Portuguese had appeared on the Malayan peninsula. A conflict with the Sultan was bound to ensue,

Spread of Islam in the Indonesian Archipelago. Also shown are the most important tribes that have remained up to the present entirely or almost entirely uninfluenced by Islam.

141

and in 1511 the port of Malacca was conquered by forces under the command of d'Albuquerque. The Sultan fled and continued the struggle against the invaders from Johore, to the south-east.

In 1520 the small principality of Atjeh in northern Sumatra succeeded in gaining its independence, and displayed such vigour that it won control of large parts of Sumatra. In the first half of the 17th century in particular, it became a notable maritime power, and under Sultan Iskandar Muda even succeeded in conquering Johore (1615).

The fall of Malacca hastened the spread of Islam along the coasts of Borneo. For it was here that Mohammedan merchants from Malacca settled when the Portuguese acquired full control over commerce there. But the Portuguese were not the only Europeans to appear in this area. They were followed by Spanish, English and Dutch merchants, who penetrated as far as the Indonesian Archipelago, where they found the products that had caused them to undertake these difficult and dangerous voyages: on the western islands pepper, and further to the east, on the Moluccas, cloves and nutmeg. A violent struggle developed for monopoly of the spice trade, in which the Dutch finally emerged as the victors.

In Holland itself the United East Indian Company (*Verenigde Oost-Indische Compagnie*) became the most important agency in the spice trade (1602). In order to obtain firm control of the market in Indonesia, the Company had to combat energetically the smugglers for whom these valuable commodities opened up tempting opportunities for profit. For this purpose factories were set up in the most important Indonesian ports, and measures were taken, such as restricting production, which were later to have extremely detrimental consequences for the wellbeing of the Moluccas in particular.

For a fairly long time the Portuguese continued to retain possession of the important port of Malacca on the Malayan peninsula, from which the maritime trade through the Straits of Malacca could be controlled. The conquest of this key point in 1641 finally gave the Dutch a complete monopoly.

The Dutch also succeeded in gaining a footing in Sumatra. When Atjeh lost power and prestige as a consequence of internal troubles, the East Indian Company conquered the areas formerly under the dominion of that kingdom, and only the northern Atjeh principalities retained their independence. In central Sumatra Malayu, the kingdom of the Menangkabau, remained in existence as an ostensibly independent state until 1825.

All these events led to decisive changes in the cultural as well as in the political field. For certain reasons, to be mentioned later, after the collapse of the Hindu kindom of Madjapahit no further concentration of power developed in Java capable of playing an important role outside that island. From the time of Malacca's supremacy onwards Malay replaced Javanese as the language of commece. This development continued even after the Malay sultanates had lost their power. Malay became the *lingua franca* of Indonesia, and to a considerable extent even in Java, where it found support from the Dutch.

Islam did not penetrate into Java until the 15th century. This island, too, maintained vigorous contact with Gujarat. The earliest known Mohammedan tomb in Java, that of Malik Ibrahim (1419), is also of the type found in Cambay. The Muslims who spread Islam by their personal influence described it as a mysterious and mystical doctrine. Thus the spread of the new religion was greatly facilitated, as has already been pointed out. Mysticism is also suggested by the name given to the apostles of the new faith: *wali*, an abbreviation for *wali Ullah*, one close to God.

Although polytheism, the deification of princes, and the caste system were rejected, the ancient ancestor cult was not only tolerated but was actually incorporated into Islamic ritual. The ban on making images of human beings or animals was not strictly observed. Thus, for example, the wayang show continued to exist, although it is not ruled out that the extreme stylization of the figures, which bore little relation to the realities of anatomy, was due to the influence of Islam. Local traditions were taken over without difficulty, and Moslems even used the existing buildings, apart from a few changes necessitated by the new ritual. Even where mosques were erected, they were built in the eastern Javanese style. Thus, for example, the entrance-gate to the mosque of Kudus, built in the 16th century, was given the shape of a 'split' or double gate, *tjandi bentar*, such as we found in eastern Java, and such as still forms the first gate of Hindu temples on Bali.

The walis have played a considerable role in Javanese thought. In the many legends woven around the most important of them, they appear as great magicians. And whilst Mohammedans are opposed to the worship of saints, in Java walis are in fact worshipped as saints, and their tombs are regarded as sacred places. They are chiefly to be found on mountains, a sign of a link with the traditional indigenous customs of ancestor worship.

In the political field the walis occupied a place that was quite unique.

Statue of a demon (Cheribon, Java). *K.I.T.* (Height 19 ins.)

They replaced, so to speak, the former Brahminic priests, consecrating the princes, and conferring upon them the title of sultan. The external signs of princely power were the so-called *pusakas*, symbolic objects such as crown jewels, sacred krisses, and suchlike. The struggle for power was simultaneously always a struggle for possession of such pusakas.

Amongst the walis there are two who are of particular importance in the history of Java as founders of hereditary dynasties, which exerted authority in both the spiritual and political fields. One of these was Prabu Sadmata in eastern Java, who exercised great influence and after his death was venerated under the name of Sunan Giri, 'the saint of the mountain' (*giri*, in Sanskrit = mountain).

In western Java a wali appears who became known under the name (probably Portuguese) of Falatehan. He originated from Pasei in northern Sumatra, and on a pilgrimage to Mecca obtained the right to bestow the title of sultan upon Tranggana, the third prince of the kingdom of Demak. This principality, on the northern coast of central Java, was founded by Raden Patah in about 1500. Within a short period of time the Muslim princes of Demak were able to encompass the ruin of the Hindu kingdom of Madjapahit. Only Balambangan in eastern Java was still able to retain its independence. Falatehan was sent by the Sultan of Demak to western Java to eliminate Hinduism from this area, too. He founded the wali dynasty of Bantam, and with fire and sword imposed a far from tolerant Mohammedanism, probably in conformity with his own convictions. He inflicted irreparable damage upon the Hindu kingdom of Padjadjaran by conquering its most important port, Sunda Kelapa, hereafter called Djajakarta, or Djakarta for short. He then subjugated the kingdom of Cheribon: it was here that he died, and was buried on Mount Djati. Under the name of Sunan Gunung Djati (*gunung* = mountain) he lived on in the memory of the people as the Great Wali. His tomb is still regarded as the most sacred of holy places in Java.

At the beginning of the 16th century it looked very much as though the Mohammedan state of Demak would be able to consolidate its authority. But Tranggana fell in an attempt to conquer the Hindu kingdom of Balambangan in eastern Java. The position of hegemony occupied by Demak now passed for a time to the sultanate of Pajang, until the kingdom of Mataram, which was also Islamic in religion, attained supremacy in 1575. In the meantime the kingdom of Bantam was able to win its freedom, and at the end of the 16th century

Mataram, Bantam and Balambangan shared sovereignty over Java. But in Java, as in other parts of Indonesia, merchants now appeared from Europe. The East India Company founded a factory in Djakarta in 1610, which led to a dispute with the British who had already settled there, and with the Sultan of Bantam. But under the command of Jan Pieterszoon Coen, the Governor General, the Company succeeded in defeating the British, Djakarta was destroyed, and a new port, Batavia, was built.

At the end of the 17th century the East India Company, by skilfully turning the disputes in Bantam to its own advantage, succeeded in bringing this kingdom under its sway. The wali dynasty of Cheribon also lost prestige at the same time.

Under the powerful leadership of Senepati (1575—1601) Mataram was able to extend its authority over large areas of central and eastern Java, but under his successor it was again threatened with collapse. Then, in 1613, a saviour appeared in the form of the greatest of all the Mohammedan princes of Indonesia, Agung (1613—1645). He regained sovereignty over the other kratons, conquered the important port of Surabaya, and extended his influence to the coasts of Borneo. With the secret intention of gaining possession of Bantam, he made repeated efforts to come to terms with the East India Company, but without success. He then attempted to attain his ends by force of arms, but this brought him into conflict with the Company. Twice Agung besieged Batavia, but on both occasions in vain. A 'cold war' resulted, which allowed the Dutch to obtain ever greater control of maritime trade, and thus inflict great losses upon the kingdom of Java.

In internal politics, on the other hand, Agung was able to strengthen his position by forcing the ruling priest-prince, a successor of the above-mentioned Prabu Sadmata, to consecrate him — a step which was essential for the religions consolidation of his authority, and at the same time to give him the title of Sultan.

Wood-carving on a gamelan instrument (Java)

His successor, Amangkurat I Tegalwangi, attempted to strengthen his authority further by imposing increased restraints upon the less influential kratons. But the consequence of this centralization was a dangerous insurrection, which he could put down only with the assistance of the East India Company.

This prince adopted an outspokenly hostile attitude towards leading Muslims. He relinquished the title of Sultan, which his father had won at the cost of such great effort, and called himself by the Javanese

146

title of *susuhunan* or *sunan,* the venerated. It may be readily understood that a prince with such an intellectual outlook could not tolerate rival influence in the form of a wali dynasty. Once again with the assistance of the Dutch, the 'ruling' priest-prince was captured and killed. It seemed as though the power of the sunan was now unassailable, but after his death the actual situation was by no means clear, since the succession was unsettled. Repeated rebellions weakened the kingdom more and more, and the political influence of the Company thus became ever greater. The Dutch had already taken possession of large parts of the kingdom when, in 1755 and 1757, the remainder of the kingdom of Mataram was partitioned into three vassal states: Surakarta, Djogjakarta, and the principality of Mangkunagara, a member of another branch of the dynasty. In 1813, under the British Vice-Governor, Sir Thomas Stamford Raffles, yet a fourth principality was created, that of Paku Alam. These small states of central Java are usually grouped together under the name of the 'Principalities'. In Europe the East India Company constantly lost influence as a result of shifts in the balance of power in the course of the 18th century — indeed, in 1795 its possessions in Indonesia were even taken over by the 'Bataafse Republiek', as the Netherlands were called under French supremacy. But for Java this did not mean fresh possibilities for development along independent lines. In subsequent decades there was no question of any of the kratons exercising real authority.

It is quite obvious that the political and economic decline of the Islamic kingdom of Mataram did not remain without effect in the cultural sphere, and it is also understandable that, in view of the unfortunate external situation that prevailed, the courts recalled the splendour of the past, since they needed external glory all the more to conceal their weakness. Islam without doubt shaped the religious life of the Javanese, and the influence of this faith was felt in practically all branches of the life of the community. In the cultural field, on the other hand, strong ties with the past could be maintained.

It is of great importance that no great Javanese works of architecture and sculpture have been preserved. Several reasons may be given for this: firstly, the prince held a completely different position under Islam; secondly, Islam prohibited the representation of human beings and animals; and the prohibition affected princes much more than the common people; and thirdly, political and economic circumstances prevented Mataram from becoming a powerful and flourishing kingdom.

147

But also the arts and crafts which had flourished so successfully during the Madjapahit era were now threatened with decline. The many wars and insurrections which took place at the beginning of the Islamic period had most disastrous consequences, especially in the northern districts of Java (Cheribon, Japara, and Kudus), and on the island of Madura. And it was precisely here that the most famous schools for wood-carvers had existed.

FIG. P. 146

It appears very probable that in Cheribon art was very considerably influenced by China. In any case wood-carving from this district exhibited Chinese characteristics, both in the motifs employed (rock and cloud motifs) and in technique (lacquer technique); Cheribon art thus became something unique.

PLATES PP. 144, 148

But under Sultan Agung the decorative arts were afforded a new

Lacquered fruit dish, wood, carved with plant motifs (Cheribon, Java). *K.I.T.* (Height 8¼ ins.)

opportunity. As we know, this prince sought to consolidate his authority in the state and to give the monarchy greater influence and prestige. For this purpose he needed a show of splendour, and here the decorative arts proved useful, and could flourish once again. The stimulus was apparently provided by Pangeran Pekik, the prince of Surabaya, who was married to a sister of Sultan Agung.

As well as the wood-carvers, the silversmiths and jewellers derived benefit from this new impetus. Their motifs were borrowed from Hindu-Javanese prototypes.

But, whatever the significance of these new tendencies may have been, Java's real reputation in the realm of arts and crafts rested upon two completely different branches: batik designs on textiles, and arms and armour.

This art of designing textiles is almost exclusively practised in Java and Madura. Wherever else in Indonesia it was fostered, the stimulus came from Java. The sole exception is the batik work produced by the Toradja, which we shall come back to later. Basically, the whole process is as follows: a fabric is dipped into the dye-vat, all those parts which are not to take up the colour being covered on both sides with a substance which does not allow the dye to seep through. The whole fabric had to be dipped into the dye because the Javanese only had vegetable colouring-matter, which needed a long time to take effect properly.

BATIK

In order to protect the fabric from colour in the parts not to be dyed, beeswax, made fluid by heating, was always used.

This art was able to attain its unique standard of accomplishment once use was made of a *tjanting*, a small copper crucible with one or several spouts, by means of which continuous lines of wax of various width could be applied to the fabric. The invention of this simple but cleverly contrived device probably dates from the 17th century, because it was at this time that the art of batik work began to flourish, and the patterns could be developed in finest detail.

The batik fabrics of the Toradja were produced in a more simple fashion, and since the Toradja led a relatively isolated existence, this method must be a very ancient one. Hot wax was applied to the fabric by means of a narrow, flattened round strip of bamboo. As can be seen clearly from the illustration on p. 152, there can be no question of continuous lines of wax. The geometrical figures have instead been composed of separate small rectangles, which have apparently been sketched out piece by piece, with the required amount of wax being applied each time by means of a strip of bamboo. This kind of batik fabric is invariably one-coloured. The design stands out against the one-coloured background by reason of its natural colour.

A similar method was originally also common in Java. From a comparison of the batik work of the Toradja with the traditional prototypes of Javanese batik textiles (Plates p. 155, 158), it is clear what possibilities were opened up by the invention of the *tjanting*. Naturally many technical knacks were still required before a pattern of such intricacy could be made. These cannot be discussed here, and we shall limit ourselves to describing the motifs, patterns and colours, referring the reader to the specialist literature on the subject for a more detailed account of the techniques employed.

Tjanting for batik.

Some of the most ancient patterns are the so-called *bandji* designs, the basic motif of which is the swastika (*bandji*). The design is formed by regularly repeating this basic motif and combining the lines in a

Fig. p. 213
certain way (for the *bandji* motif, see also section on Bali).

The decoration as a whole in this pattern has grown organically from the individual parts, each of which have a meaning of their own. The motif is primary, the geometrical segmentation of the space ancillary. But the usual design was just a symmetrical interplay of lines, with

The various patterns
certain motifs being incorporated into the geometrical figures (rectangles, rhombs, circles, etc.), which were thereby formed. These patterns can be divided into two main groups:

a) patterns with a horizontal and vertical geometrical arrangement;
b) patterns with a diagonal geometrical arrangement.

Group (a) can be subdivided according to the geometrical form of the motifs employed:

i) *Tjeplokkan*: the motif is rosette-shaped (circular, oval, or square);
ii) *Ganggong*: the motif is star- or rhomb-shaped;
iii) *Kawung*: the pattern is derived from intersecting circles, with the elliptical spaces thus formed being filled in with certain small motifs;
iv) *Tambal*: this pattern strongly resembles a crazy quilt. The motifs found are fairly varied;
v) *Polèng*: the chequered pattern. The unique point about this pat-

Plate p. 129
tern is that it is never found on articles of clothing, but only on the garments worn by certain puppets in the wayang show.

This classification is not complete, but merely gives a survey of those patterns which can be easily recognized. The groups mentioned comprise dozens of variations, each pattern having a name of its own. Amongst the motifs employed we find flowers and leaves, animals and objects, all of them in a flat ornamental stylization. Group (b) of the patterns mentioned may be classified by the collective term *garis-miring* in so far as the bands running diagonally are not bordered by wavy lines. If this is the case, then it is called the *parang* pattern.

FIGS. P. 154

Characteristic of these latter are fairly broad, parallel diagonal bands bordered by wavy lines and alternating with narrower bands. These small bands mostly have small rhomb-shaped decorative motifs, but also other geometrical figures as well. From the wavy border there sprout forth linear patterns which cover the broad bands and alternate regularly with the others: next to the ornament which springs out from the lower wavy line and does not touch the upper border, there is always a similar ornament, but upside down.

These are simple linear motifs, sometimes with tendrils and hooks, as well as stylized leaf and flower motifs. The most beautiful style amongst the parang patterns is the so-called *parang rusak* pattern. Only persons of princely rank were allowed to wear it. But not only for this reason does it deserve to be called a princely pattern: from an aesthetic point of view, too, this pattern is by far the most beautiful example of batik work executed at the princely courts of central Java.

PLATE P. 155

Those batik fabrics characterized by a freer interpretation form a group of their own. The motifs are always formed by intertwining leaf or flower motifs, producing a rhythmic arrangement. These patterns are called *semèn*.

PLATE P. 158

In the semèn patterns flowers and leaves are invariably found, also sometimes in conjunction with animals, the *mirong* and/or the *sawat* ornament. The mirong ornament consists of a single or double wing motif, whilst the sawat ornament has a double wing with a bird's tail spread out like a fan. Perhaps this is reminiscent of Shiva's eagle, *garuda*.

FIGS. PP. 153, 154

FIG. P. 153

It is worth noting that the tumpal motif, too, appears on the borders of some groups of patterns. Here an ancient symbol has survived.

Mention may also be made of the so-called imitative patterns, or *nitiks*. By characteristic short broad lines various designs employed in weaving are imitated. It need hardly be pointed out that this is in complete contrast to the typical features of batik art, the continuous

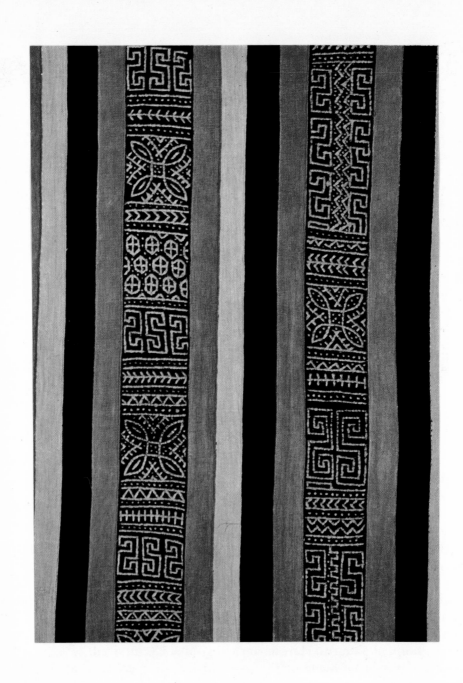

Detail of head-cloth, cotton. Pattern executed by ancient technique of applying dotted lines of wax. (Galumpang, central Celebes). *K.I.T.*

lines. They are mentioned here not because of any particular value they had, but because they owed their origin to the very causes that led to the development of batik art as a whole. In the 17th century painted textiles were imported into Java from India (Malabar) in such quantities that attempts were made on economic grounds to stimulate domestic production of coloured fabrics, with the result that batik textiles now became a much sought-after export. Finally, reference may be made to batik work from Cheribon, on which typical Chinese motifs, clouds and earth symbols, were to be found. The colours used, too, differ from those that are usual. Nuances of colour such as are found here do not ap-

Sawat motif: garuda, stylized (Java).

pear on other batik fabrics.

As already mentioned, the earliest batik fabrics are one-coloured; they have a colourless drawing on a dark blue ground. For this blue ground indigo was used — a light-resisting colouring-matter obtained from the leaves of various plants of the genus *indigofera* by means of fairly complex processes. It was only later that multi-coloured batik fabrics were produced. In the 'Principalities' preference was given to the colour combination of indigo, soga brown and white. Soga is obtained from the bast of certain trees, but this particularly beautiful colour will not adhere to the fabric without the use of a fixative.

In districts outside the 'Principalities' yellow and red were also used. The art of dyeing cloth red was introduced to Java by Indian Muslims from the 18th century onwards; it required particular care because the colouring-matter had to be rubbed into the fabric. The red dye is thus applied before the blue. Those who do not know Java at first hand can hardly visualize the matchless beauty — a veritable visual feast — exhibited at the kratons of central Java, especially at

Manuk déwata, bird of paradise (Java).

festivals. The batik articles of clothing worn on such occasions bear witness to a truly aristocratic sense of beauty and a unique taste in textile design.

Many articles of clothing were also produced by the batik method: in addition to the traditional head-cloth, the dye is applied subsequently. This process, known as *plangi,* produces carrying things in, *slendang,* and the breast-covering worn by women, *kembèn,* mention should be made of the festive garment worn by men, *dodot,* and by women, *sampur,* each four to five yards long and of magnificent design.

The old batik fabrics testify to a centuries-old civilization, in which the dignity of the prince depended on ostentation and beauty, and the sacred ancient patterns suggested, more than anything else, the social position of the wearer. Batik became a real national craft. Though bound by tradition, it nevertheless offered ample opportunities for personal interpretation and individual expression.

Figure of small bird (Java)

But there is yet another way of designing textiles in Java and other districts of Indonesia. First of all certain motifs are drawn or stamped, each individually, on to the fabric, which is usually silk. Then the figures are sketched in outline by means of tacking thread. When the threads are pulled tight, small loops appear which are then bound round with plant fibre. When the fabric is dipped into the dye-vat, the parts protected in this way do not take up the dye. Many colours can be applied on one and the same fabric; and nowadays an aniline dye is applied subsequently. This process. known as *plangi,* produces especially attractive results, with a broad range of colour shades.

THE ARMOURER'S CRAFT

Naga (mythical snake) motif (Java).

As has already been mentioned, in many parts of Indonesia the armourer's craft was far developed. The weapons were frequently more than mere implements, but had a deeper significance, a definite func-

154

Batik work. Pattern: *parang-rusak klitik*. Figures accentuated by gilding (*prada*) affixed with clear-cole. (Java). *K.I.T.*

tion of an almost religious nature. Particular attention was paid to the manufacture of the hilt and scabbard as well as the blade, and such weapons were often fine works of art.

The kris The *kris* constituted the peak of achievement of the Javanese armourers. Just as Java cannot be imagined without its wayang plays, gamelan orchestra, and batik fabrics, so also one cannot envisage it without its national weapon. The kris is of special importance both from a ceremonial and a religious point of view. The masterly skill shown in the making of these weapons reached an acme of perfection with the finest specimens.

The Javanese armourer, *empu*, was not merely a highly respected expert in his craft, but much more. To forge a kris was for him a solemn act, as is shown by the complicated ceremonial which had to precede the actual work. The smithy then became a consecrated place, and the empu re-enacted here the ceremony in which, according to ancient tradition, the gods had once entrusted weapons to man. In Java many tales are still told in which the main role is played by the magic force latent in a certain kris. In the Pararaton, the tale of Ken Angrok already referred to, Gandring, the murdered empu, lays a curse upon the kris, which brings death to the children and grandchildren of the founder of the Singhasari kingdom.

There are two types of Javanese kris which may be clearly distinguished from one another. The kris referred to above has a hilt, fashioned separately, and often splendidly embellished, which is held fast by PLATE P. 160 means of an iron tang at the guard of the blade, thus forming a whole. The blade itself is asymmetrical, and can be either straight or wavy. This weapon is also provided with a scabbard.

There also exists a kris-shaped dagger, smaller than the kris just mentioned, with hilt and blade forged out of a single piece of metal. The hilt invariably bears a simply worked figure of an ancestor. This weapon is called *kris-madjapahit,* but this does not necessarily imply that it appeared in the time of that dynasty.

Little is known for sure about the antiquity of the kris, or of the relationship between the two types mentioned. The idea behind both types was undoubtedly similar, but it cannot be proved that the common two-piece kris was a development of the one-piece kris-madjapahit. But one may point to some of the relevant facts.

On the bas-reliefs of Borobudur, an inexhaustible 'source' of information on Javanese life in the eighth century, the kris is not to be found. Nevertheless one cannot conclude from this for certain that this weapon was unknown at that time. For in the space under the main stupa a kris-madjapahit has been discovered! It remains an open question when it was placed there.

The wayang-purwa figures do not bear a kris. At the time when this type of wayang play evolved, stimulated by eastern Javanese literature, this weapon apparently did not yet play the important part it did later.

The male wayang-gedog figures, on the other hand, do indeed carry a kris. But this type of wayang play did not develop until later.

The most ancient kris with a date on it bears the year 1264 'Shaka', which corresponds to 1342 A.D. This kris is of the common type still in existence today, and has been worked with great artistry. This leads almost certainly to the conclusion that this craft must have already been known by then for quite some time.

A kris-shaped dagger is to be found for the first time in the bas-reliefs at Panataran. This suggests that this weapon existed during the Madjapahit period, because it was under this dynasty that the important buildings of this complex were erected, and no further bas-reliefs were added at a later date. Chinese accounts from the early 15th century mention it as a general custom in Java to carry a kris.

But the 'ordinary' kris was also to be found on Bali, and it is just as important here; the Balinese armourer, too, has the same social and spiritual status as the empu in Java. For this reason, therefore, the kris must have become known on Bali during the eastern Javanese period, and also have been held in particular esteem.

In other parts of Indonesia, too, the 'ordinary' kris is to be found. It is generally assumed that it came into vogue in those districts at the time when Madjapahit attained the zenith of its power.

Distribution of the kris

In southern Celebes the hilt has changed its shape. Whilst the hilt of the Javanese kris is straight and only gently curved, the one from southern Celebes is sharply curved. This variation can be explained by the fact that different basic forms determined its development: in Java the human figure, but in southern Celebes an animal figure. The kris found in Malacca also displays a certain affinity with that from southern Celebes, whilst the sizes that are most commonly met with bear Javanese names. Even the armourer himself is designated by the Javanese word *pande*. (Specimens from Java and southern Celebes are illustrated in the plates on pp. 160 and 163).

From all this it may be concluded that at a time during the Madjapahit dynasty when Java's cultural influence was particularly strong,

Batik work. Pattern: *semèn*; border composed of *tumpal* figures. (Java). *K.I.T.*

the kris attained the extraordinary significance it has retained up to the present day in Java and Bali. Thus it is also understandable that the princes of the kingdom of Mataram bestowed their favour upon armourers. For with no other weapon could the authority and majesty of a prince be better symbolized than with the kris, the beauty of which reflected the prince's own splendour, and the origins of which went back beyond the sacred tradition of Madjapahit to the customs associated with a primitive cult.

We have still to examine two points: the special processes used in forging the blade, the so-called *pamor* work, and the iconography of the kris.

The process referred to is as follows: ordinary iron and nickelous iron (meteoric iron) are cut and folded in a special way, so that certain patterns are formed on the surface of the blade. For this bars of ordinary iron and also bars of nickelous iron are placed one upon another in a certain order, and then are cut and folded. The metal bar thus obtained is then split in a special manner by the armourer, who punches holes or recesses in it, or forges it into a spiral, after which it is all cut and folded once again. When the blade is finished, but the pattern is not yet visible, the metal is treated with arsenic or acetone. This acts upon the nickel steel only, thus making it bright, and the design comes to light. Since the result is not apparent until the acid has taken effect and the blade is finished, the empu must know all the tricks of his trade, and have ample experience.

The best nickelous iron originally came from several meteorites found in Java. From the late 19th century onwards nickelous iron from southern Celebes has mostly been used, but it is of inferior quality. This explains why nowadays the technique of pamor work has lost some of its former excellence.

The blade can be either straight or wavy: in both cases the mystical snake, *nāga*, can be recognized as the prototype. On the straight type the snake is depicted in a state of repose and contemplation, and on the wavy type in a state of motion. For the Javanese the blade was, and in many cases still is, more than a symbol. For him the relationship between the kris and the snake is a very close one: in order to enhance the mystical power of his kris, he may bring the blade into contact with the entrails and brain of a snake.

A snake is generally also found on ornamented blades. That this is a very ancient motif is clear from the fact that the kris already mentioned which bears the date '1264 Shaka' has a small snake on both sides of

Kris with wavy blade, encrusted with golden figure of *nāga* (mythical snake). (Java). *K.I.T.* (Length 14½ ins.)

the blade. A particularly fine specimen is shown in the illustration on p. 160. The figure incrusted in gold adroitly matches the shape of the kris.

A particular magic force is attributed to the snake: as nāga it plays a privileged part in Hindu mythology (cf. chapter on tjandis), as well as in the magic symbolism of many isolated Indonesian tribes.

PLATE P. 76

But the blade is also decorated with other mythological figures, such as the *kāla* figure and Vishnu's eagle, *garuda,* as well as leaf motifs.

Yet another symbol deserves to be considered. Lower down on the convex side of the blade we often find a figure which suggests the trunk and mouth of an elephant. This probably was intended to invest the kris with the strength of the elephant in some magic way.

The hilt has undoubtedly developed from a human figure. Wherever it can still be recognized, it is generally a demonic figure, *raksasa.* This was surely designed to ward off evil spirits, in the same way as the raksasas erected at the entrance to temples. But in many cases the hilt has been kept so simple in shape that the original figure can hardly be recognized any longer; it is not completely ruled out that this simplification may have been due to the influence of Islamic thought. This is also indicated by the fact that we do not find this simplified shape on Bali. But on the inner side of the crooked hilt one generally finds a very simplified representation of kāla heads. It may also be mentioned that the Javanese always call the individual parts of the hilt after parts of the human body.

The hand-wrought scabbard, too, is a far from unimportant accessory. The dagger and its scabbard belong together like body and soul. Generally the scabbard is kept simple, but we also come across some with superb ornamentation. In such cases the scabbards may be polychrome, or have an extra outer scabbard made of metal, with some of the figures embossed. A characteristic feature is always the extended top, the so-called 'shoe'. This part is generally devoid of ornamentation, and its beauty lies in its shape, which resembles nothing so much as a ship with its stern built up high. Costly sorts of wood, frequently grained, are used for this purpose, their colour and grain often being brought out by polishing.

It has already been mentioned that certain krisses were often regarded as charged with magic power, which could ensure and establish a prince's authority. These were sacral heirlooms, *pusakas,* which were accorded general veneration. But some krisses had value as pusakas only within a particular family. A pusaka-kris is always treated with special reverence, and even sacrifices (e.g. of incense or viands), are offered to it, which are thought to enhance its magic power.

The princely pusakas also include other weapons which testify to the consummate artistry of Javanese armourers. As an example of this, we reproduce a lance-head, on which gold has been used to incrust a human figure. If one compares this with the figure on p. 131 it can easily be recognized as Semar, the first of the three Panakawans from the wayang-purwa plays; this represents an old Indonesian ancestral figure.

PLATE P. 166

THE JAVANESE GAMELAN

The word gamelan is derived from *gamel*, a hammer, and thus the gamelan orchestra is composed almost exclusively of percussion instruments. The high level of musical achievement represented by these orchestras is due to the strong sense of tempo and rhythm possessed by the Javanese.

The music produced with these instruments naturally sounds somewhat strange to the European ear. The scales are divided into intervals unfamiliar to the Westerner. Modulations are not to be found in gamelan music; melodies are not based on a fixed key-note. Since modern music, with its tendency towards atonality, has opened up new perspectives, it has become easier for us to understand Indonesian gamelan music, and we have perhaps even come some distance towards it.

The scale   In Javanese music there are two tone systems, *sléndro* and *pélog*. They are subdivided into instrumental and vocal *sléndro* and *pélog*.

The instrumental sléndro is always five-toned, the octave being divided into more or less equal intervals. This scale corresponds approximately to our: d - e - f sharp - a - b - (d). In the vocal sléndro there are also five semitones.

The instrumental pélog is likewise five-toned, but the intervals are unequal. Its notation would be approximately: d - e flat (+) - f - a - b flat - (d), with the flat notes sounding somewhat higher than ours. This pélog is termed *pélog-bem*. If one starts with the keynote a, then one obtains the series: a - b flat - c - e (—) - f - (a), with the e sounding somewhat lower than ours. This scale is called *pélog-barang*. At times a sixth, or even a seventh, tone are added. The vocal pélog, again, has several more tones.

Every gamelan orchestra is tuned to a certain scale, for the pitch of most of the instruments is fixed.

The pélog is presumably the most ancient scale, dating back to the

Kris, scabbard and grip in gold embossed with plant motifs. At the bottom of the grip *tumpal* motifs. The gold is alloyed with base metals to obtain a reddish-brown colour (*suasa*). (Southern Celebes). *K.I.T.* (Length 15¾ ins.)

pre-Hindu era. The sléndro, it is thought, became known in central Java about the eighth century A.D.

Sléndro and pélog evoke different sensations, rather like our major or minor key. The sléndro is chiefly employed as accompaniment at wayang-purwa performances, and is cheerful, or even festive and solemn. The pélog is used in the music at wayang-gedog performances, and evokes a more melancholy mood.

Gamelan music is not really an art in its own right; if gamelan concerts are indeed sometimes performed at the kratons, this contradicts the essential character of this type of music, which practically always plays a merely auxiliary role. Thus in the wayang-purwa, for example, the movements of the puppets, the voice of the dalang, and the musical accompaniment are all blended into a single entity.

But gamelan music is not only played at wayang shows. The dances in the wayang-topèng and wayang-wong are executed to the rhythmic strains of the gamelan; this kind of music is indispensable at festivals, processions, and on other special occasions.

Gamelan music is polyphonic: certain instruments play the nuclear theme, others the ornamental variations and counter-melodies, whilst others keep and determine the tempi, and a fourth group regulates the musical paraphrasing and interpunctuation.

Comparison with Western polyphonic music, as it reached its zenith in the monumental works of Johann Sebastian Bach, is not really admissible. Western polyphony has its strict rules, and is constructed almost mathematically, whilst the polyphony practised by the gamelan players is much freer. For this reason the musicologist Jaap Kunst can even speak of 'heterophony'.

The instruments   Gongs play a significant part as paraphrasing instruments in gamelan music. They occur in various sizes and fulfil various functions.

The *gong-ageng*, a large gong suspended from an upright wooden frame, marks the end of the longer phrases into which the melodic line is divided. The *kenong*, a large gong which lies horizontally, terminates the divisions of the phrase, whilst the *ketuk*, a small horizontal gong, marks the subdivisions of each division denoted by the kenong. The gongs have a magnificent long-echoing note, only the ketuk having a flat and short note. It may also be noted that the terms used for the instruments are onomatopoeic: *ketuk* — short and dull; *gong* and *kenong* — deep resounding notes.

The instrument whose particular function it is to mark the tempi is the large drum, or *kendang gending*. These kendangs consist of a conical or full-bellied resonating chamber, with skins stretched across the two open sides, and resting upon cross beams. They are beaten with both hands. Besides the kendang gending a medium-sized drum, *kendang tjiblon,* is used in the gamelan, whilst the smallest one is termed *penuntung.*

The most important instruments used in playing the nuclear theme belong to the group of *sarons.* These consist of convex metallic resonating keys, which are beaten with small mallets. The *rebab* serves the same purpose; this is a two-stringed instrument, played like a cello. One of the finest instruments is the *gendèr*: small key-shaped bronze slabs are suspended freely by two cords in a row. Under each slab there is a resonating tube, tuned to the same pitch, which gives the tone the necessary resonance. As soon as a slab is struck, (the instrument is played with two small round sticks), the same hand acts as a damper.

The gendèr is especially suitable for developing the nuclear theme, and accompanying the dalang as he sings.

The same purpose is served by the *gambang,* a trough xylophone, with wooden keys which are similarly struck with round sticks. This instrument has a peculiarly soft and full tone.

The instruments mentioned form the typical gamelan orchestra, which plays at wayang shows. In larger orchestras other instruments are also to be found which are used for special purposes, such as the gong-chimes, *bonangs,* consisting of double rows of small gongs resting on a horizontal frame, which serve to bring out the melody fully with a clear note.

The psaltery, or *tjelempung,* which is plucked, is an instrument of a special type: it has a rather large trapezium-shaped resonator, standing on four legs. There is a bridge across the whole width, to which many double strings are fastened on the bias. These are arranged at equal intervals up to the peg-box at the top, which usually has the shape of an oblong spiral. This instrument is plucked with the fingers.

Finally reference may be made to the only wind instrument in the gamelan orchestra, a flute, *suling.*

The gamelan orchestra also comprises male and female soloists, as well as a chorus, which invariably sings in unison. The singers always sing with a nasal *timbre,* and turn their heads away from the audience during the performance.

The most beautiful and popular gamelan orchestras are to be found at the kratons of central Java. The court of Djokja has a very ancient

The most important gamelan orchestras

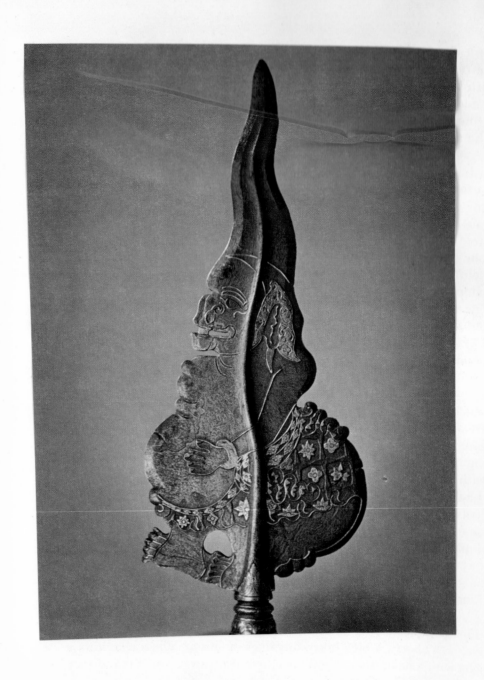

Head of ceremonial spear with figure of *Semar* encrusted in gold. (Java). *K.I.T.* (Length 25½ ins.)

gamelan, venerated as a pusaka. According to tradition this orchestra was founded already at the kraton of the kingdom of Madjapahit. It is tuned in the sléndro key, with only three tones. This gamelan is one of the so-called *sekati* gamelans: these orchestras were only allowed to play in *sekatèn* week, which the Javanese devote to commemorating the birth and death of the Prophet. Here one can see a typical link with Islam. Islam apparently only tolerated this one type of gamelan, and also only did so in order to facilitate conversion to the new faith.

In the cultured circles of the kratons gamelan music flourished anew. In this matter, too, Islam made itself felt, but its influence could not stop this evolution.

In the reign of Sultan Agung in particular, new compositions, instrumental as well as vocal, arose. But one must bear in mind that there could be no question of any individual touches; this music is a typical collective activity, the nature and purpose of which are readily understood by every member of the community.

The art of the dance reached its zenith in the ceremonial court dances **DANCING** at the kratons of central Java. The accompaniment was provided by the prince's *pélog* gamelan: a dalang gives a spoken introduction, and then male and female choruses sing. These dances are very ancient, and have a special sacral significance, but nevertheless the influence of Islam is noticeable here, too. Thus these dances are performed during the celebration of the *garebegs*, Mohammedan sacrificial festivals. These are group-dances, in which girls of noble birth, but not the daughters of the prince himself, are privileged to participate.

The so-called *bedaya* dance is performed by nine girls at a time, representing the nymphs of the goddess of the South Sea (by which is meant the sea to the south of Java), whilst the so-called *serimpi* dance is performed by a group of four girls, representing the heroines of the *Ménak* romance. Also in this case a connection with Islam is apparent, as we shall see when we turn to literature.

The dances are stylized down to the last detail: each single movement has its particular significance, each gesture being performed with a wonderful repose and with feminine charm cultivated to perfection. In no other form of art is the unique Mohammedan civilization of Mataram and the subsequent 'Principalities' so evident as in these ceremonial dances. They exhibit in most accomplished perfection courtly dignity, complete self-control, and devotion to symbolical detail.

Of equal distinction and beauty are the wayang dances, which occur in the wayang-purwa and the later wayang-wong.

In both these types of wayang show the puppets are replaced by human performers; whilst the masked actors in the wayang-topeng do not speak and the dalang has a task similar to that in the wayang-purwa, in the wayang-wong, on the other hand, the players themselves, who are not masked, speak the words, and the dalang is not so important.

PLATES PP. 169, 172
The masked dances from the wayang-topèng are clearly influenced by Hinduism, but in their conception are linked with the primitive masked dances in Java. The ceremonial, and frequently magic, character survived. Hindu influence is primarily evident in certain stylistic elements in the dance. Thus the symbolic gesture of the hand, *mudrā*, is taken from Hinduism, as is also the deferential greeting, *sembah*, and the meditative seated posture, *sila*, with the legs crossed under the body.

As can be seen from illustrations and from the bas-reliefs of Borobudur and Prambanan, the vigorous character of Hindu dancing was transformed by the Javanese into an individual style, corresponding to their own ideas, and during the last centuries of the Hindu-Javanese period a special style for the topèng dance crystallized.

As in so many other branches of art, the political troubles of the 15th and 16th centuries had a most unfortunate effect upon the dance. Once again it was the cultural stimulus from the kraton of Mataram that infused these ceremonial and wayang-wong dances with new life.

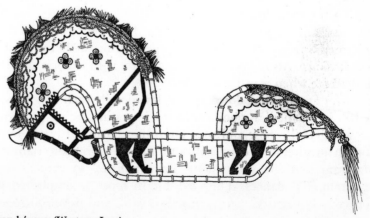

Djaran-képang (Western Java).

Wayang-topèng mask representing the noble character. Employed in performance of the Pandji romances. (Java). *K.I.T.*

This also explains why, after the partition of the kingdom of Mataram into three vassal states (1755 and 1757) the art of dancing evolved in quite a different fashion at the courts of Djokjakarta and Surakarta respectively. And though these two schools have influenced each other, the difference between them is still recognizable. Dancing at the court of Mangkunagara conformed stylistically to that at Djokjakarta.

In wayang-wong, as it evolved during the later 19th century, the style of the dances incorporated into it is on the whole similar to those of the wayang-topeng. But whilst no group dances occur in the latter case, this is the general rule in the wayang-wong. These groups always consist either entirely of men or entirely of women, the female parts sometimes being performed by men. It is precisely in these group-dances that the difference in the character of female and male dancing is most apparent. Dances of women are characterized by restraint, which makes every gesture extremely composed and graceful. The movements are as a rule centripetal and more involved than those in the mens' dances. In dances representing giants or demons in particular, the movements of the men are virile and provocative.

Only one dance has been adopted by wayang-wong from wayang-topèng; it is called *kiprah,* and is the most beautiful of them all. It is a solo dance in which the prince expresses his joy at the victory he has won. In the wayang-topèng this dance can also be performed by a woman, and has a different meaning. Here it is a love-dance: the prince dresses himself and makes ready before meeting his beloved. Also in the wayang-wong the dances are accompanied by gamelan music, with the kendang-tjiblon giving the rhythm. The gong marks the beginning and the end of each strophe of the dance.

In the wayang-wong the spoken word, the music and the art of movement are blended into a single whole. The repertoire is drawn from the same sources as the lakons of the wayang-purwa.

This type of wayang testifies impressively to the high standard of culture prevailing at the court of Mataram, which to some extent survived subsequently in the kratons in the 'principalities'.

Folk-dances In addition to the dances described above, which must be classed with the courtly art of the kratons, there are folk-dances of many kinds. Most of these are accompanied by gamelan instruments, such as the *djaran képang*: two persons dance with figures of horses plaited from stalks of bamboo. Their movements give the impression that they are 'riding' these horses.

Fig. p. 168

In western Java an instrument of strange construction, a rattle known as *angklung*, is used for accompaniment. In a bamboo frame several vertical bamboo tubes of a certain length are suspended freely. They are hollow at the bottom, and when the instrument is shaken they strike with two small protuberances sideways against a slit made in the bottom frame-tube.

FIG. P. 171

Every instrument emits a note of a certain pitch, and is tuned in octaves. In order to play a tune, as many instruments are needed as there are notes of various pitch in the melody. Each angklung player shakes his instrument when it is his turn to play his note. This rattle is very ancient, and was presumably already known in the neolithic era. As already mentioned, the Javanese language was replaced in the other

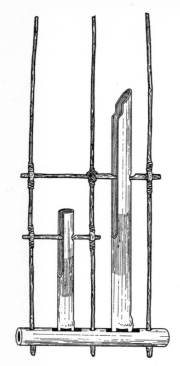

Angklung (Western Java).

LITERATURE

parts of the Archipelago by Malay, which in the course of time became the *lingua franca* for the whole of Indonesia.

From the cultural point of view it was of great importance that a notable literature developed in Malay. The subject-matter was partly borrowed from eastern Javanese literature as found in the lakons. But apart from this there were also literary works both in prose, *hikayat*, and in verse, *sjair*.

In the evolution of Malay literature we can distinguish two periods: first the classical period, which reached its climax about 1500, and then the post-classical era, which lasted until the beginning of the 20th century.

In the classical period those works in particular deserve mention which could be called legendary-historical, such as the Hikayat Hang Tuah, (which tells the story of Hang Tuah, the national naval hero of the Malays), and the Hikayat Sadjarah Melayu, based on the chronicles of the Malayan princes. This was courtly literature, and the language used in these works is considered a model of pure and

Wayang-topèng mask: demonic character (Cheribon, Java). *K.I.T.* (Height 14¼ ins.)

unadulterated Malay. In the post-classical period many works of a narrative character developed, both in prose and verse (sjair); the style as well as the content are influenced by Arabic, Persian and Indian works. The Hikayats are long-winded compositions, marred by a luxuriant uncontrolled romanticism, without the slightest attempt at regularity: descriptions of princes and princesses, of audiences at the princes' courts, and of seductions follow one another in disorder, and there is no lack of magic weapons — or even of flying horses.

The 'Tales of Amir Hamzah', the adventures of a Mohammedan knight of that name, were very popular. *'Amir Hamzah'*

The Malayan poet Abdullah bin Abdulkadir Munsji, who lived in the early 19th century, is a writer of a more independent turn of mind. He became known chiefly through his autobiography, the Hikayat Abdullah, and a traveller's tale, the Pelayaran Abdullah. These works have a very personal imprint, and are distinguished by their lively style. Atjeh possesses historical works such as the Hikayat Malem Dagang, which records the heroic deeds of Sultan Iskander Muda, the conqueror of Johore. These were often turned into epic poems.

Also Macassar and Bugin have their own chronicles. These peoples originally inhabited southern and south-western Celebes, and occupy a special place in Indonesian history. Excellent seamen, they sailed the whole Archipelago and founded states of their own, often situated far distant from their homeland. Where political complications arose, one can be almost certain to find representatives of these tribes involved. They penetrated to the east and west coasts of Borneo, where the Buginese established small aristocratic republics, and even as far as Malacca.

In their chronicles they show a strong tendency to idealize events, but the dates in them are accurate.

In Javanese literature we find a conservative traditionalism maintained by the so-called *pudjanggas*, the court scholars and poets, who had a special predilection for the pre-Islamic era. It is due to their influence that in their historical accounts in verse of the Islamic era, known as *babads*, pre-Hindu, Hindu and Islamic features are intermingled.

Muslim epic poetry is represented by the Hamza romance (the equivalent of the tales of Amir Hamzah), known to the Javanese as *Ménak*. In other works there is no trace of a positive influence of Islam.

It will have been noted that we have devoted a particularly large amount of space to Javanese art. This has its full justification, since Hindu influence was at its strongest and most enduring in Java, and at many courts such a notable cultural tradition developed that, even after a period of retrogression and decline, art in various forms was again able to flourish on a considerable scale. The influences radiating outwards from these kratons enriched the Javanese cultural scene greatly. These courts were able to keep up the splendour of the 17th, 18th and 19th centuries.

We have still to mention another, smaller, island situated to the east of Java: Bali. It remained untouched by Islam, and has retained its Hindu character up to the present day; for this reason it deserves a chapter to itself.

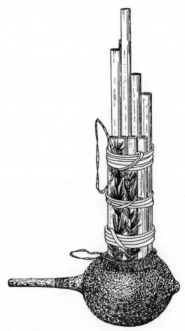

Kledi (Dayak).
Sarawak, northern Borneo.

XI. MUSIC AND DANCING ON ISLANDS
OTHER THAN JAVA AND BALI

The peoples that immigrated into the Indonesian Archipelago from South-east Asia during the neolithic era must have already had a highly-developed and varied musical culture, probably comprising some elements dating back to still more ancient times. These peoples spread throughout this vast realm of islands, coming into contact with the aboriginal inhabitants. In some areas they exercised an influence upon one another, whilst in other parts the various peoples lived in complete isolation, so that in the course of many centuries prior to the Christian era the differences between them became ever more marked. Influences from many countries — India and China during the first millennium A.D., then the Near East, and from the 16th century Portugal and the Netherlands — have at various times all helped to create in Indonesia an incomparably rich treasure-house of native music. Although certain common characteristics do exist, it is these local differences which make Indonesian music so exceedingly varied and attractive.

Sumatra

The music of this large island is of particular interest both as regards the instruments used as well as the style of composition, since many of the influences referred to above can be traced most clearly here. Islam, which attained considerable influence over large parts of Sumatra, brought with it from Gujarat elements of Persian and Arabic culture and had an unmistakable effect upon musical instruments. One kind of wooden shawn was even given a name, *serunai*, which hardly differs from the original Persian term, *surnai*. In addition to this primitive type of oboe, there are two different kinds of drum, and the *rebana*, similar to a tambourine, which is also popular in Mohammedan areas outside Sumatra. A lute with three double strings and one single string also originates from this area, as does a bamboo flute. In southern Sumatra, in addition to instruments of Arabic origin, we also find others, such as various kinds of gong and drum, which suggest Javanese influence. Gamelan instruments of this type are, however, tuned in a tone system that is common in Siam and Burma.

The structure of the instrumental music points to the influence of China and Further India, whilst the songs suggest Arabic, and even early Portuguese, influence. The last-named are called *krontjong* songs. These melodies are in our major scale, and seem very romantic to us. Songs of this kind are in vogue in other districts of Indonesia, too, probably having been transmitted either by indirect or direct channels.

Nias On the island of Nias we also come across large and small gongs which originated from Java. Characteristic of this island are the magnificent drums with skins either on one side or on both; those with a skin on only one side are often of enormous size and occasionally reach almost ten feet in length.

But the most remarkable instrument on Nias is a sort of bamboo 'buzzer'. It consists of a hollow bamboo cane, that part held in one's hand serving as a resonator, with two holes opposite each other. Below these holes the cane is slit lengthwise. When this part is struck with a knuckle of the other hand, (or, where two 'buzzers' are played simultaneously, on the knee-cap), a buzzing note of a fixed pitch is produced. If both holes are closed the note produced is lower by a major second. On Nias the player uses two 'buzzers' simultaneously, one instrument being smaller than the other, and produces two notes, the interval between them being a major third. If the notes c and d are sounded with the larger instrument, the smaller one adds e minor and f sharp. It is on this tritone that most of the songs of southern Nias are constructed.

We are deliberately dealing here only with southern Nias, since northern Nias lost almost everything indigenous as the result of the introduction here of a rigorous form of Christianity. All local cultural achievements were regarded from a one-sided European point of view, and were eliminated as quickly and thoroughly as possible. It was not, of course, the intention of the missionaries to impoverish the cultural life of the people; they merely believed that they could replace what they considered 'objectionable' elements by the values of their homeland. Trumpets thus took the place of the traditional instruments, and were used to accompany the hymns introduced by the missionaries from Europe.

Soon warning voices were raised within the missionary society itself which had selected Nias as its zone of operations. But for northern Nias the consequences of their activity had already proved disastrous. This very ancient instrument, the bamboo 'buzzer', dates from the early megalithic period. It probably reached Indonesia from Yunnan by way of the Philippines. At present an instrument of this kind is still to be found on the Sangi and Talaud islands north of Celebes,

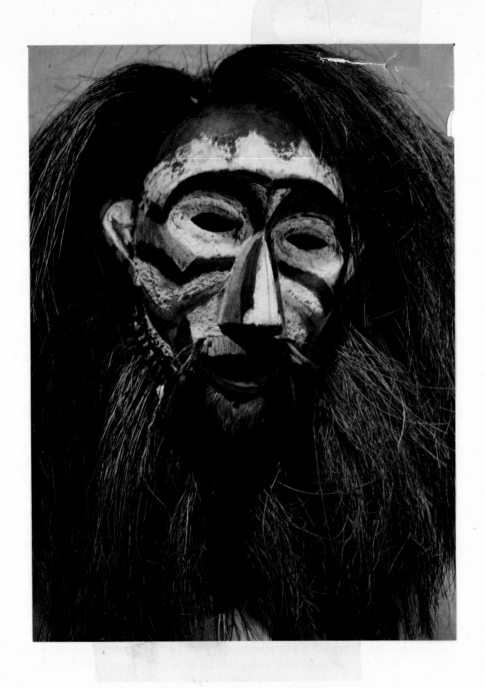

Death-mask (Timur Batak). *K.I.T.* (Height 11½ ins., breadth 7½ ins.)

on Celebes itself, in Borneo and even on the islands to the south-east; it thus also exists in eastern Sumbawa.

An instrument typical of the Batak districts is a very well-constructed lute with two strings made of palm fibres, which are plucked. We also come across large and small gongs, which are partly built in this area and partly imported from Java. The Toba Bataks have a group of drums tuned to different pitches of the scale in use there. As far as we know, rows of drums tuned in this way only exist in the Batak districts and in Burma. These drums are beaten with sticks; the music thus produced, with its carefully measured rhythm and canonical development of the melody, appeals to European ears.

In Atjeh we may mention a three-stringed bamboo zither and a vase-shaped drum with a single drumhead.

Borneo On Borneo we find instruments which are quite out of the ordinary, especially amongst the Dayaks who live in the interior of this island. In the districts settled by Malayans and Chinese indigenous music is unknown, and there are also no instruments of special interest. In the south, in the area of Bandjermasin and Martapura, Javanese influence dating from the time of Madjapahit supremacy can be observed. The musical instruments in use belong to the same type as the ancient gamelan instruments of eastern Java.

In some villages in the south-west the western Javanese angklung is met with.

In northern Borneo there are large, often magnificently cast dragon gongs, as they are called, doubtless patterned on those of China. The most noteworthy musical instrument amongst the Dayaks is the *kledi,* which is especially popular with the Kenja and Kayan tribes. This bagpipe-like instrument we have already seen depicted on the bronze drum from Hanoi mentioned in the section on Dong-Son culture, as well as in a bas-relief on the Borobudur. We are accordingly dealing here with a very ancient instrument: it is by no means ruled

FIG. P. 174 out that the Dayaks already had the kledi when they arrived from Further India. This instrument consists of six or eight small narrow pieces of bamboo cane, from which the nodes have been removed. These bamboo canes are inserted at the bottom into an oval hollow gourd, to which a mouthpiece is attached and air blown in. These six or eight tubes have a reed which is 'suprajacent', so that they only sound when the aperture is closed. Since the air pressure in the gourd can be regulated, a certain note can be sustained — the lowest, which then forms a sort of bagpipe drone. With the other five or seven bamboo tubes a simple melody can be produced. However simple this instrument may seem, its sound is surprisingly beautiful, and similar to that of an organ.

There is another instrument only known in the interior of Borneo, a large flat lute with two rattan strings, which are plucked. The wooden resonance-box is often painted, with a splendid effect.

Of the other instruments still in use one may also mention the goblet-shaped drums, drums with one skin made of heavy hollowed-out tree-trunks, as well as gongs with broad rims, which have been imported from Java.

Of this island only three districts will be examined in detail: southern Celebes (the people of Macassar and the Buginese), central Celebes (the Toradja), and the northern peninsula of Minahassa.

Celebes

The inhabitants of Macassar and the Buginese are renowned for their chanted heroic epic poems, in which the story-teller accompanies himself on a lute with two strings, played with a bow.

Another type of lute, which also has two strings, is not played with a bow but plucked. This instrument is of a more pleasing slender shape, and is frequently decorated with magnificent fretwork.

We also come across the *rebana* here, as is usual in Islamic areas.

Furthermore, mention should be made of a long bamboo flute with six holes, a primitive oboe in the shape of the *serunai* to which reference has already been made, as well as a large drum with two heads, the larger of which is beaten with a curved stick, but the smaller one with the hand. Besides these relatively melodious instruments a large number of objects are used in southern Celebes to make noises to exorcize evil spirits, particularly at the birth of princes' children.

The singing of the Toradja sounds monotonous, as it is restricted to the compass of a few notes. The singer is usually accompanied on three one-stringed lutes, played with a bow, their resonators being made from coconut-shell or of wood. In addition there are bamboo flutes, short transverse flutes as well as longer ones. As one would expect, these instruments are magnificently engraved, and also decorated with poker-work in the old style. The vertical flutes often have a resonating cone made of buffalo horn.

Finally one may mention the bamboo 'buzzer' which we came across on Nias Island.

In Minahassa, just as on northern Nias, everything in the way of native art has disappeared. Here, too, when Christianity was introduced, the missionaries failed to appreciate that a culture can be destroyed, but it cannot be artificially rebuilt. Of the little that has survived, one may mention the harvest songs for four voices or more, sung polyphonically.

Wherever Christianity became established in Celebes, the bamboo transverse flute with four, five or six holes is generally to be found; it is often played by schoolchildren. This instrument originates from Ambon in the south Moluccas; Christianity was introduced here as early as the sixteenth century by the Portuguese, and was later spread further in Protestant form by the Dutch.

Moluccas Nowhere else in Indonesia is such a general renunciation of native traditions to be found as here, on these Christianized islands. Relics of the ancient culture only exist sporadically, with the result that in this whole area the musical instruments used are practically the same. In the islands of the northern Moluccas — Ternate, Halmaheira, Batjan and Tidore — instruments are known which were spread by Islam, and which we have already referred to in the section on Sumatra above.

On the Moluccas there are also to be found goblet-shaped drums, imported gongs, one-stringed lutes played with the bow, as well as bamboo zithers.

The Kei islands, situated in the south-east, are musically the least impoverished. The songs there are constructed diatonically, and are sung in various metres — even up to five-quarter, and are particularly attractive.

Lesser Sunda Islands In complete contrast to the poverty of the Moluccas, the group of islands to the east of Java can boast of great musical wealth. The first of these islands, Bali, will be dealt with separately; it has also exercised a great influence upon the neighbouring island of Lombok. On Sumbawa there are, in addition to influences from Java, also instruments that were introduced with Islam. One may note the fine violins, built in the pitch of violas.

The island of Flores occupies a very special place. The various tribes settled here display individual characteristics both in their musical instruments and in their singing. This island, too, became almost completely Christianized, but the art of the natives was spared. In the districts of Endé and Lio very harmonious diatonic harvest songs are popular. The singing of the people of Manggarai resembles yodelling, whilst in other districts even three- and four-part singing is known. A rather remarkable relic of Western influence upon eastern Flores exists in the shape of folk-songs originating from 17th-century north-western

Polychrome dance mask, wood (*hodo apah*). (Mahakam district, eastern Borneo). *K.I.T.*
(Maximum breadth 20¾ ins.)

Europe, which have survived in a form almost unmodified by time. The Portuguese and Ambonese, too, have also left traces of their presence here.

As far as musical instruments are concerned, Flores possesses indirectly blown bass flutes, which are only to be found on this island, and also bamboo zithers, bamboo slit-drums, small gongs, pan-pipes, very primitive one-stringed lutes played with the bow, and a very simply constructed xylophone.

Much of the music played by the inhabitants of the central districts of Timor corresponds to that on Flores, although it lacks the same rich variety of form. The inhabitants of the coastal districts, on the other hand, were exposed to various foreign influences, and have thus lost much of their individuality. From the neighbouring island of Roti they have adopted a particularly fine instrument, a bamboo zither, *sesando*, with between ten and thirty-six strings of copper wire and a hemispherical resonator made of leaves of the nipah palm.

On the island of Alor the most notable instrument is the kettle-drum, *moko*, already referred to, which plays a special part in bride purchase. There are also small Jew's harps (mouth-harps), bamboo flutes, drums with one head, and, on practically all the islands, small gongs, which were presumably imported from Java.

Finally, reference may be made to the 'vibrated-shriek' songs of the women of the island of Sumba. This is certainly a relic of ritual customs; with songs of this kind they must have welcomed their husbands after a successful head-hunting expedition.

DANCING   The dance is common to the civilization of all peoples at all times. Man thought that in rhythmic movements of his body he possessed an excellent medium through which he could enter into contact with supernatural powers. Where belief in magic is prevalent, men hope to exert influence upon *mana* most effectively by means of dances. For magic is a desire and striving to implement one's aspirations and wishes by means of conspicuous display. "In a dance all the important desires and fears of the clan or tribe are represented rhythmically. The same applies to music. It is an attempt to propitiate the menacing cosmic forces, or to subject them to the will of the tribe by means of expressionist rhythm, etc." [1]

The aim desired, it is thought, can be attained by completely abandoning oneself to this compulsive rhythm, by surrendering oneself to the constantly repeated and metrically phrased strains of the accompanying instruments, and finally by succumbing to an ecstasy bordering upon frenzy. The main thing is not graceful gestures or beauty of movement but rather complete fusion with the rhythm of the music. The dance is here a ritual proceeding which has a definite purpose. In this way there developed harvest dances, dances to ward off illnesses or other misfortunes, *danses macabres*, etc. On occasion masks are worn to emphasize one's desire to escape 'beyond oneself'. In Indonesia it is once again those tribes living almost in isolation from the outer world who maintained longest the dance in its original ritual form.

Of truly breath-taking beauty are the masked dances formerly performed by the Bataks for those who died without leaving male descendants. The masks worn for such dances are amongst the most magnificent to have been made by men for a magic purpose. It is remarkable how human and moving in their immediacy these masks are, especially if one merely observes the face.

Masked dances

PLATE P. 177

An absolutely different approach is reflected in the masks of the Dayaks. Any naturalistic resemblance is dispensed with, the mouth protrudes like a snout, showing four laniary teeth, and the demonic character is unmistakable. The linear decoration is similar in style to the ornamentation common amongst the Dayaks. A human aspect is retained only in the ear-pendants: the Dayaks, too, wear heavy ear-pendants, often resulting in distended lobes.

PLATE P. 181

Very many dances are executed in the most primitive fashion as round dances, in many cases by women and maidens. From the Batak districts the ceremonial *sibaso* dance, which is performed by the Toba women, deserves to be mentioned.

Southern Sumatra and the adjacent area of central Sumatra is the scene of dances performed by unmarried girls, who are draped in heavy vestments interlaced with gold, and wear upon their heads a crown adorned with gilded laurel leaves. These dances are usually accompanied by five or six small gongs resting upon crossed ropes in wooden stands. These dances, too, have been influenced by foreign styles: their magic-evoking character has yielded to graceful restrained female charm.

On northern Nias a complete stop was put to native dancing at the instigation of the missionaries. Only in the southern half of the island did some of the old war dances, snake dances, and graceful round dances survive.

Of the numerous dances of the Toradja the best known are those performed at funeral ceremonies. The ritual, with its strange and often grotesque customs, attracted attention already at an early date. And when a distinguished person was snatched by death, the 'festivities' were complicated and lengthy. Their climax came with the sacrifice of several buffaloes and the burial of the corpse in a grotto set high up in a sheer cliff face. An important element in the death rites was the round dance, or *ma'badong*.

In our survey of music we have already mentioned that the musical culture on the island of Flores is particularly varied, and here the dances are also quite different in type. In addition to masculine war-dances and ritual sacrificial dances, there are several round dances, and also dances performed by young girls, which are characterized by an exquisite grace.

As mentioned before, dancing, like music, was greatly modified by external cultural influences, both in form and in manner of execution. This is very evident, for instance, in south-eastern Borneo. The instruments which are common there belong to the ancient eastern Javanese gamelan; and we find the same Javanese influence, dating from the Madjapahit era, in the dances performed by young girls. Indonesia is exceptionally rich in music and dancing, which, after all, go hand in hand. But this wealth is exeedingly sensitive to change for good or ill. Only where the people are aware of the value of what they possess can they attempt to keep in check the levelling materialistic tendencies apparent everywhere in the world. The problems arising from this will be dealt with more fully in the last chapter.

[1] Prof. Dr. C. Tj. Bertling, 'Sociale werkelijkheid bij de primitieven'.

XII. BALI

Through a strange freak of history Bali, which like the neighbouring island of Java had adopted so much from Indian culture, and was certainly no 'forgotten area', remained almost entirely untouched by Islam. In the whole of Indonesia it is only on this small island, some 2100 square miles in area, that Hinduism has survived up to the present day. Without doubt this was to a large extent due to the fact that the kingdom of Balambangan on eastern Java, with its Hindu-Javanese culture, was for a long time able to resist the pressure of the Mohammedan kingdom of Mataram. *Hinduism*

On Bali a culture developed of a unique character: Hindu, Buddhist, Hindu-Javanese and ancient Balinese elements merged to form a 'unity in diversity'. Little is known about the first contact with Indian civilization on Bali, as is also the case in Sumatra and Java. Although Chinese references exist, dating from the first half of the 6th century, which presumably relate to Bali, it is not until the 8th century that we have more accurate information.

To the south of Pèdjèng clay tablets have been found with a Buddhist MAP P. 185

sacred text in a script probably dating from the 8th century. But the first documents bearing a date do not appear until the 10th century; at that time Indian civilization must have already been in existence here for some centuries. A significant find is a document carved in stone dealing with the foundation of the bathing-place Tirta Empul, dating MAP P. 185 from the year 962, written in the language common on Bali at that

186

time. But from 989 onwards documents appear which indicate a gradual Javanization of the island.

As has already been pointed out in the chapter on the spreading of Indian culture, the first clearly established union between the dynasty of Mataram (which had then withdrawn to eastern Java) and the ruling prince of Bali was brought about at the end of the 10th century. This prince, Udayana, married the Javanese princess Mahéndradatta; in 1010 their son Airlangga was crowned king of Mataram and both kingdoms were united under his sceptre.

After his death Bali came under the sovereignty of the kingdom of Kediri, but remained fairly independent under the rule of Airlangga's descendants. But as a result of the close dynastic link between the two islands, Bali became flooded with Javanese culture. This is shown, for instance, by the style of the cliff tjandis of Tampaksiring, dating from the 11th century, as well as the type of characters used in inscriptions, which largely correspond to the architecture and script of eastern Java at the time of the Kediri dynasty.

PLATE P. 186

It is remarkable that these tjandis are not free-standing buildings, but are hewn out of steep cliffs, so that each stands in a recess of its own. Next to these recesses a hermitage was also built into the cliff.

This above mentioned political independence continued until Kertanagara, the most powerful prince of the Singhasari dynasty, acceded to the throne. In 1284 he took the last descendant of Airlangga to rule in Bali to Java as a prisoner, and governed Bali from there. Kertanagara was murdered in 1292, and Bali adroitly utilized the opportunity provided by the political dissension in eastern Java to regain its liberty. But it was once again subjected when Gadjah Mada raised the Madjapahit dynasty to a new summit of power. He ordered the Javanese to establish a settlement on Bali, thus ensuring that Java's influence upon this refractory island should be permanent. The consequences of this measure were to prove more far-reaching than its *auctor intellectualis* could foresee: when the mighty kingdom of Madjapahit collapsed and many valuable art treasures were lost in Java, eastern Javanese culture was able to maintain itself on Bali. As has been mentioned earlier, many literary works which appeared in eastern Java were re-discovered on Bali.

In the events of later years the Kingdom of Gèlgèl now emerges. Its rise must be dated to the 14th century. Attempts to extend its authority over neighbouring areas, the Hindu Balambangan and the island of Lombok to the east of Bali, finally bore fruit, but in 1651 this kingdom broke up into several small districts as a result of intrigue and internal dissensions. Balambangan retained its link with Bali until 1772, whilst Lombok remained subject to the Balinese until 1894. The loss of the above-mentioned territories was the result of Dutch expansion. After several unsuccessful attempts between 1846 and 1849, which led only to the conquest of the northern part of the island, Bali finally fell into Dutch hands in 1908.

From this brief historical sketch it can be seen that up to the latter half of the 10th century Bali was directly exposed to Indian culture; that in the subsequent period Java's influence is clearly discernible; and that after the decline of the kingdom of Majapahit Bali developed along independent cultural lines.

Religion, society and temples Bali has justly been called the island of a thousand temples. And although this may sound a little like a travel brochure, it is not really so misleading, for the temples on Bali are of more than mere external importance.

In the first place, an examination of temples and temple customs affords one an insight into religious thought on the island. But in addition to this the temples, with their varied functions, give one an idea of the complex social conditions that prevailed on Bali, whilst the architecture and decoration of these sacred buildings is often on a most impressive scale.

The style of temple architecture is determined by ancient pre-Hindu ideas to a greater extent than is the case in eastern Java. Undoubtedly eastern Javanese influences have left a certain imprint upon the style, but they have not ousted local influences. The ornamentation and decoration, on the other hand, display marked Hindu features. The PLATE P. 189 Balinese temple is a terraced building; as is the case in the temple complex of Panataran, the various buildings do not give the impression of forming a composite whole. But on Bali, to an even greater extent than in Java, one is struck by the lack of adherence to any recognizable system, either as regards design or use of material. In Balinese temples the most remarkable feature is the often profuse exuberance of ornamental decoration.

"Hindu sculpture found a favourable climate in which to develop on Bali, as it did also in Java. Already at an early date the stone terraces, sacrificial recesses, temple walls and gateways of Balinese temples were decorated with arabesques and spirals, demons' heads and images of deities. Ornamentation was at first subdued, and integrated into the buildings with fine sense of proportion, but in the course of time

Tjandi Kubu Tambahan. Terrace stairway with entrance-gate. On the gate a baroque ornamentation in *paras* (Bali).

these tendrils and spirals became more florid and exuberant at the hands of Balinese artists. Decoration came to play an ever more important part in the design as a whole. The artist was seized with an irrepressible impulse to create a superfluity of petals and leaves, until the temples seemed almost smothered in a veritable orgy of stone flowers and garlands.

In central Bali the gateways are broader, with massive spiral ornamentation — mighty supports for the sculpture-bedecked walls of the temples and princes' palaces. In the north of the island the slender temple gateways with their more elegant pointed antefixes tower high above the walls and sacrificial recesses." [1]

Plan of the temples

Whilst the magnificent monuments erected in Java by the princes of the central Javanese period differ in style, material, and also to a certain degree in purpose, from the simple sanctuaries of the *désa*, the buildings of these two types on Bali remained more akin to one another. Thus the mountain sanctuary of Besakih, the temple of the kingdom of Gèlgèl on the southern slope of Gunung Agung (*gunung* = mountain), dating from the 14th century, has the same plan as

PLATE P. 193

many village temples in Bali. Besides the *pura* Besakih, several other sacral buildings from that era have survived. Some of these, such as Sad Kahjangan, are amongst the most majestic temples that exist. In addition to the Besakih, the mother temple or chief sanctuary, one may also mention the Panataran Sasih of Pèdjèng, where the bronze drum, the famous 'Moon of Bali' already referred to, is preserved and venerated. The layout of such a temple, *pura*, (its simplest form, the *pura-désa*, is to be found in almost every village) is basically as follows:

The temple as a whole consists of three open courts, enclosed by walls and connected with one another by gates. The first one is entered by means of a 'split' gate, *tjandi-bentar*. It can be most easily envisaged as two halves of a small tjandi, which are so far apart that there is a

PLATE P. 196

wide enough passage between them. Gates of this type are also met with in eastern Java, and are also depicted on bas-reliefs found in Desa Trawulan, which is situated on the same spot where the ancient capital of Madjapahit formerly stood. Curiously enough, the old mosque at Kudus, a 16th-century Islamic building, also has a similar gate.

From this first court, in which, incidentally, the Balinese staged their popular cock-fights, one passes into the second court through a cover-

PLATE P. 196

ed gateway, *paduraksa*. This gate is one of the most splendidly decorated structures of the whole temple complex, its plan being based on that of a tjandi. In the second court there stands the great assembly-hall, *balé-agung*, where the elders of the community meet, and where certain rites are also performed. Here, too, is to be found the signal drum, *kulkul*, made from a hollowed-out cylindrically-shaped piece of wood, split lengthwise. This court is completed by several sacrificial recesses and sheds for the slaughter of sacrificial animals.

The third court, to which one also gains access through a gateway, is the temple proper. There are no idols here. The Balinese imagine their deities as residing upon the peaks of the many volcanoes which tower up in the interior of the island. A stone seat for a deity, *padma-sana* (*padma* = lotus), has indeed been erected here; this spot, for the most part lavishly decorated, is where the deity invoked is thought to be present, invisible to human eyes, during the ceremony.

In a similar way, in the neolithic era, certain megaliths served as seats of ancestors.

Here tower up the symbols of the celestial mountain, *meru*, the seat of the gods. With their roofs piled one upon another like a multi-storeyed building, they dominate the landscape of Bali. A meru indicates the rank which its deity holds among the other gods. The higher the god, the more roofs there are. Their number is always uneven, with the highest number being eleven. This eleven-storeyed meru is dedicated to Shiva, the Māha-Déva (Supreme Deity), who resides upon the Gunung Agung. Merus to Brahma and Vishnu have nine storeys. The stone base is generally lavishly decorated with sculptures. In the uppermost storey stands an urn of clay containing offerings inscribed with magic words.

Next to the merus stand countless small shrines and recesses for offerings. The fact that on Bali art is closely connected with the religious outlook of the people is shown by the existence of a place of sacrifice to Déva Bagus Mantja Gina, the tutelary deity of the five crafts: iron-, copper- and gold-working, wood-carving and painting. Traces of Hinduism are indeed clearly apparent here, but the population has retained the primitive ancestor cult as the essential function of the temple. This is also quite clear from the fact that the Balinese also has his own domestic temple, *sanggah*, with recesses for offerings and shrines for sacrificial acts required in the ancestor cult. But Hinduism has left its imprint on these domestic temples, as is shown by the existence of sacrificial recesses, *pasimpangan*, for the Mountain God and the Sun God, Surya. The word *pasimpangan* means 'a place where one abides a while', i.e. where the deity stays temporarily amongst men during the ceremony.

Merus

PLATE P. 193

Actually a better name for this sacred spot would be 'household temple'. For the smallest unit within the désa is not the family in our restricted sense of the term, but a patriarchal community comprising descendants of the same father, grandfather, or even great-grandfather. The courtyard in which this family group lives communally is surrounded by a wall, and the terrain is divided into three areas, as in the pura. From the village street one gains access through the gate of the courtyard into the first area, in which one finds stalls for cattle, barns for rice, sheds for tools, etc. In the second area adjoining the first are the living quarters, whilst the shrine of the household is accommodated in the third area.

Associations for irrigation
Thus the ubiquitous village temple and the household shrine demonstrate the close relationship that exists between the social life and religious conceptions of the Balinese. This is evidenced still more clearly in the temple of the cooperative association for irrigation, *pura-subak,* to be found in most désas. In Bali rice is the main crop, and the Balinese is expert in its cultivation. From 'Tafelhuk' in the south MAP P. 185 right up to the slopes of the range of volcanoes in the interior of the island there stretch the *sawahs,* terraced fields, fed by an extraordinarily complicated system of irrigation, the work of many centuries. The distribution of water to the various fields, and the maintenance of the irrigation installations can naturally only be effected without friction when the owners of the sawahs collaborate closely, for each one is dependent upon his neighbour. In general the members of the désa get along with one another quite well, but it does sometimes happen that their fields are not exactly co-terminous with the territory of the désa, or that a village draws water from several irrigation systems. Such matters fall within the competence of the co-operative association for irrigation, the *subak,* which also has its own temple. If for some reason it should not have one, then one or more recesses for offerings in the village temple, *pura-désa,* are reserved for it. They are dedicated to the goddess of rice and fertility, Devi Shri, who is also venerated in this capacity in Java. Here we have a characteristic example of the way in which primitive conceptions have acquired Hindu features. Shri, the shākti of Vishnu, became the goddess of fertility, PLATE P. 200 as symbolized in rice. In decorative art we frequently come across the *tjilih* figure, a simplified representation of Devi Shri.

Temple to the dead
But in addition to the three sanctuaries mentioned, *pura-désa, sanggah,* and *pura-subak,* every désa has yet another temple, the purpose of which points to a completely different aspect of Balinese religious

thought. Near the cremation ground (cremation was adopted from the Hindus) stands the temple to the dead, *pura-dalem*, dedicated to Batari Durga, the shākti of Shiva, the goddess of death. For although the Balinese believes that he has the protective blessing of his numerous deities, nevertheless he feels himself threatened by demons and evil spirits. By means of sacrifices to Batari Durga he seeks to escape the threat of calamity.

In addition to these désa temples (we may still mention the temple to the Mountain God, *pura-bukit*, and to the Sea God, *pura-segara*, which are not to be found everywhere), there are countless other holy places, the significance of which extends beyond the confines of the locality in which they are situated. For example, there are many fountain puras, amongst which the temple of Tirta Empul near Tampaksiring deserves to be mentioned. The water from this fountain is deemed to have a special purifying power. Every year sees the population of Gianjar bringing their everyday objects here to be blessed.

The mountain sanctuary *pura* Besakih, the temple of the kingdom of Gèlgèl, 14th century. View looking towards the entrance. In the centre eleven-storeyed *meru* dedicated to Shiva. (Bali).

The water from such fountains with a cleansing effect is also used in the funeral rite.

Finally, one may mention the temples situated in the neighbourhood of the lakes in the volcanic craters, such as those near Lake Batur, Lake Bratan, and others. These lakes, from which the rivers were thought to take their source, were naturally the object of particular veneration on the part of men who imagined their gods to live on the peaks of volcanoes, and who were completely dependent upon abundant water for their rice cultivation.

Priests The actual ceremony in the temple of the community is not performed by a fully-qualified Hindu priest, a *pedanda*, but by a *pamangku*, a sort of lay priest from the village, who is at the same time curator of the temple. It is only at the special festivities which inaugurate the annual purification of the village from demons and evil spirits that the pedanda appears and blesses the offerings with holy water. The fact that he has thus no direct connection with the villagers is the consequence of the specific social system which became established on Bali after the introduction of the Hindu caste system. Whilst in India differentiation between the castes developed into an almost unbridgeable stratified social system, Bali still has in the main the classical division: the three castes, *triwangsa*, i.e. the Brahmans (with the title Ida), the Kshatriyas (title: Tjokorde or Déva), and the Vaishyas (title: Gusti) stand in contrast to the original indigenous population of Bali, *wong ksamèn*, who are allotted to the *shudra* group as casteless. We shall not go into the sub-divisions of the three castes, the many groups amongst the shudras, the origin of which is generally recorded in *presastis*, sacred documents written on lontar leaves, and shall merely point out that the five crafts mentioned above, the *pantjagina*, provide an example of the way in which such groups were formed. These presastis are kept secret, but in so far as they are made known, they show that the Balinese have a well-developed feeling for their own dignity, and certainly do not consider themselves inferior in rank. The few members of castes living amongst the rest of the population occupy no privileged place in the life of the village, although their rank is respected.

Daily life The daily life of the villagers takes its course in house, field and market under the patriarchal supervision of the authorities of the community and the subak. In the older-established villages the upper class is formed by the patriarchs of those families descended from the founder of the village, the *kromo-désa*. They manage the economy of the village, and the other inhabitants owe them obedience.

In the more recent types of désa authority is exercised by a so-called *klian*, who is elected at the village meeting, the centre of village life, and who is deemed to hold his authority from the gods. Not only must they constantly take care of the material needs of the community, but they must also observe ceremonies to maintain contact with ancestors, gods and tutelary spirits, and to keep off demons and evil spirits.

The women of the village are in charge of the sacrifices deemed indispensable for many varied purposes, such as the proper cultivation of the fields, the averting of dangers when a journey is undertaken, and especially all the landmarks in human life which are considered important and subject to magic influence: birth, first cutting of nails and hair, filing of teeth, piercing of ear-lobes, and subsequently contracting of marriage, and finally death.

Ceremonies do not always take place within the closed group which comprises the household. Important events concern the whole village, and on such occasions the village temple becomes the point around which everything revolves: for instance, at the odalan festival, to commemorate the building of the temple, at the njepi, the day on which the village is cleansed from demons and evil spirits, and the harvest festival, for the course of which the authorities of the subak are naturally responsible. And finally everyone participates in the cult of the dead and the cremation of corpses, for death is a most mysterious transition to another life, and it intervenes in a man's life more deeply than anything else.

Ceremonies

On such occasions Balinese art displays a wealth and variety that are unique in the world. Colourful offerings, piled up high, are carried by the womenfolk on their heads, and are presented with reverential and graceful movements; fascinating temple dances are performed, many of serene beauty, and others of an enthralling primitive force, with rhythmical movements of torso, arms, and hands. Then there is the splendour and lustre of the magnificent fabrics and the merry, melodious strains of the gamelan. At open-air performances old legends are acted out in all their terror and demonic force. And finally we find wondrous effigies built upon carrying-poles which play their part in the cremation ceremony, and in which the Balinese demonstrates his strongly-marked sense of beauty and his ability to create artistic decorations despite the simplicity of the materials at his disposal. And in so far as these festivities take place in the temple, the gateways and walls provide a fitting background to this colourful, animated scene of enchanting splendour.

It is impossible to describe here in detail all the customs and artistic attainments associated with this ceremony. I am well aware that these few remarks can give only a very inadequate picture. The reader may be referred to the extensive literature that exists about this uniquely rich and fascinating island.

Applied art in connection with the pura The walls and gates and other parts are constructed of brick or of other natural stone, *paras*. This paras is a fairly soft type of stone, which can be carved easily but which weathers much more rapidly. Thus many of the fine old buildings and sculptures have been lost to us. But as the Balinese is morally obliged to maintain his temples in proper state, much is also being restored and fine new works are constantly being produced. Thus sculpture in stone is still today a flourishing living art. The balance between the building itself and its ornamentation has admittedly been spoilt in many cases, because

Pura-désa Pasaban. Rear view of main entrance, *paduraksa.* To the right a side-entrance, a 'split' gate, *tjandi-bentar.* (Bali)

196

the decorations are florid to an extreme, often obscuring the general appearance of the building. Despite this often baroque-like exuberance, the artistry is nevertheless enchanting, since the artists have apparently given full vent to their taste for ornamentation and passion for creation. PLATE P. 203

As has already been mentioned, the Balinese do not place any images in their sacrificial recesses and temples. But formerly such images were indeed fashioned, particularly during that period when a stimulus was provided from eastern Java, i.e. between the 11th and 15th centuries. Most of these images have been found in a narrow strip of land between two small rivers, the Pakerisan and the Petanu, extending from the south coast up to the mountains (cf. Map). It was presumably in this district that the kingdom of Pèdjèng was situated, with its centre at Beduluh-Pèdjèng, where at one time King Udayana resided. This was the classical period, characterized by sculptures of princes in the image of gods at the spot where the ashes of the prince or his consort were interred. The question arises whether this is original Balinese art or sculpture carved under the influence of eastern Java. In support of this latter assumption it may be noted that the cliff tjandis of Tampaksiring, referred to earlier, are distinctly akin in style to Javanese tjandis. Nor do these sculptures mean so much to the Balinese; they regard them much in the same way as the Mohammedan Javanese do similar sculptures in Java. When Bali developed along independent lines, at any rate, these stone idols no longer played any significant part — although the Balinese do erect demonic figures in stone, *totogs-batu,* in order to protect their temples and homes from demons and evil spirits. MAP. P. 185

This does not of course mean that the Balinese have not created any idols; but these either serve rather as an additional embellishment, or else are carved of wood, in which case they are not designed for a temple, *pura.*

Sculpture belongs to the craft of wood-working, one of the five crafts, *pantja-gina.* There is much affinity in technique between the working of rather soft paras and wood. Thus it is not surprising to find the lavish ornamentation of Balinese wood-carving in the paras sculptures as well. The former have not been worked with such elaboration, but they nevertheless also testify to the same sense of decorative effect. *Wood-carving and sculpture in wood*

Ornamental wood-carving is to be found in the homes of members of the three castes. Furthermore, the three wooden supports of the carefully-built rice-barns are also richly decorated with figures of a PLATE P. 214

magic character, such as images of Devi-Shri, winged lions (*singas*), etc. Ornamental wood-carving is also extremely popular on the wooden lower parts and supports of gamelan instruments. With his predilection for pronounced effects, the Balinese artist painted his carvings gaily with lime-water colours. This also had the effect of making life difficult for the wood-worm!

The art of sculpture in wood also flourished, the themes being drawn from Hindu symbolism and the Hindu pantheon, as was also the case with decorative wood-carving. These wooden figures show very little feeling for space. They are usually in frontal style and as rigidly symmetrical as possible. They owe their particular charm rather to

their polychromatic ornamentation.

Such figures were also frequently used as stands for krisses, evidence of the deference paid to this weapon.

Besides the more traditional sculptures which remain entirely within the limits of Hindu religious thought, figures are also met with which may be called profane. In the wooden sculptures of Batuan various scenes from everyday life have been reproduced in a pertinent and often humorous manner. These works arose from an attitude of mind which facilitated penetration by the secularized West, a process that began several decades ago.

Work of smiths As in Java, so also on Bali the kris is the armourer's greatest achievement. On this island, too, this craft is held in high esteem, and is regarded as a gift of the gods. The Balinese, with his pronounced predilection for splendour and ostentation, knew how to give these objects an individual *cachet*. The blade is mostly fashioned in pamor work, but the figures are more accentuated than is the case in Java. This is partly due to the fact that the meteoric steel used here has a higher nickel content. But on Bali the armourer makes the design show up more clearly by polishing the blade, so that the lustrous pamor nickel is set off better against the background of blue-black steel.

On the hilt a human figure is represented, usually a *raksasa*, to ward off evil spirits. These hilts are not so stylized as those on Java; the figures are much more lifelike.

Ivory, precious and semi-precious metals are employed with considerable technical skill and choice taste.

Gold and silver work The Balinese love pomp and splendour, and like to use precious metals for making Hindu devotional objects, jewels, vessels for holy water, etc., and also for articles used in everyday life. Various techniques are known, but it is in the very difficult art of engraving gold that the Balinese goldsmith particularly excels. The reason why this technique is so difficult is because one slip of the graver is sufficient to ruin the technical perfection of the work, and thus its particular attraction and value; the only thing that can then be done is to polish the whole surface anew.

For their figures the Balinese engravers draw mostly upon the inexhaustible source provided by the Hindu pantheon.

A special pattern is to be found on the pinang scissors with which hard pinang nuts, an ingredient of the sirih quid, are cracked. Here, too, one finds the swastika motif, the *bandji*, as on Javanese batiks.

It is true of Bali, as of everywhere in Indonesia, that with precious metals it is their form, colour and pattern that are appreciated more than the value of the material used, and artistic effect more than the value of the actual material.

In Java painting was neglected after the Hindu-Javanese period, but *Painting* on Bali it has remained a living art. Episodes from literary works particularly those inspired by Hinduism, such as the Bhāratayuddha and Rāmāyana, were painted in lime-water colours on domestic woven textiles, flat beaten bast, wood, gourds, bamboo vessels, and ceramic objects. These paintings are two-dimensional in conception, with the PLATE P. 218 same person sometimes being represented in various situations simultaneously. Under the influence of Western works, Balinese painting evolved along completely individual lines. In their choice of themes, painters, like wood-carvers, turned from the sacred to the profane, from the world of gods and demons to the world of men. In form the transition was effected from the two-dimensional to the three-dimensional, retaining a strong predilection for the ornamental, particularly in the shape of trees and flowers.

A particularly valuable and characteristic achievement of Balinese *Temple plays* native art is the open-air play, in which the Balinese is able to display *and -dances* in a most impressive manner his sense of dramatic form. Plays of this type are tremendously effective, not only by reason of the grotesque figures employed, but even more so by the skill with which the actors express their feelings in gestures. The realism of these plays often inspire the spectator with terror, but the strains of the gamelan ensure that a rhythmic effect is maintained.

No setting could be more appropriate for such a performance than the temple court, no atmosphere so ideal as a tropical evening when the light from the torches and the wood fire make the movements of

Cotton fabric, *lamak*: detail, supplementary warp weaving technique. Design: stylized *tjilih* figure, over it sun motif, *tumpal* on both sides. (Bali). *Collection of J. and L. Langewis.*

the play, with its eery silhouette effects, seem still more lifelike. The main characters in this play are demonic figures, such as a woman named Rangda, and a legendary monster, Barong.

The play in which the widow, *rangda*, appears is based upon an ancient legend which goes back to the time of King Airlangga. In those days, we are told, there lived in Girah a widow by the name of Tjalon-Arang, who had a daughter of dazzling beauty. But the mother was suspected of dabbling in the black arts, and thus no young suitor dared to ask the young maiden for her hand, although she was of great virtue. Embittered, Rangda decided to take revenge upon the men who had caused her daughter suffering by their reproaches against her, Rangda.

One night she repaired to the pura-dalem and besought the goddess Durga to bestow demonic power upon her, so that she might destroy mankind. Durga granted her request, and with several other women she set about her diabolical work. Within a short time the flourishing and prosperous district had been turned into a place of death and terror. The distress was so great that it even came to the ears of King Airlangga, who decided to intervene; he sent soldiers to kill the witch, but only a few of them returned; the others had been slain by Tjalon-Arang through her demonic power.

Thereupon Rangda resolved to pursue her campaign of annihilation with still greater zeal. For this purpose she allotted the four quarters of heaven amongst her cronies, reserving for herself the centre and zenith for her destructive work.

King Airlangga, realizing that he was faced with demonic powers, and that his warriors were powerless, called upon a hermit, Shri Baradah, for assistance. The latter was able to arrange a marriage between his disciple Bahula and Tjalon-Arang's daughter. But when Bahula noticed that his mother-in-law went nightly to the pura-dalem, he realized what was the source of her demonic power, and stole her magic books, giving them to his teacher. Shri Baradah was now in a position to break Rangda's demonic power. At first he succeeded in reclaiming her companions, and finally in killing Tjalon-Arang with the magic power of his glance.

In its popular version this legend has been provided with a supplement, according to which Tjalon-Arang is none other than the mother of King Airlangga, the Javanese princess Mahéndradatta, who accused her son of murdering her husband Udayana. She is then said to have decided to take vengeance and destroy Airlangga's kingdom.

It can hardly be ascertained to what extent this legend may have been based upon historical fact. But one may point to a remarkable sculpture of Durga as Goddess of Death and Witchcraft, which is believed to be a sepulchral monument for Princess Mahéndradatta. This statue, found near Kutri, is one of the finest works of sculpture dating from the era of the Beduluh-Pèdjèng kingdom.

It does not take much imagination to see that this legend provided an excellent dramatic subject. The gripping sensation which the play, and especially the demonic figure of Rangda, produce upon the spectator will never be forgotten by anyone who has been fortunate enough to have attended one of these performances. The demonic mask of the principal figure, with its truly terrifying features, its dis-shevelled white hair and long fiery tongue, is characteristic of the artistic sense of a people like the Balinese, who feel themselves continually threatened by diabolical forces. The figure of Barong is also demonic: he usually appears in the shape of a monster rather like a bison, manipulated by two men. In this play, to an even greater extent than in the Tjalon-Arang play, the whole action is dominated by this monster. When it moves across the stage in the flickering light, it seems uncannily lifelike. Barong is the counterpart of Rangda, and also appears in other forms, for instance, in the stage version of an episode from the eastern Javanese Ardjunavivāha, as the *damalung*, or wild boar: it is shot simultaneously by Shiva and Ardjuna, which subsequently gives rise to further complications.

Comparison with Javanese wayang

If one compares these dumb-shows with the similar ones in Java, the wayang-wong and the wayang-topèng, those on Bali strike one as being much more dynamic. In just the same way, Balinese dancing differs from the Serimpi and Bedaya dances in Java already referred to. On Bali, too, dancing consists of stylized movements, but it has more verve, and is, so to speak, more 'warm-blooded'. The same applies to gamelan music, which forms a single entity with the dance.

The *légong* dance is performed by two or three maidens, whilst the dalang comments on the individual phases of the dance, and speaks the relevant parts. The exeedingly attractive restrained movements require complete bodily control on the part of the dancers, which is attainable only after years of training.

Quite different in style is the *djangèr* performance: in this young men and maidens form a large square; two rows of men sit opposite one another, with the girl dancers forming the two other rows. The actual

The *pura-désa* at Bangli. An example of overdoing of ornamentation. The principal figures represent (from the bottom upwards): Ardjuna, Raksasa, Garuda, Vishnu and Shiva, flanked by Durga and Ganesha. (Bali).

symbolic dance itself takes place within the square; it is led by a man known as the 'dag'. The young men seated round about accompany the action in the centre of the square with rhythmic movements.

Neither of these dances have a religious background. This, however, it the case with the *sanghyans*, in which the girls dance in a state of ecstasy, celestial powers being thought to manifest themselves in the dancers.

In the *ketjak* dance many male dancers take part. This also shows the marked talent the Balinese have for representing a dramatic situation. This dance depicts episodes from the Rāmāyana. The scene in which the monkey host is called to arms by its king, Hanuman, is an uncommonly impressive scene, a masterpiece of stage management, with the rhythmic movements of countless torsos, arms and hands, interspersed with the cries of the dancers, affording a performance of breath-taking excitement.

Wayang and gamelan

The wayang plays also have their accepted place in the life of the Balinese, along with the Tjalon-Arang play, Barong plays, and the various dances, of which we have only mentioned the best known. It has already been stated that the open-air plays in Bali bear comparison with the wayang-wong and wayang-topèng in Java, although the former do not belong to these types of wayang. This is only so when plays in which masks are worn derive their subject-matter from such 'classical' epic poems as the Rāmāyana, the Mahābhārata and the Pandji cycle.

Very many masks are in use, for not only is the number of performers very great, but each actor has different masks for different appearances, the facial expressions of which are adapted to each situation. This, of course, makes exacting demands upon the artistry and skill of the craftsmen who fashion the masks.

A comparison of the figures on these masks with those on the *topèng* masks illustrates the differences in outlook between artists in Java and Bali. Javanese art often displays a finesse, and at the same time a serene composure which, so to speak, is elevated far above everything mundane. But the Balinese artist draws directly upon his own experience; his masks often represent changing human moods.

The wayang-wong (*wong* = man) comprises only those plays in which no masks are worn, and the subject-matter is drawn from the Rāmāyana; plays based on the Mahābhārata and Bhāratayuddha are called *wayang-parwa*. The Javanese wayang-purwa is only known on Bali by name of *wayang-kulit*. In addition to the 'classical' repertoire, the

Tjalon-Arang legend, characteristically enough, is also performed as a 'shadow play'.

In all the plays mentioned the gamelan is absolutely indispensable. As in Java, so also on Bali, several gamelan systems are met with, each differing according to the purpose it serves. Despite their general similarity, there are also conspicuous differences between them, both in the composition of the orchestra and in the individual instruments. As already mentioned, Balinese music is more lively than Javanese. Thus gamelan music on Bali is fuller and more melodious. A reasonably complete description of the instruments customary and their use in various types of orchestra would need much more space than is available here, and only a few details can be given. *Gamelan*

In the Balinese gamelan the *gendèr* occupies a conspicuous place. The resonating tubes placed beneath the keys give the instrument a full sonorous tone, which is apparently highly esteemed on Bali. For this reason there is a striking number of different types of gendèr. In gamelan-wayang, which provides the musical accompaniment to the wayang-wong, the wayang-kulit, and the wayang-parwa, four sorts of gender are used, and in the gamelan-angklung even a minimum of six and a maximum of ten. This gamelan music is played on special and out-of-the-ordinary occasions, as, for instance, when the relatives are fetched in a festive procession for the cremation ceremony. This orchestra takes its name from four angklungs which correspond to those common in western Java.

An entirely independent phenomenon, quite unknown in Java, is the *gamelan-djòged*. In this all the instruments are made of bamboo, so that this orchestra sounds flat, and induces a cool, somewhat macabre mood.

The most highly esteemed orchestra is the gamelan-gong, which is capable of producing a considerable fullness of tone, and is therefore particularly suitable for use at festive events, such as processions, temple feasts, etc., which take place in the open air. At such festivities the cheering effect of the music is more important than its beauty, for the orchestra also comprises noise instruments such as a sort of crescent of bells and small cymbals.

An instrument of a unique type is the *réjong*, consisting of two deep gongs, fastened vertically to each end of a stick. The réjong is not met with in Java, but was probably known in the eastern Javanese period of the Hindu-Javanese era, since we find them depicted on the bas-reliefs at Panataran.

Quite different in type from the gamelan-gong is the *gamelan-semar-pagulingan*, the music of which has an intimate character. The name indicates this, as *pagulingan* means something like 'comfortable repose'.

Cremation No other ceremonial custom affords the Balinese so many opportunities of giving vent to his artistic sense as the cremation rites. This custom was adopted from Hinduism, and traces of Hinduism can be seen in the manner in which the ceremony is performed, and in the symbols to be found on the most important objects associated with it. But the Balinese understood the art of investing the whole ceremony with a completely unique character. The great cremation festivities are the occasions on which typical Balinese popular art reaches its zenith. The religious background is formed by faith. The purging power of fire and the cleansing power of water enable the soul to attain the land of souls; the ashes are scattered into the sea or into a river. For this reason it is usual to cremate a person without further ceremony, i.e. without previous burial. But as the expense of a cremation is naturally very high, the deceased is in many cases first interred; the cremation follows later when sufficient funds are available. But when a distinguished personage is cremated on Bali, this opportunity is readily used to consign to the flames simultaneously the mortal remains of poorer relatives.

The whole proceedings take place in several stages. The ceremonies begin with the lying-in-state of the deceased in a pavilion, *balé-bandung*, in the courtyard of his home. If his remains have already been interred, then the skeleton, which is exhumed and cleaned, takes the place of the corpse. The pavilion is most lavishly equipped with magnificent fabrics, small mirrors and gaily-coloured bands, flowers and gilded foliage, strings of beads and paper decorations. Diverse objects used by the deceased during his lifetime, and also articles to protect him from evil spirits and demons after death, are placed in the temporary coffin or next to it. All baskets, vessels, etc., containing these necessaries are provided with a magic sign, generally the lotus flower, *padma*.

Some of the articles deposited have some bearing upon the re-birth of the deceased; they are intended to help bring it about that this re-birth should take place under the most auspicious conditions. From the very first day a group of three small baskets, *pesang-djati*, stand next to the bier, tied together with veins of leaves, containing small packets of victuals, titbits, and suchlike. The most important of these

Polychrome lion, *singa*, wood. Traditional style. (Bali). *K.I.T.* (Height 19¼ ins.)

is a bamboo shoot which, owing to its vitality, is regarded as an effective magic symbol promoting re-birth (cf. the tumpal motif).

Underneath the bier a human figure of Chinese coins, *ukur*, is placed.

The length of the body and limbs correspond to those of the deceased. Chinese influence on Bali can be traced in various districts.

Near the balé-bandung there are also generally two recesses for offerings, one for the Sun God, Surya, and one for the deceased person himself.

The ceremony mentioned cannot simply take place on any day; a day must be selected for each ceremonial act which is magically propitious. This applies particularly to the day when the cremation takes place.

The above by no means gives a full picture of the proceedings; no mention has been made, for example, of the ceremonies performed when holy water is fetched from the sacred fountain, when someone dies abroad and the mortal remains are not at hand, the customs which assist the wandering soul on its way to the balé-bandung, or finally, the preparations for the actual cremation ceremony.

The second part is formed by the ceremonies that are performed when the mortal remains of the deceased person are taken to the cremation ground. The great cremation ceremonies have more about them of a spectacle, with a great hullabaloo, than of a solemn occasion. But it would be wrong to draw the conclusion that the people present have no sense of the religious character of the proceedings. The seriousness of the occasion is not merely displayed by external restraint. Of greatest importance, for its symbolism and as evidence of typical Balinese native art, is the cremation tower, or *badé*. The whole structure can reach the height of 50 or even 65 feet, and rests upon a base in the shape of an enormous tortoise, encircled by a snake, *nāga*, whose lavishly adorned head projects from the front of the badé. The base consists of two cubes, the upper one receding a little. On the cross-ribs large bunches of paper flowers are fastened. On the upper cube there is an open platform, on which the corpse or skeleton rests, and the whole structure is topped by a series of receding roofs, like a pagoda; the number of roofs is uneven, as was the case with the merus.

The symbolism is based on a myth which reached Java and Bali from India: Vishnu commanded the gods to churn from the cosmic ocean the nectar with which they were to make themselves immortal. For this purpose they were to use the cosmic mountain, *mandara*, as a churning stick, and the snake Vasuki as a churning rope. Vishnu himself assumed the form of a tortoise, and held up the cosmic mountain with his body.

On Bali this symbolism was then merged with primitive conceptions derived from the ancestor cult. The two cubes represent the cosmic mountain, whilst the bunches of flowers symbolize trees. Thus this part of the structure can be seen as a rendering of the terrestrial sphere. The deceased is 'not yet in heaven, but no longer on this earth', still bound to earth, yet still far from heaven.

Numerous heads of demons are affixed to the badé to ward off evil spirits. Finally, one can see on the front of the upper cube a stylized representation of Vishnu's celestial eagle, *garuda*, which is to carry the purged soul up to the celestial fields.

These ornaments derive for the most part from Hinduism. In addition the Balinese decorate the cremation tower with paper ornaments, mostly flowers; the bandji motif (swastika) is to be found on the edge, at the corners. The social status of the deceased is indicated by the number of storeys of the roof; Brahmans who are not priests and Kshatriyas are entitled to eleven, Vaishyas at the most seven. Ordinary mortals from the villages must rest content with just a single meru roof. For the Brahmanic priest, the pedanda, a special cremation tower is built: it is actually only a throne without a canopy; its name, *padmasana*, is familiar to us from the description of the pura.

The badé is basically a lavishly decorated bier, on which the corpse or skeleton is conveyed to the place of burning. Thus the common term 'cremation tower' is not really acurate.

The mortal remains are carried up a runway placed against the tower, which is also richly decorated, and across a bridge into the top of the tower; the entrance to this runway is formed by a wide-open demon's mouth.

Once all the ritual requirements have been carried out in full, the badé is brought to the place of burning in a ceremonial procession as though it were an occasion for rejoicing. Innumerable women, all attired in gaily-coloured garments, walking in long files, carry on their heads small jars of holy water and offerings piled up high. The clear strains of the gamelan-angklung resound, and on the bamboo platform on which the badé rests, and which is propelled by dozens of bearers, several gendèr players are also seated. Young men carry with them long poles, from which flutter gaily-coloured fabrics (their import has already been discussed); spearmen perform war-dances, and hundreds upon hundreds of curious men and women, clad in festive attire, follow in the procession.

Particular reference must still be made to one custom, connected with certain primitive native conceptions: during the procession, amidst loud cries, the badé is turned round and round, and also to and fro, several times, the intention being that the spirit of the deceased should lose its way. Several male relatives of the deceased are in charge; they are seated on the platform of the badé, and take care that the enormous structure does not topple over when it is turned. This procedure is connected with customs observed in primitive times designed to ward off demonic spirits. Similar customs are also to be found elsewhere in Indonesia.

The cremation proper
The third part of the ceremony is the actual burning. On arrival at the cremation ground, *sema*, the procession moves three times around the spot where the coffin to be burned has been erected. As in the case of the badé, the workmanship of the coffin indicates the social status of the deceased. The Brahmans and upper nobility have a coffin in the shape of a bull or a cow. Formerly this was an exclusive privilege of the Brahmans, and a distinction was made between the pedandas and members of this caste who were not priests. The pedandas were given a white coffin, the others a black one.

Members of the lower nobility are entitled to a coffin in the shape of a winged lion, *singa*, whilst ordinary villagers only have a simple coffin, though sometimes it is decorated with the head of a bull or a cow, in which case the decoration is also kept simple.

After the procession has moved round three times, another lavishly decorated bamboo runway is placed against the badé, and the shroud which covers the corpse, and which is inscribed with sacred texts, is first removed; then the corpse, which is encased in bindings, (or the skeleton), is removed, being passed from hand to hand down a long line of helpers.

The pedanda now performs the most important ritual acts. Whilst he recites prayers, the so-called *mantras*, the bindings are cut; he takes the jars of holy water and sprinkles the deceased with the magic water. Various effigies and offerings are placed in the coffin, which is now closed and tied round with the *nāga-banda*. The latter is a long narrow strip of gaily-coloured cotton, adorned with tinsel and paper decorations. During the procession to the cremation ground, where, as already mentioned, the pura-dalem is generally situated, a naga-banda hangs down from the spot where the corpse lies, and the rela-

Polychrome rider and mount, wood. Traditional style (Bali). *K.I.T.* (Height 18 ins.)

tives hold on to it firmly. If the deceased was a member of a caste, this strip is in the shape of a snake, *nāga*.

The great moment for setting off the pyre has now arrived. The bundles of twigs piled up beneath the coffin, or coffins, are set alight. The badé is then stripped of all its decorations by the young people, and is burnt together with the offerings for which there was no room in, or next to, the coffin.

Right at the end, when it is certain that the very last pieces of bone have been completely burnt, the ashes are collected and placed in coconut shells, wrapped in a special way, and are then scattered into the sea or into a river.

Usually on the day after the body has been burnt, these ashes are carried in another procession to the sea, or if this is not feasible to the largest river in the vicinity. For this purpose a bier of a very simple kind is constructed, and the ashes are then committed to the cleansing water. This constitutes the end of the cremation ceremonies.

Hardly anywhere else in the world has a religious rite attracted sensation-hungry foreigners as this pageantry on Bali. Originally it took place entirely within the community, and thus had its own dignity, but now it has in many cases been degraded to a mere spectacle by foreign tourists, an item in some travel agent's programme, "Come and see Bali in three days!" The contact between the Balinese and the outside world has by no means been always for the best.

Weaving The five crafts mentioned above, *pantja-gina*, were exclusively reserved to men. Weaving, on the other hand, as everywhere in Indonesia, is performed by women. In this craft, too, Bali can boast of very fine achievements. It is understandable that silk is given preference over cotton on this island where men and women have such a pronounced predilection for colour, splendour and brilliance. Silk fabrics are to be found here with simple patterns of bands and rhombs, but also some in which gold and silver threads are richly interwoven with patterns, often very complicated ones, of extraordinary beauty. Nowadays aniline dyes are almost exclusively used. The ground of the fabrics is usually red; against this the patterns, in lighter colours such as yellow, green, pink, purple and white, stand out well. Gold and silver threads are often also woven in.

Three kinds of fabrics may be specially mentioned here, for their importance as regards the technique employed, as well as for their general significance.

Tenganan In the village of Tenganan, south-west of Karangasem, ancient native customs survived for a long time, with Hindu influence being little evident. Textiles are produced here known as *gring-sing*, which means an illness-averting fabric (*gring* = illness, *sing* = not). It is thus unmistakably a fabric to which magic powers are ascribed. The technique is not known anywhere in the whole of Indonesia outside this one désa. The threads of both the warp and the weft are treated by the ikat method. On a very simple loom cotton fabrics are produced with magnificent motifs, mainly flowers and human figures. Utmost care must be taken when carrying out the preliminary dyeing, as otherwise the colours will not be distinguished clearly and the desired pattern will not be obtained.

Kain-prada
Detail of
design (Bali)

On Bali, too, there are to be found textiles with designs in gold, *kain-prada*. The motifs are reproduced in clear-cole on the fabric, on which a ground-colour has already been applied. Then the whole fabric is covered with gold-leaf or gold-dust, which adheres to the gummed parts. After it has been left to dry, it is quite easy to remove the surplus gold. The principal motif in the kain-prada is always a stylized lotus flower, whilst the border is decorated with the bandji. This material is worn by female temple dancers and is immediately recognizable by its striking and accentuated motifs.

Kain-prada

Fig. p. 213

Lamak The *lamak* has both a very special ornamentation and a very special ceremonial purpose: one of the great festivals of the Hindu-Balinese year is the New Year feast, *galungan,* regarded by the Balinese as a day of renewal and purification. On this occasion the lamak is indispensa-

PLATE P. 200 ble for decorating the offertory altars. The curious thing is that part of the material always hangs down from the opening of the sacrificial recess. For the word lamak means: something longish, which must hang on something, and also hang down by one corner.

Lamak also denotes the gilded oblong ornament in leather, a stiff vest covering the chest, which forms part of the costume of the légong dancers; this also indicates 'something that hangs down'.

On Bali the term *lajah* is used, meaning the same as lamak, but also

Door-panel, wood, polychrome, with lion, *singa.* Balinese influence. (Lombok). *K.I.T.* (Height 14½ ins., width 15¼ ins.)

'tongue'. If we recall for a moment the figure of Rangda, we see that the demon's mask always has a long tongue, decorated with flame motifs hanging far down the chest. This elongated tongue, hanging down, is also to be found elsewhere: probably it is a magic symbol PLATES PP. 64, 132 designed to ward off evil forces.

On closer examination perhaps the connection between the words *lamak* and *lajah* may prove scientifically a hypothesis which at present can only be a matter of conjecture: that the traditional usage of lamak material has derived from a similar function.

To understand more fully the significance of these ornaments, we may assume that every object which unmistakably serves a ceremonial purpose contains symbolic signs in its decoration. As has already been mentioned, it is, however, not ruled out that the original form has been greatly modified in the course of centuries.

We shall limit ourselves here to the ornament which appears on the circular embroidered decoration, always placed centrally, which is frequently met with on the lamak (cf. Plate on p. 200). For certain reasons this ornament is thought to be a so-called tjilih figure, rendered almost unrecognizable by stylization, a mystical figure connected with Devi Shri, the goddess of agriculture, fertility and weaving.[2]

The sacral significance of the lamak is specially emphasized by its colours — red, white, yellow and dark blue. For these colours play an important symbolic role in Balinese mythology. For this reason alone we may see in this fabric a cover for the offertory table, with symbolical magic ornaments closely connected with the sacred rites.

In this connection reference may also be made to the presence of the tumpal motif, the significance of which has been sufficiently treated in the last part of Chapter IV.

It may be concluded that the ornaments on the lamak indicate primitive symbols which continued to live on in a genuine and powerful tradition.

The Tjalon-Arang legend mentioned above without doubt reflects an era which abounded in catastrophes. Perhaps in those far-distant days this island was stricken by a severe earthquake, and the population was sorely afflicted by famine and plague. The Balinese saw themselves as threatened with destruction by demonic powers.

Bali, so greatly blessed in many respects, knows well this threat from mysterious forces, concealed deep down beneath the deceptively calm surface of the lakes in the volcanic craters. In 1917 the island was once again struck by a severe earthquake. Thousands of temples were destroyed; and in those years when Bali was 'discovered' by tourists, the island was indeed impoverished. The 'Last Paradise' was a country whose inhabitants had only recently begun to restore their puras in honour of the gods without whose succour man is doomed to destruction.

[1] J. C. Lamster in 'Bali', 1932.
[2] Bulletin CXIX, Abt. Culturele en Physische Anthropologie, Koninklijk Instituut voor de Tropen, Amsterdam, Nr. 53, 'Lamak and Malat in Bali and a Sumba loom', Prof. Dr. Th. P. Galestin, L. Langewis, and R. Bolland.

XIII. INDONESIA
IN THE 19TH AND 20TH CENTURIES

On the 31st December 1799 the Charter of the East Indian Companies (Verenigde Oostindische Compagnieën) expired, and the Batavian Republic took over its possessions and debts. But the colonies which the Republic thereby obtained were in a far from flourishing state. The alliance with France (in 1810 the Republic itself became part of France under King Louis Bonaparte) involved the country in what was to all practical intents and purposes continuous war with England; commerce steadily declined, and more and more territories fell into the hands of the British. An officer, Herman Willem Daendels, was appointed Governor-General of the Asian Territories, in the hope that Java, at least, could be retained in Dutch possession. He did indeed take important military measures (for instance, the construction of a road 600 miles long across Java from the west coast to the east, which was later to prove extremely advantageous for the economy of the island), but his clumsy handling of the princes of Java made any assistance on their part doubtful, to say the least. In 1811 Daendels was recalled by King Louis Bonaparte, and a few months later, after a short struggle, Java was occupied by the British. *Political situation*

The administration was entrusted to the Vice-Governor, Thomas Stamford Raffles. In one respect he stood head and shoulders above the previous Dutch governors. During his administration, which lasted less than five years, he devoted himself with great energy and much success to scholarly activities, and presented the results of his studies in his 'History of Java'. Particularly noteworthy was his lively interest in the Hindu-Javanese architectural monuments, which had by then already fallen into ruins. This English interregnum came to an end in 1816, and Java, together with its adjoining islands, was restored once again to the Kingdom of the Netherlands (Convention of London, 1814, and Treaty of London, 1824). William I now became the ruler of the colonies.

During the Napoleonic period Holland had sunk to a nadir, both economically and culturally. The decisive factor in colonial policy was now therefore the attempt to overcome these economic difficulties as quickly as possible, the means for this being provided by the colo-

Painting on wooden sacrificial vessel. Rape of Sita (from Rāmāyana). (Bali). *K.I.T.* (Height 7½ ins.)

nies, and in the first place Java. Interest in cultural matters scarcely existed, and Raffles' fine example found no emulator for some time to come.

Agrarian policy In 1818 the administration was entrusted to Governor-General Van der Capellen. The trouble and friction which he experienced in his agrarian schemes involved him in conflict with the princes and magnates of the so-called 'principalities'. For they had leased land to European settlers in return for large loans. The Governor-General now declared illegal all leases with a term of more than three years and an advance amounting to more than six months' rent. But the lessors of the land were generally living in style, had already spent most of their loans, and thus found themselves in considerable difficulties. The attitude to the Dutch administration had long been hostile, and the result was a devastating war under Dipo Negoro, the 'Java War', which raged from 1825 to 1830.

The Dutch were disappointed in their hopes to obtain from their colonies the necessary means of escaping from their own economic difficulties. On the contrary, by 1828 the colonies were indebted to the extent of some 40 million guilders, partly as a result of the need to put the colonial administration in order. This meant that armed force had to be used in Palembang, on the Padang plateau, and elsewhere.

In 1830 a start was made in introducing the so-called 'Cultuurstelsel', *'Cultuurstelsel'* which at first was only intended to be applied on Java and Madura. This proceeded from the basic assumption that the government was sole owner of all the land, and that the population could only lease it. But instead of paying rent, the inhabitants of each village were to put a fifth of their land at the disposal of the government and cultivate on it products destined for the European market. This system certainly also had its positive sides, in that the population learned to cultivate new kinds of crops, but it imposed heavy burdens upon the peasants. For Holland, on the other hand, it produced considerable financial benefits.

But at home the Netherlands were now developing more and more along liberal lines, and thus the opposition to such a colonialist economic policy increased, with the result that in the latter half of the 19th century an entirely new course was instituted in colonial policy. The obligation to cultivate certain products was gradually lifted. The agrarian law of 1870 was based upon totally different principles: only natives could own inalienable property in land, and only virgin land could be leased by Netherlanders and Dutch companies.

This short survey of colonial history is necessary in order to account for the extreme impoverishment of the population, the princes and magnates included. For this in turn was one of the most important reasons for the decline of certain arts and accomplishments.

Still more important for Indonesia was the development of modern means of communication. Within a short space of time large areas of the country were caught up in the dynamic economy of the West. Innovations and changes in the economic life of Europe made Indonesia an important supplier of valuable raw materials and at the same time a highly-valued market for its industrial products.

This process was facilitated by the opening of the Suez Canal (1869) *Suez Canal* and the modernization of means of transport. The number of plantations, invariably administered by Europeans, increased considerably, especially in Java and Sumatra. This encouraged the development of agriculture, which in turn fostered the growth of many other branches of industry. All this presented Indonesia with problems which could not be grasped fully, and which undermined the whole social and economic structure, as well as the religious and cultural life of the Indonesian population.

Money economy In ever-increasing tempo the money economy of the West penetrated into Indonesia — at first into the most important areas, but later even into the remote districts — everywhere superseding the natural economy which had hitherto prevailed. The economic structure of the existing communities changed accordingly: whereas previously the individual had lived according to the requirements and advantage of his community, as *adat* and tradition demanded, he now strove more and more for personal gain. Economic activity no longer served the will and needs of the community exclusively, but was now to an ever greater extent conditioned by the aims and purposes of men who lived far beyond its confines. That which various external cultural influences had been unable to achieve in the course of many centuries now came to pass: the self-sufficiency of the communities could no longer be maintained under the pressure of revolutionary changes in economic life. But a closed undifferentiated civilization cannot undergo such a radical change in certain aspects only; the inevitable and irrevocable consequence is a general 'revolution of values'. In a closed community *adat* and tradition, social relationships, religion and art are all so closely inter-connected that once such a community is stricken in its foundations they cannot retain their vigour or value. Where an art serves a particular function within the community, and where the artist not only has a definite social position but is also assured of his economic livelihood — such an art inevitably loses its *raison d'être* once the tie between artist and community has been dissolved and a work of art, the significance of which is no longer understood, is all too easily discarded as valueless. Or if a work is still aesthetically appreciated, such appreciation will hardly be so deep-rooted or widespread that the decay of native forms of art could be halted thereby.

The development sketched above may be clearly traced in the decline in the art of weaving. The textile industries of the West (in which one may include Japan) saw welcome opportunities for the marketing of their cotton prints in the rapidly increasing population of Indonesia (approx. 70 million inhabitants in 1940). The imported product was much cheaper than that manufactured by hand within the coun-

try. It takes at least several months to make a lavishly designed ikat fabric, and a sarong in batik needs its six weeks of patient labour.

In Java attempts were made to simplify the batik process for economic reasons. Instead of applying the wax pattern upon the fabric with the aid of the *tjanting*, stamps of copper were used. Thus the 'repeats' in the pattern could be applied in wax with a single action. Workshops appeared, generally managed by Chinese, in which a considerable part of the work was performed by men. The traditional dyes, often obtained only by complicated processes, were replaced by imported aniline dyes. To inexpert eyes the batik fabrics produced in this way cannot easily be distinguished from those made by hand; nevertheless the former were not so highly treasured. Where the traditional patterns were still used, this was done exclusively to increase the sales of such fabrics; for the batik craftsmen now had to compete with imported goods which bore the same designs.

Mechanization of batik technique

From a purely economic point of view this course of events was not only inevitable, but even something to be welcomed. However, batik as folk-art was thereby ruined.

The technique of batik work could be mechanized to a certain extent by using wax stamps. The ikat method, on the other hand, does not permit such a simplification and acceleration of working methods. For this reason it was quite out of question for it to compete with imported goods. In addition living conditions were very bad for those tribes which were engaged until comparatively recent times in ikat work, and in particular ikat of the warp. The inevitable consequences soon followed: everywhere this unique method of ornamental textile design declined sharply. The old fabrics are still greatly admired, but in not too distant a time they will suffer the consequences of their impermanence: only a few specimens will be preserved in museums to testify to this vanished native art.

In the present century attempts have been made to promote artistic weaving, for example, the floating weft technique, by introducing improved looms, and indeed the decline has been checked. But in modern Indonesia the creation of an indigenous weaving industry will finally make the popular craft of weaving superfluous. It need hardly be mentioned that articles of clothing in which gold and silver threads are worked are too expensive nowadays.

Even on Bali, where native art is held in higher esteem than anywhere else in Indonesia, there has been an obvious decline in weaving as a craft. Thus R. Bonnet, an artist who lives and works on Bali, wrote as

Man with dog and squamiferous animal, wood, uncoloured. Modern (Bali). *K.I.T.* (Height 7 ins.)

long ago as in 1936: "No other art has been impaired as much as weaving by imports and foreign influences — for a change, not by tourists. During the past few years there has been a deterioration in the magnificent art performed by the women of Bali, which expressed the joy and prosperity of the people. Every year Bali now spends thousands of guilders on imports of pyjamas, sweaters, pullovers, shirts, printed *kains* (materials) and cottons. These inferior, often absurd and unhygienic mass-produced goods are ousting the artistically folded head-cloth, bare shoulders, magnificently coloured *saputs* or *antengs,* and domestic woven *kains* — this exquisite and invariably dignified national costume. Thus the art of weaving has little hope left here" ('Beeldende Kunst in Gianjar').

Accomplishments in other fields have also become less important, or have vanished completely, as a result of the economic and other reasons referred to. In Java, where some two-thirds of the Indonesian population live (in 1940, approx. 50 million of the total population of 70 millions), the economic difficulties of the last century were particularly severely felt. Wealthy customers from the Indonesian upper classes were far fewer in number. Later, especially after 1870, when there was a considerable boom in agriculture, industry and commerce, their place was taken by merchants and people with a European upbringing, who were too attracted by modernity to commission exquisite artistic textiles in the traditional style. Only in Japara in central Java did merchants have their houses decorated with large wood-carvings, the motifs of which were derived from those of the Hindu-Javanese period; but this exception in one single place could of course not check the decline of wood-carving as such. The gold- and silversmiths and armourers were even worse placed in these inauspicious times. The armourer's craft even perished entirely. The *empu* families, the possessors of traditional skills and accomplishments, have died out during the course of the 20th century.

Wayang, music and dancing found a secure haven at the courts, *kratons,* of the 'principalities'; it was here alone that cultural life continued to be inspired by ancient tradition. But elsewhere, and especially in the large towns (for urbanization has become an ever more serious problem during the present century) the taste for traditional artistic performances diminished considerably, especially after the introduction of the cinema. The influence of this modern means of entertainment can hardly be over-estimated. It brought the people into contact with a completely strange world, a world full of violent

Decline of the arts

passion and artificially contrived tension; upon the uneducated classes in particular, the effect could not be other than bewildering. Subsequently the sound-films introduced Western music (and not always the best!) and dancing; these films mostly provided merely light entertainment, and the younger generation of Indonesians was particularly susceptible to these new pleasures.

But apart from the influences mentioned, one may instance other reasons for the decline of traditional forms of artistic expression amongst peoples that had lived for so long in a world of their own. For these peoples were for a long time regarded as economically unimportant, and were therefore not involved in colonial power politics either *de facto* or *de jure*; in the latter half of the 19th century, however, they could no longer be left out of account. When James Brooke established an independent 'sultanate' in northern Borneo in 1851, this was one of the first alarm signals which pointed to the fact that the policy of 'non-intervention' was actually conjuring up a real danger. The threat became more acute after the opening of the Suez Canal. The fear that foreign Powers might gain a footing in Atjeh, which had been detached from the Dutch sphere of influence by the Treaty of London in 1824, caused the British to allow the Dutch a free hand in this area (Sumatra Treaty of 1871). Thereupon the Dutch became

Atjeh War   involved in a very costly and tedious war with Atjeh, which was not brought to a conclusion until 1904. In other areas, too, the Government had to intervene with armed force in order to assert its authority. Not until 1911 was the entire Archipelago united under Dutch sovereignty, with the exception of North Borneo and North Timor, which remained respectively under British and Portuguese rule.

Consequences of   But now the Protestant missionary societies, as well as the Roman
Christianization   Catholic mission, saw in the 'heathen' inhabitants of Indonesia a fertile field of activity. The Protestant mission began its work at the beginning of the 19th century in northern Celebes (Minahassa). The population of this area was followed by other peoples: the inhabitants of Nias, the Bataks, Dayaks, Toradja, and the peoples of various islands in the Lesser Sunda group. The Catholic mission did not become active until much later on Flores and Timor, but later extended its sphere of operations considerably, particularly during the present century. The Portuguese had already made a start with the Christianization of the Moluccas and the Sangi and Talaud Islands to the north of Celebes. Their work was continued in Protestant form under the aegis of the East Indian Companies. As already mentioned in

Chapter XI, the manner in which the missionaries carried out their work led in certain areas, especially in the 19th century, to the almost complete elimination of native art in all its aspects. It was thought that only by doing so could the idolatry reflected in this art, and which it served to encourage, be effectively suppressed.

Gradually a different attitude obtained the upper hand, especially after a clearer understanding had been reached of the many problems which missionary activity raised. For example, could one make use of existing cultural achievements for the benefit of church art, and incorporate them into it? In Java Doctor J. Schmutzer undertook some experiments in this direction, which, however, did not prove particularly fruitful. No doubt ornamental decoration can be incorporated more easily than sculpture, and music more easily than dancing. But however all this may work out in practice, the immediate gain, which should not be underestimated, is that the existence of the problem has at least been recognized by Catholics and Protestants alike, and that they now approach native art with greater understanding.

As in the sphere of colonial policy, a different view was now taken of the moral responsibilities of the Dutch Government towards the Indonesian population. Of course, it took a long time before this new approach made itself felt in the colonial administration. Not until the beginning of the present century had matters progressed so far that one could speak of an 'ethical policy'. *'Ethical policy'*

But practice showed that the new course upon which the Government embarked with the adoption of this policy was not the only one that counted. Influences exerted by the aristocratic native *élite* also played an increasingly important part, for the members of this class sought to have their say in the framing of policy in many different fields. They considered Western culture indispensable, and the introduction of a proper educational system on Western lines as the first step. This 'awakening', however, did not have any effect upon the broad masses of the population. The village communities still adhered to *adat* and tradition, at least at first; one reason for this was the agrarian law, which left the population in undisturbed possession of their agricultural land.

In establishing an educational system the Government sought to create schools with a Dutch spirit and with Dutch as the principal language used. *Educational system*

Although, in conformity with the 'ethical policy', education was not restricted to the aristocratic upper class, but was extended to the rural population as well, and instruction was given in the vernacular, it was precisely this educational system which brought with it the threat of alienation from indigenous cultural values, of 'uprooting'. For Western education lacked a positive religious basis: it did not conform to the religious and mystical outlook of the Indonesians, but was in the main directed to the pursuit of material ends, and thus easily upset and even dissolved customs and ties sanctioned by ancient tradition.

Yet this education also had its positive side. It created the essential prerequisites that enabled Indonesia to become part of the modern world — a development which could not be halted and which could only be facilitated, materially and intellectually, by education.

The fact that in this process the ancient art of the Indonesian people was being undermined was not only clear to many Indonesians who were aware of the value of their cultural heritage, but also became apparent to the authorities. Instead of contenting themselves with merely writing many learned books and articles, the authorities now made attemps in several ways to check the cultural decline, and in these efforts the schools were designed to play a significant part. In 1937 batik was added to the curriculum in girls' schools in the 'Principalities'. In Bali schools began to be built in traditional style, with ornamental wood-carvings. In 1939 attempts were made in primary schools in the 'Principalities' to base gymnastics upon Javanese dance postures, which led to the training of teachers in Javanese dancing. The training courses were held in the kraton of Djokjakarta under the supervision of Pangéran Tédja Kusumo, an uncle of the reigning Sultan, Amangku Buwono IX.

Acting upon a proposal of the Java Institute and its director, Pangéran Prof. Hussein Djajadiningrat, an applied art school with boarding accommodation was opened in 1938, also in Djokjakarta, in conjunction with a museum that already existed there. Furthermore, instruction was given to silversmiths and wood-carvers in places where these crafts had traditionally been practised. The motifs were modelled upon those of the Madjapahit era. Obviously the articles manufactured had also to be sold on the market. For this reason objects were designed which were of value also to non-Indonesians, i.e. the free market had to provide the means with which these activities could be carried on.

Special preventive measures were also necessary to preserve from further decay the fine objects that had survived the passage of centuries. In Batavia, as it was then called, a museum of antiquities was founded,

I. Dewa Gdé Soberat: Landscape (Detail). Modern (Bali). *K.I.T.* (Size 4 ft. 4¾ ins. × 5 ft. 7 ins.)

and collections were also built up by private individuals. One of these collections, formed in Holland, which the 'Nederlandsche Maatschappij van Handel' commissioned Doctor of Law F. W. van Eeden to make, became so large that the Haarlem Museum was no longer able to find room for it, and search had to be made for suitable alternative accommodation. The choice fell upon the Colonial Institute in Amsterdam with its museum, founded in 1910, now known as the 'Koninklijk Instituut voor de Tropen' and 'Tropen-Museum', where the collection expanded with time until it attained its present unique comprehensiveness.

Restoration of monuments In the same spirit restoration work has been undertaken on buildings dating from the Hindu-Javanese era. As has already been pointed out in Chapter IX, Borobudur was one of the monuments restored in this way; work was also done on part of the Prambanan complex, so that the main temple, the Lara Djonggrang, was returned to its original beauty. This great undertaking was commenced before the last war, and completed after 1945. Also other monuments were restored as far as possible.

When one considers that at the end of the last century stones from the ruins were used for paving roads or building sugar factories, one can imagine how difficult it was to reconstruct the monuments in their totality, and that in many cases the task was insoluble.

Art on Bali As far as restoration work is concerned, Bali occupies a special place, for on this island artistic traditions were still vigorous and intimately linked with the religious life of the people. This art was based upon exceptional technical skill and an innate feeling for refinement of line and colour. But here, too, popular art was now threatened by economic changes and totally different mental attitudes, especially amongst the younger generation. I have already mentioned the decline of weaving. But the sculptors of Bali responded to the new influences from the West in their own individual way. Western European artists discovered Bali's unique beauty, and several of them resolved to settle and work here. The work of the Mexican ethnologist and caricaturist Covarrubias, whose attention was drawn to 'megalithic' ornamentation by a German artist living on Bali, Walter Spies, inspired a Balinese wood-sculptor to produce a sculpture in an extraordinary style: a very slender figure with elongated arms, totally different from the traditional way of representing the human form. This style made a great impression upon other sculptors. The very slender form, and the attempt to reproduce the quintessence of the subject by the maximum austerity and simplicity, gave the works of these artists a very special *cachet*. Also as regards choice of material, and abstention from painting the figure, they followed a path of their own, totally different from that of traditional works.

After this first attempt, other forms and styles were developed which all displayed a distinct Balinese note. Balinese painters, too, as already mentioned, could not fail to be influenced by Western art. They created a new style in which influences of traditional painting were also apparent, particularly the decorative elements. Modern materials have also opened up new technical opportunities.

PLATE P. 222

PLATE P. 227

These wood sculptures and paintings did not serve to decorate *puras,* or even the artist's own environment. He cut himself off from his community, which gave him inspiration, but no longer security. He was forced to sell his works outside his own island of Bali, and thus had to use the services of an agent. Thus in many cases he received only a small part of the proceeds of the sale of his work, which was all the more unfortunate since every sculptor and painter on Bali thinks it quite in order to copy the works of others — a characteristic and fully justified feature of a communal existence, in which the work of the individual artist is common property.

All the world over it can be observed how the tourist industry promotes the manufacture of all sorts of shoddy trash. But this presented a very real and grave danger for Balinese artists, who, although very gifted, had in general little sense of style. Fortunately this danger was recognized in time. The association 'Het Balimuseum' did valuable work in this field by trying in various ways to keep the art of sculptors, painters, gold- and silversmiths at the highest possible standard, and by assuming the function of agent in selling original works. But however valuable these Balinese works of art may be, the tie to the community was now no more. The artist had abandoned the religion- and tradition-bound community within which art had hitherto developed, and a secularization of art was thus easily brought about: the all-embracing unity of style, which is the characteristic feature of non-personal art, was greatly endangered.

In Java, too, painting was doomed to decline with Hindu-Javanese culture. In the 19th century the works of Raden Saleh (1814—1880) aroused particular interest. He was an excellent painter of animals, but also did portraits and landscapes. He was not, however, a true representative of Javanese art, since his works were too greatly influenced by the West, both in form and content.

229

From the very beginning modern Indonesian painting took a different course in Java. In all attempts to express freedom of personality through emancipated art, one can feel the passion and impatience of revolution. This development is only to be understood when seen against the political background after the first World War.

Already in 1904, under the impression of the Japanese victory over Russia, a national tendency could be discerned, at first expressed in the development of a consciousness of identity as members of the Mohammedan community. Hundreds of thousands of Indonesians found in the Islamic society 'Sarekat-Islam' a means of putting their new ideals into practice. Originally this movement did not have a revolutionary character. Its statutes provided that only those means were to be used "which do not transgress the laws of the land and the Government", but after the first World War, when the victorious Powers proclaimed the right of all peoples to self-determination, various organizations formed which were politically active and which had a strong nationalistic and more or less revolutionary outlook.

Moreover, partly under the influence of this movement, important changes were made in the system of government. Indonesians were steadily given a greater part to play in various offices and committees. The greatest concesssion was the 'People's Council', with its limited legislative functions, laid down by law in 1916. But the right of Indonesians to voice their opinions still remained limited, and in the extreme nationalist groups the movement of resistance grew ever stronger. The outbreak of the second World War accentuated the conflicts still further, especially since the Government refused to countenance any political reform for the duration of the war. In the meantime preparations had to be made to withstand a Japanese invasion, for which it was necessary, amongst other things, to establish an Indonesian militia. The nationalist members of the People's Council declared themselves ready to collaborate in this only if the Government held out the prospect of independence for Indonesia. In response to this pressure the Government promised to hold a Round Table Conference after the war.

When the Japanese actually invaded, the military preparations proved totally inadequate. After a short but bitter resistance, capitulation became inevitable. The fact that the Government and administration broke down so suddenly was of the greatest psychological importance. When after the war for various reasons a vacuum ensued, the more radical elements utilized the opportunity to proclaim the Republic of Indonesia. This introduced a four-year period of complex struggles and negotiations at the national level, until finally the Round Table Conference of 1949 resulted in recognition of the independent State of Indonesia under President Soekarno.

Round Table Conference

It may readily be understood that young artists took sides in the events taking place about them, for they were all immediately affected by them, each in his own individual way. In 1938 there was founded in Djakarta (as Batavia is now called) the Painters' Union, 'Persagi', under the energetic leadership of S. Sudjoyono. This association campaigned violently at meetings and in print against a style of painting which sought to reproduce only the beauties of the Indonesian landscape, and against the sale of paintings to Europeans. The painter, they held, must devote himself to his art with the whole force of his personality. In Bandung the leading figure was the painter Affandi, a more restrained but forceful and energetic artist.

PLATE P. 233

The artists mentioned did not turn their backs upon the latest tendencies in Western painting. They were undoubtedly personally acquainted with the unique collection of paintings by the great Impressionist and Expressionist masters which had been formed by the connoisseur P. A. Regnault, and which was exhibited in several Indonesian cities with the assistance of the 'League of Artistic Circles of the Netherlands-Indies'. Nevertheless, they attempted to protect their students from Western artistic 'isms', and tried to give Indonesian painting an individual character of its own — a worthy aim which, however, proved unattainable, especially when many young Indonesian painters travelled to Europe after the war, came into contact with Western art, and were able to exhibit their own works. It should not be overlooked that these young artists had never left Java before, and that most of them had still not really acquired a style of their own, so that they absorbed all the more eagerly the influences of Western art.

This explains why the works of Indonesian painters of this period (one may mention Agus and Otto Djayasuminta, Basuki Resobowo, Hendra, Henk Ngantung, Kerton, Baharudin, Emiria Sunasa, M. Apin, Sundoro, Sudarso and Trubus) display many varied stylistic tendencies. Naturally many paintings treat themes connected with the struggle for independence.

After the political reconstruction new Indonesian painters came to the fore, such as O. Effendi, Zaini, Kusnadi, Sutiksna, Suromo and Surono. Of these O. Effendi and Zaini have stimulated painting to embark upon new paths. Less influenced by revolutionary tendencies, they aim at a simple primitivism, although influences of abstract painting can also be seen in their work.

Whatever one may think of the value of the works of these Indonesian painters, it is amazing how rapidly emancipated painting could develop in a mere twenty years in a country which had known practically no individualistic artistic expression. The attempt to create a national art in the shortest possible time by throwing in all available forces attained surprising and significant results.

Modern literature The lines on which modern Indonesian literature was to develop first became clearly visible in 1933 in the work of a group of writers generally referred to by the name of the journal with which they were associated, 'Pudjangga Baru' ('The Young Poet'). Just as in the political field the first independent movements sought to adopt Western civilization, seeing in it the essential prerequisite for the progress to which they aspired, so also in the literary field the leading figure on 'Pudjangga Baru', Takdir Alisjahbana, called upon the Indonesian people to put out feelers towards the West and to absorb the dynamism and vitality of the Western world. In his most important work, the novel 'Lajar terkembang' ('Under Full Sail'), he contrasts dynamic individualism with the tradition-bound static attitude of earlier generations. He lays emphasis upon the definition and development of personality; there is nothing here of the self-criticism and self-pity of some novels from the epoch prior to 'Pudjangga Baru'. On the contrary, the struggle against the ties of *adat* no longer presents any problem to modern authors. This is also clearly shown by two works which must be mentioned in addition to 'Lajar terkembang', the novel 'Belenggu' ('Chains') by Armijn Pane and the play 'Manusia Baru' ('The New Man') by Sanusi Pane.

Nevertheless there are also marked differences in the views of these authors. Takdir Alisjahbana is a radical; he rejects everything traditional and strives for innovation in all things. Sanusi Pane, on the other hand, seeks a synthesis: what is valuable in the heritage of the past is to be harmonized with the demands of the present. His views are illustrated in his collection of poems 'Madah Kelana' ('Songs of an Itinerant Companion') and his translation into Indonesian of 'Ardjunavivāha'. Of lyricists Amir Hamzah occupies pride of place in this period.

The poetic works of Muhammed Yamin, of Sumatra, also exhibit an adherence, to some extent deliberate, to traditional cultural values,

Affandi: Self-portrait entitled 'Tida senang' ('Dejection'). Modern (Java). *K.I.T.*

for, although he indubitably favours modern individualism, his debt to classical literature is undeniable.

In the columns of the journal 'Pudjangga Baru' a vigorous discussion developed around the question how a national Indonesian culture was to be attained. The contributions to this polemic were later published under the title of 'Polemik Kebudajaan' ('A Polemic on Culture') by the Balai Pustaka ('Kantoor voor Volkslectuur').

Balai Pustaka This institute, which had been founded as early as 1908 by the Government, developed into an independent concern in the 1920s. In establishing a system of education, the Government had to consider the provision of popular reading matter. Its aim was to make available literature adapted to various levels of development in all the languages of the Archipelago, for in the primary schools instruction was given in the vernacular of each district. Works were published chiefly in Malay, Javanese and Sundanese, the languages spoken by the largest groups of the population. That this aim was not easily attainable may be readily appreciated when one considers that there are some 250 languages in Indonesia. In the course of time more than 1600 works appeared in editions of between 500 and 100,000 copies. Translations of Shakespeare, Cervantes and Dostoyevsky appeared, as well as reading matter of a less advanced standard, and in addition recourse was had to the rich treasure-house of native culture.

Use has been made above for the first time of the term 'Indonesian' to denote a language. As has already been mentioned when discussing Java during the Islamic period, Malay became the *lingua franca* of Indonesia. This language proved particularly suitable as a means of communication between the many peoples of Indonesia. Naturally there appeared many variations in spoken Malay, but this was less the case with the written language. With the progress of intellectual development and education in Indonesia, this language was even described as 'algemeen beschaafd', or 'generally educated'. Malay was to serve as the language through which the new cultural values were to be transmitted to the peoples of Indonesia and bring them closer together. 'National consciousness' was aroused, and closer links be-
Awakening tween the various peoples now became an obvious and essential pre-
of national requisite for the attainment of the aims which the Indonesians set
consciousness themselves. As a result of the general craving for unity, the Indonesian language, 'Bahasa Indonesia', was accepted throughout Indonesia. People were convinced that national unity could only come about when they had a national language which would open up properly

for the first time communications between all areas of Indonesia and the outside world. Thus it may be readily understood that the authors of the 'Pudjangga Baru' group wrote in 'Bahasa Indonesia'; the Balai Pustaka was an extremely efficacious means of perfecting 'Bahasa Indonesia' and disseminating it throughout the country.

'Bahasa Indonesia'

In addition to the circle of writers gathered around 'Pudjangga Baru', there was another group whose influence was significant. The most important journals in which these authors published their works were 'Pedoman Masjarakat' ('The Social Compass') and 'Pandji Islam' ('Flag of Islam'). This last title shows the contributors' leanings: they sought to assure Islam its proper place in the new society that was evolving. The best-known author of this group is Mamka, whose works have a pronounced romantic flavour. Whereas the contributors to 'Pudjangga Baru', led by Takdir Alisjabana, looked primarily to the West, the last-named group looked towards Egypt.

After the second World War the literary scene was dominated by a new generation of authors who had a completely different approach. The pressure exerted during the occupation by the Japanese, who rendered impossible any free literary activity, and the ensuing struggle for independence, invested their works with a harshness and single-mindedness which left no place for sentimentality or symbolism.

Chairil Anwar

The most prominent of these authors was the lyric poet Chairil Anwar, with his collections of poems 'Deru tjampur debu' ('Lumber and Dust') and 'Kerikel tadjam' ('Sharp Gravel') and the prose writer Idrus. The youthful Anwar founded with his associates a group of artists known as 'Gelanggang' ('Arena'), which in 1950 addressed a manifesto to all Indonesians. A single sentence from it will serve to illustrate the outlook of these artists: "Indonesian culture will be formed by all the voices resounding from all corners of the world, and will evoke a response that will re-echo with an original voice". And it concludes: "The criterion by which we judge all that surrounds us is the attitude of men who are convinced that there exists a mutual interaction between the artist and society".

Anwar atracted many authors to his banner. But he died at the age of only 27, and his death robbed Indonesia's literary life of one of its inspiring geniuses. Amongst the journals which also deserve to be singled out are 'Mimbar Indonesia', 'Sisat' and 'Indonesia'.

Amongst more recent authors there are naturally many who are still in search of an individual style. The art critic on 'Mimbar Indonesia', H. B. Jasin, exercises great influence and has therefore a most responsible task. There are also several authors who have already arrived at a style of their own, such as Achdiat K. Mihardja, Rivai Apin, Siti Nuraini, Asrul Sani, Usmar Ismail, Dr. El Hakim, and Uruy Sontany, whose historical novel 'Tambera' is notable for its particularly well-defined characterization. Intense activity is being displayed in all spheres of literature. The attempt is being made to provide a response "with an original voice" to all the problems with which the Indonesian artist is faced.

It is a heavy responsibility that he has to bear. The old traditional popular art exists no more, and the country threatens to become culturally impoverished. The task is now to create the basis upon which a people that has experienced so many varied influences from different quarters during its past may now establish for itself a rich new cultural future.

APPENDICES

CHRONOLOGICAL TABLE

2500 B.C.
Immigration of Indonesian tribes from Yunnan (South China); neolithic era.

1500 B.C.
Neolithic culture. Megalithic culture (monumental style)

500 B.C.
Penetration of Dong-Son and Late Chou culture
Development of decorative art. Megalithic culture (dynamic style)

	JAVA	BALI	SUMATRA	OTHER ISLANDS
100	A.D. Commencement of Indian colonization			
400	First Hindu kingdom in western Java (Taruma)		Chinese accounts of existence of centres of power	Hinduized kingdom in Borneo
600	CENTRAL JAVANESE PERIOD		KINGDOM OF MALAYU (Djambi, eastern Sumatra) KINGDOM OF SHRIVIDJAYA Palembang, centre of Buddhist learning (Hīnayāna Buddhism) *Stone buildings*	
	First traces of a Hindu centre of power in central Java			
700	Shivaist kingdom of King Sandjaya (circa 732)			
	Tjandis on Dieng Plateau	First traces of Buddhism	Large-scale expansion of Shrividjaya Conquest of Malayan peninsula (775)	
	SHAILÉNDRA DYNASTY (778) Mahāyāna Buddhism *Tjandi Kalasan* *Tjandi Pawon* *Tjandi Mendut*			
800	*Borobudur* *Tjandi Sewu* MATARAM DYNASTY (864) *Prambanan complex*		Shrividjaya becomes Javanese protectorate Authority of Shailéndras transferred to Sumatra	
900	EASTERN JAVANESE PERIOD (927)		Shailéndras ruling over Sumatra and Malayan peninsula	
	Mpu Sindok (928—950)	KINGDOM OF PÈDJÈNG (Beduluh-Pèdjèng)	Mataram invades Shrividjaya (992)	
	Earliest literary works *Parva Rāmāyana*	Charter of foundation of Tirta Empul King Udayana ∞ eastern Javanese princess Mahéndradatta Son: Airlangga		

238

JAVA	BALI	SUMATRA	OTHER ISLANDS
1000			
Invasion of Shrividjaya (1006)	Eastern Java and Bali united under a single crown	Shailéndras of Sumatra invade Java (1006)	
Airlangga (1010—1049)	*Javanese cultural influence on Bali*	Decline of power of Shrividjaya	
Kakawin: Ardjunavivāha (Mpu Kanwa)	*Cliff tjandis of Tampaksiring*	Malaya again at the helm of power	
Partition of kingdom into Kediri and Djanggala (1045)	*Commencement of classical period*		
KEDIRI DYNASTY (1045—1222)	Bali again virtually independent after 1049		
1100			
Flourishing of literature Kakawin: Rāmāyana? Kakawin: Bhāratayuddha (Mpu Sedah and Mpu Panuluh; 1157)			
1200			
SINGHASĀRI DYNASTY		Malayu recognizes Javanese suzerainty under Kertanagara (1275) COMMENCEMENT OF ISLAMIC PERIOD Samudra: first Islamic State	
Ken Angrok (Radjasa, 1222—1227) *Tjandi Kidal (circa 1240) Tjandi Djago (1268) Tjandi Singhasāri* Kertanagara (1268—1292) Attack by Chinese fleet (1293)	Bali subjected by Kertanagara (1284) Bali independent again (1292)		
MADJAPAHIT DYNASTY (1294—1520)			
1300			
Raden Widjaya (Kerta-radjasa, 1294—1309)		Malayu driven back into interior of island (Menangkabau)	
Panataran complex Gadjah Mada; chief minister (1331—1364)	Conquest by Gadjah Mada	KINGDOM OF PASEI	
Javanese colony established on Bali (1343) Hayam Wuruk (1350—1389)	Javanese colony (1343) *Strong Javanese influence on Balinese culture*		
Maximum expansion of Madjapahit *Kakawin: Nagarakertā-gāma* (Mpu Prapansha)	Kingdom of Gèlgèl		Most of Archipelago in the hands of Madjapahit
Flourishing of all the plastic and applied arts	*Mountain sanctuary of Besakih*		

JAVA	BALI	SUMATRA	OTHER ISLANDS
1400			
Decline of Madjapahit	*Independent development of Balinese culture*	KINGDOM OF MALACCA	
		EXTENSIVE SPREAD OF ISLAM	
CONVERSION TO ISLAM COMMENCES Malik Ibrahim (1419) *Pararaton (Prose)* Wali dynasty in eastern Java (Prabu Sadmata)		*Development of Malay literature Classical period Hikayat Sadjarah-Malayu*	
1500			
SULTANATE OF DEMAK (Raden Patah) Portuguese conquer Malacca (1511)		Portuguese conquer Malacca (1511)	
END OF HINDU-JAVANESE PERIOD (*circa* 1520)	Conquest of Lombok	KINGDOM OF ATJEH (1520) Authority extended over whole of Sumatra	Moluccas Christianized by the Portuguese (Franciscus Xaverius)
COMMENCEMENT OF ISLAMIC PERIOD		*Evolution of Amir Hamza romance*	Spread of Islam on coast of Borneo
Wali dynasty in western Java (Bantam and Cheribon; Falatéhan) Foundation of Djakarta Decline of Hindu kingdom of Padjadjaran Bantam independent			
ISLAMIC KINGDOM OF MATARAM (1575)			
Senepati (1575—1601) *Cultural decline* European merchants establish factories in western Java			
1600			
Establishment of Dutch East Indian Company (Verenigde Oost-Indische Compagnieën, 1602) Djakarta laid waste; Batavia built		Iskandar Muda of Atjeh (1607—1636) *Hikayat Malem-Dagang*	Southern Celebes converted to Islam (Macassars and Buginese)
COMMENCEMENT OF SUPPREMACY OF EAST INDIAN COMPANY	Decline of Kingdom of Gèlgèl Balambangan conquered	East Indian Company conquers Malacca (1641) Decline in power of Atjeh	*Chronicles*
Sultan Agung of Mataram (1613—1645) Attempted consolidation of authority Conflict with East Indian Company	Several small autonomous districts		

JAVA	BALI	SUMATRA	OTHER ISLANDS
Decorative arts, music and dancing again flourish (Pangeran Pekik) *Pudjangga Institute; Babads (rhymed historical tales) Ménak (Hamza) romance*		East Indian Company conquers new districts of Atjeh *Malay becomes lingua franca of Indonesia*	East Indian Company takes Celebes (1669) **Buginese** found independent states outside Celebes
Sunan Amangkurat I Tegalwangi (1645—77) End of Wali dynasty in eastern Java Internal troubles in Mataram			
1700			
Increased influence of East Indian Company Mataram partitioned into 3 vassal states: Surakarta, Djokjakarta and the vassal state of the Mangkunagara (1755, 1757) East Indian Company replaced by 'Batavian Republic' (1799)	Bali loses Balam-bangan (1768)		
1800			
Governor-General Herman Willem Daendels Great highroad Provisional British administration (1811—16) Thomas Stanford Raffles *(shows much understanding Javanese culture)* Vassal state of the Paku Alam			
ASSUMPTION OF SOVEREIGNTY BY KINGDOM OF NETHERLANDS (1816)			
Treaty of London (1824) Atjeh remains independent Agrarian difficulties Java War (1825—30, Dipanagara) 'Cultuurstelsel', 1830 *Decline of popular art*	Dutch expeditions (1846—49)		

INDONESIA

1850   Sarawak (North Borneo) independent 'Sultanate' under James Brooke (1851).

Change in colonial policy: extension of Dutch power over Indonesia.

Opening of Suez Canal (1869).

Sumatra Treaty (1871). Holland obtains a free hand in Atjeh. Atjeh War (1873—1904).

Ever-increasing involvement of Indonesia in world commerce. Development of plantations and large-scale agriculture, especially in Java and Sumatra.

Expansion of money economy, and consequent disruption of the closed agrarian communities. *Further decline of popular art.*

Agrarian law (1870). Rights of native population to cultivated land safeguarded.

Increased Catholic and Protestant missionary activities. *Popular art jeopardised.*

1900   'Ethical policy' introduced.

Restoration of Borobudur (1907—11) by Dr. Th. van Erp. Ever-increasing interest in Indonesian culture (i.a. safeguarding and restoration of works of art).

Japanese victories over Russia (1904). Awakening of national consciousness.

Education on Western lines.

Sarékat Islam.

Conquest of Bali (1908). *European influence on wood-carving and painting on Bali.*

Indonesia entirely in Dutch hands (1911) except for North Borneo (British) and North Timor (Portuguese).

World War I (1914—18). Demands for right of national self-determination. Increase in national sentiment. Nationalist organizations.

Establishment of People's Council (Law of 1916).

Considerable expansion of education on Western lines and promotion of popular art, particularly in Java and on Bali.

Greater understanding for and academic interest in the importance of popular art amongst Catholic and Protestant missionaries.

Pudjangga Baru (first literary grouping of Indonesian writers, 1933).

Development of Bahasa Indonesia into national language: recognized by People's Council (1936), and vigorously promoted by the Bureau of Education (Balai Pustaka), founded in 1908.

Persagi, first group of Indonesian painters (1938).

World War II (1939—45).

After the war: great efflorescence of painting and poetry.

Round Table Conference (1949).

INDONESIA AN INDEPENDENT STATE (1949).

BIBLIOGRAPHY

This bibliography is confined to the most important works. The number of monographs and articles in periodicals is so great that it is not possible to list them all. But several of the works mentioned below contain extensive bibliographies, to which reference can be made for information with regard to specialized fields.

L. *Adam*, Primitive Art, Pelican Books. London 1949

Z. *Ali*, Islam in the world, Lahore 1947

A. *Alten*, Some remarks on rural industry in Indonesia, no place, 1955

Batiks in Indonesia, Djakarta 1952

H. *Beckh*, Buddhismus. Buddha und seine Lehre, Berlin 1919–20 (2 Bde.)

H. *J. Benda*, The crescent and the rising sun (Indonesian Islam under the Japanese occupation, 1942–1945), The Hague 1958

A. *J. Bernet Kempers*, The bronzes of Nalanda and Hindu-Javanese Art, Leiden 1933

C. *C. Berg*, Inleiding tot de studie van het Oud-Javaansch, Soerakarta 1928

C. *T. Bertling*, Sociale werkelijkheid bij de Primitieven, Amsterdam 1947

F. *D. K. Bosch*, Het vraagstuk van de Hindu-kolonisatie van de Archipel (Inaugural lecture), Leiden 1946

H. *Th. Bossert*, Ornamente der Völker — Eine Sammlung angewandter Schmuckformen aus Afrika, Asien und Indonesien, Australien und Ozeanien, Nord-, Mittel- und Süd-Amerika, Tübingen 1955

G. *H. Bousquet*, Introduction à l'étude de l'Islam indonésien, Paris 1938

C. *Brockelmann*, Geschichte der Islamischen Völker und Staaten, München-Berlin 1939

A. *Bühler*, Materialien zur Kenntnis der Ikattechnik (Int. Archiv für Ethnographie, Bd. 43, Leiden 1943)

M. *Bührmann*, Das farbige Schattenspiel, Bern 1955

Catalogi van de tentoonstellingen van moderne Javaanse schilders, Djakarta, 1947–48, Amsterdam 1948

E. *Conze*, Buddhism — Its essence and development, Oxford 1953, 2.

C. *K. Coomaraswamy*, A History of Indian and Indonesian Art, London 1927 (with extensive bibliography)

M. *Covarrubias*, Balinese Art (Asia, vol. XXXVII, 1937)

N. *A. Douwes Dekker*, Tanah Air Kita

J. *P. Duyvendak*, Inleiding tot de ethnologie van de Indische Archipel, no place, 1940

J. *S. Furnivall*, Netherlands India, no place, 1938

Th. *P. Galestin*, Indonesië, Algemene Kunstgeschiedenis, dl. 6, Utrecht 1951

Th. *P. Galestin*, The story of the Buddha on the Stupa of Barabudur (Ned. Indië — Oud en Nieuw), 1933

Th. *P. Galestin*, L. *Langewis* and R. *Bolland*, Lamak and Malat in Bali and a Sumba Loom, Amsterdam 1956

Handbuch der Weltgeschichte, dl. 1, 2 en 3, Amsterdam — Antwerpen 1957

H. *von Glasenapp*, Der Buddhismus in Indien und im Fernen Osten — Schicksale und Lebensformen einer Erlösungsreligion, Berlin-Zürich 1956

G. *Goedès*, Les états hindouisés d'Indochine et d'Indonésie (Histoire du Monde, tome 8) Paris 1948)

H. *Goetz*, India — Five thousand years of Indian Art (Art of the World Series), London 1959 (with extensive bibliography)

J. *Gonda*, Letterkunde van de Indische Archipel, no place, 1947

J. *Gonda*, Letterkunde van de Indische Archipel, Int. Archiv für Ethnologie, Bd. 19 und 20, 1910 und 1913

A. *C. Haddon* and L. *E. Start*, Iban or Sea Dayak Fabrics and their pattern — A descriptive catalogue of the Iban fabrics in the Museum of Archaeology and Ethnology Cambridge, Cambridge 1936

B. *Harrison*, South-East Asia, Hongkong 1954

H. *R. van Heekeren*, The bronze-iron age of Indonesia, The Hague 1958 (with extensive bibliography)

H. R. van Heekeren, The stone age of Indonesia, The Hague 1957

A. R. Hein, Die Bildenden Künste bei den Dajaks auf Borneo — Beitrag zur Allgemeinen Kunstgeschichte, Wien 1890

A. R. Hein, Die Verwendung der Menschengestalt in Flechtwerken (Mitt. d. Anthrop. Gesellsch. in Wien, Bd. XXI) 1891

A. R. Hein, Ornamente der Dajaks, Vortrag gehalten in der Haupt-Versammlung des Vereins österreich. Zeichenlehrer am 15. Dez. 1888, Wien

R. von Heine-Geldern, Introduction to the catalogue of the exposition »Indonesian Art«, New York 1948

R. von Heine-Geldern, Prehistoric research in the Netherlands Indies, New York 1955

R. von Heine-Geldern, Über Krisgriffe und ihre mythischen Grundlagen (Ostasiatische Zeitschr. Jg. 18, Nr. 6) 1932

A. N. J. Th. à Th. van der Hoop, Indonesische siermotieven, Batavia 1949

A. N. J. Th. à Th. van der Hoop, Megalithic remains in South Sumatra, 1932

C. Hooykaas, The old-Javanese Rāmāyana Kakawin with special reference to the problem of interpolation in Kakawins, The Hague 1955

C. F. Iklé, Ikat technique and Dutch East Indian ikats, New York 1934

Indonesia to-day, Djakarta 1951 (Min. of Information)

Indonesian Art, Jogjakarta 1955 (Min. of Educ. and Culture)

Indonesien in seiner Kunst — Sonderausstellung des Museums für Völkerkunde Wien, Vienna 1957

J. H. Jager Gerlings, Sprekende Weefsels, Amsterdam 1952 (with extensive bibliography)

J. E. Jasper en Mas Pirngadie, De inlandsche Kunstnijverheid in Ned. Indie, dl 1 (het vlechtwerk), dl. 2 (de weefkunst), dl. 3 (de batikkunst), dl. 4 (de goud- en zilversmeedkunst), dl. 5 (de bewerking van niet-edele metalen)

H. H. Juynboll, Neuere Literatur über die Kunst von Niederländisch Indien, Berlin 1915

J. Kats, Het Javaansche Tooneel, dl. 1, De wajang poerwa, 1923

R. A. Kern, De verbreiding van de Islam (Geschiedenis van Nederlands-Indië onder leiding van F. W. Stapel, dl. 1), Amsterdam 1938

J. P. Kleiweg de Zwann, De oudste mensheid van de Indische Archipel, 1943

G. H. R. von Koenigswald, Remarks on some prehistoric cultural contacts of the Indonesian region, Rome 1956

G. H. R. von Koenigswald, Über Sumatranische Schiffstücher und ihre Beziehungen zur Kunst Ozeaniens, Basel 1951

N. J. Krom, Hindu-Javaanse geschiedenis, no place, 1931

J. Kunst, De inheemse muziek en de Zending, Amsterdam 1957

J. Kunst, De Toonkunst van Java, 2 delen, The Hague 1934

J. Kunst, Die 2000jährige Geschichte Süd-Sumatras im Spiegel ihrer Musik, Basel 1952

J. Kunst, Einiges über die Javanische Musik, 1926

J. Kunst, Hindoe-Javaanse muziekinstrumenten, Weltevreden 1927

J. Kunst, Music in Flores, study of the vocal and instrumental-music among the tribes living in Flores, Leiden 1942

J. Kunst, Music in Nias, Leiden 1938

J. Kunst, Muziek en dans in de buitengewesten, Amsterdam 1946

J. Kunst, The cultural background of Indonesian music, Amsterdam 1949

J. Kunst, The music of Bali and its emotional appeal, (Britain and Holland, 1, no. 3), London 1949

J. Kunst and C. J. A. van Wely, De toonkunst van Bali, Weltevreden 1925

R. M. Loeb and R. Heine Geldern, Sumatra, its history and people. The archaeology and art of Sumatra, Vienna 1935

J. A. Loeber, Das Batiken — Eine Blüte Indonesischen Kunstlebens, Oldenburg 1926

J. A. Loeber, Techniek en sierkunst van den Ind. Arch., (serial publications)

G. Mahn, Der Tempel von Boro-Budur, eine buddhistische Studie, Leipzig 1919

A. Malraux, Des bas-reliefs aux Grottes Sacrées, 1954

P. A. A. Mangkoenagara VII, De Wajang koelit en

de daarin voorkomende symbolen en mystiek, 1933

R. L. Mellema, Wayang puppets, Amsterdam 1954

H. J. van Mook, Indonesië, Nederland en de wereld, 1949

P. A. J. Moojen, Kunst op Bali, 1926

A. W. Nieuwenhuis, Kunstperlen und ihre kulturelle Bedeutung, Leiden 1903

G. J. Nieuwenhuis, Über den Tanz in Niederländisch-Indien (Beiträge zur Ethnologie des Malaiischen Archipels) Leiden 1916

C. A. O. Nieuwenhuyze, Aspects of Islam in post-colonial Indonesia (Five essays), The Hague 1958

W. O. J. Nieuwenkamp, Bouwkunst van Bali, 1926

W. O. J. Nieuwenkamp, Beeldhouwkunst van Bali, 1928

A. Pana, Kort overzicht van de moderne Indonesische literatuur, 1949

Th. Pigeaud, Javaansche volksvertoningen, 1938

Oosthoek's Encyclopaedie, deel 8, Indonesie, Utrecht 1950 (with extensive bibliography)

W. H. Rassers, Inleiding tot de bestudering van de Jav. Kris (Mededeling der Kon. Akademie v. Wetenschappen, afd. Letterkunde, Nieuwe reeks, dl. 1, no 8) 1938

W. H. Rassers, Over de oorsprong van het Javaansche tooneel (Bijdr. Taal,- Land en Volkenkunde, dl. 8) 1931

C. Sachs, Die Musikinstrumente Indiens und Indonesiens, zugleich eine Einführung in die Instrumentenkunde, Berlin-Leipzig 1923

H. B. Sarkar, Indian influences on the literature of Java and Bali, Calcutta 1934

L. Scherman, Die javanische Batik-Technik und ihre vorderindischen Parallelen, München-Berlin 1910

E. Schlager and T. Meyer, The Barong dance in Bali — Description, music and choreography

J. D. E. Schmeltz, Indonesische Prunkwaffen — Ein Beitrag zur Kunde des Kunstgewerbes in Indonesien und der ethnologischen Bedeutung des Kris, Leiden 1890

J. Schmutzer, J. J. ten Berge and W. Maas, Europeanisme of Katholicisme, Utrecht 1927

B. J. O. Schrieke, Het einde van de klassieke Hindoe-Javaansche cultuur op Midden-Java, Amsterdam 1941

S. Schueller, Christliche Kunst aus fernen Ländern, Düsseldorf 1939

F. W. Stapel, Geschiedenis van Ned. Indië, 1930, 2nd ed., 1946

A. Steinmann, Das Seelenschiff in der Textilkunst, Basel 1945

A. Steinmann, Die Ornamente der Ikat-Gewebe von Sumba, no place, no date

F. W. Stutterheim, Cultuurgeschiedenis van Indonesië, deel 1 en 2, Groningen, Djakarta 1951

F. W. Stutterheim, Leerboek der Indische cultuurgeschiedenis, Groningen 1935

F. W. Stutterheim, Studies in Indonesian Archaeology, The Hague 1956

Thio Goan Tjoan, Agama Buddha, Djakarta, Groningen 1954

M. Vlekke, Geschiedenis van de Ind. Archipel, 1947

B. A. G. Vroklage, Das Schiff in den Megalith-Kulturen Südostasiens und der Südsee (Anthropos Bd. XXXI) Vienna 1936

F. A. Wagner, Sierkunst in Indonesië, Groningen 1949

F. A. Wagner, Wat Indië ontving en schonk, hoofdstuk »Kunst« (Wereldbibliotheek) Amsterdam 1946

C. H. S. Ward, Buddhism 2 vls. (Great religions of the East) London 1947—1952

H. van Weeren-Griele, Indonesian art, New York 1947

P. Wirz, Die magischen Gewebe von Bali und Lombok, Bern 1932

K. With, Java — Brahmanische, Buddhistische und eigenlebige Architektur und Plastik auf Java, Hagen 1920

H. Wouters, Volken en Volkenkunde, Amsterdam 1958 (with extensive bibliography)

K. Wulff, Sang Hyang Kamahayanan Namtranyya; Ansprache bei der Weihe buddhistischer Mönche aus dem Altjavanischen übersetzt und sprachlich erläutert, Copenhagen 1935

B. de Zoete and W. Spies, Dance and drama in Bali, London

adat

This form of an Arabic term, common in Indonesia, means 'custom', but also indicates the aggregate of customs, usages and institutions based upon mythical conceptions. Juridical implications are not necessarily involved.

babad

Historical tale in verse from the Islamic period of Javanese history; Old Javanese, Hindu-Javanese and Islamic influences may be identified in it.

badé

On Bali, a high structure made of bamboo, wood and paper, in which the mortal remains of a deceased person are taken to the place of cremation. The whole structure usually consists of three parts, representing earth, air and the mountain of heaven. This symbolism is greatly influenced by Hinduism (cf. also meru).

bandji

A swastika, a very ancient decorative motif, which has survived both in Java (in batik patterns) and on Bali (in metal-working and on cremation towers). It was most probably introduced from China, and is the well-known magic sign of good fortune and prosperity.

batik

A technique of applying certain designs on textiles in colour. The fabric is dipped into the dye, which is not absorbed by those parts of the material, which are covered with wax on both sides, to represent the pattern.

dalang

Leading figure in wayang puppet-shows (cf. wayang) common in Java and on Bali. He directs the performance, speaks the words of the play, and manipulates the puppets.

floating weft technique

In this technique the thread forming the pattern is woven in simultaneously with the thread which holds the fabric together (as a cross-thread). The latter is the ordinary weft thread. For this purpose the warp threads are provided with shed sticks.

gamelan

The term originally meant 'hammer', and gamelan the Javanese and Balinese orchestra, which, apart from a single exception, consists of percussion instruments. The scales employed differ greatly from ours in the West. The orchestra performs the function of illustration and accompaniment.

hikayat

Prose work in Malay, relating the adventures of the national heroes of the Malayan kingdoms or containing chronicles of the relevant princely houses. Heavily romanticized; unimportant as a work of art (insignificant composition).

ikat

The term literally means 'to bind'. A technique of ornamenting a fabric. Thin fibres are wound around a thread before weaving, to protect these bound parts from absorbing the dye into which the threads are dipped. Three kinds may be distinguished: ikat of the warp, ikat of the weft, and ikat of all the threads, i.e. both warp and weft.

kakawin

Old Javanese poetic work, modelled on the Indian kavyas. The subject-matter is drawn from Indian epic literature, the metre is prescribed, and has also been adopted from the kavyas. These works produce a very artificial and intellectual effect.

kāla

Literally, 'badness', 'evil'. In a figurative sense, the demon himself.

kāla head

Head of a monster affixed over temple gates and recesses to ward off demonic forces by magic means. In shape reminiscent of a stylized lion's head.

kidung

Old Javanese poetic work, the metres of which are modelled predominantly on Javanese prototypes. The content also displays marked Javanese influence.

Mahā-kāla

This name is attributed to Shiva in his incarnation as Supreme Destroyer (Mahā = greatest, highest, most noble). Cf. also Māhā-Déva, Shiva as Supreme Deity (Deva = Deity). Mahā-Guru: Shiva as principal teacher (guru = teacher).

makāra figure

Mythological fish and elephant figure. In the involuted trunk it generally bears a flower-bud. It appears in places of worship in Java, generally together with a kāla head (q.v.).

mandala

Literally, a magic circle; figuratively, a shrine designed for meditation. Thus Borobudur, for example, is a mandala.

meru

Mountain of heaven upon which the gods reside. Javanese tjandis and places of worship in Balinese puras, also termed merus, should be regarded as symbolic of the mountain of heaven (cf. tjandi and pura).

mudrā

Symbolic gesture, as found with statues of Buddha, and elsewhere.

nāga figure

Naga = snake. The naga figure frequently bears a crown. The snake is regarded as charged with magic power, as are also, for example, the crocodile or lizard. In places of worship in eastern Java the naga figure replaces the makara figure customary elsewhere. The blade of the kris also resembles a snake.

pamor work

This technique, also called damascene process, is used in forging a weapon, particularly a kris. Ordinary iron and (meteoric) nickelous iron are cut and folded in a certain way. When the blade is finished, it is treated with acid so that the nickelous steel obtains a bright surface, and the desired pattern appears on the blade.

paras

A comparatively soft natural stone, used together with brick by the Balinese in the construction of temples. Paras is very easily worked, but weathers fairly rapidly.

parva

Literally 'oldest', i.e. the earliest Old Javanese literary works, written in prose. The subject-matter is drawn from Indian epic poetry.

pedanda

On Bali, a Hindu priest of the highest caste, that of the Brāhmans. The pedanda-Buddha is also met with.

pélog

Believed to be the oldest scale used in gamelan music (q.v.). It has five notes to an octave, and corresponds approximately to: d — e flat (+) — f — a — b flat — (d) and a — b flat — c — e — (—) — f — (a); the vocal scale has several additional semitones.

pilih technique

This weaving technique closely resembles the floating weft technique, except that in this case the thread forming the pattern is passed through the threads of the warp where necessary with the aid of a long spool (pilih = to select).

pudjanggas

Scholars and poets at Javanese kratons during the Islamic period who displayed much understanding for Hindu-Javanese culture.

pura

The terraced temple, common on Bali, with three storeys enclosed by walls. Lavishly decorated gateways lead to the terraces, the third of which is the highest in every sense of the word. Here are to be found the recesses for offerings, shrines and merus (q.v.).

raksasa

Giant figure, generally armed with a large club, to ward off evil forces. Usually erected on either side of the entrance-gates to temples.

sarung

Literally, 'quiver', 'container'. In particular, a term for a quiver-shaped woman's garment worn in Indonesia to clothe the body from the waist down.

singa figure

Singa = lion. On Bali the singa figure is always a winged lion. The Toba Bataks place the stylized head of a monster in front of their houses; this is also called singa (cf. Singapore = lion city).

sjair

Poetic works in Malay.

sléndro

A scale used in gamelan music (q.v.), probably introduced into Java in the 8th century. Like the pélog, it has five notes, and can roughly be notated as follows: d — e — f sharp — a — b — (d). The vocal sléndro also has five semitones (cf. pélog).

tantris

Narrative poetic works in the form of kidungs (q.v.), the themes of which were borrowed from Indian fables.

tjandi

The term means 'sepulchral monument'. In Java the term is used to indicate Hindu monuments consisting of a base, temple and temple roof. The temple proper in its simplest form contains a single chamber, to which access is gained by means of a stairway leading up alongside the base. The tjandi contains a statue of a god or a deified prince, and an urn with the ashes of the prince, or his consort, in whose memory the whole structure was erected.

tjanting

A small copper crucible for wax, with a diameter of approximately 1 cm. (½ in.) and one, or sometimes two, spouts. The implement is provided with a short bamboo handle and is used to apply a wax pattern upon a fabric (batik work q.v.).

topèng

A mask used in a certain kind of wayang show in which the parts are played by masked actors. The words are spoken by the dalang, not the actors (cf. dalang, wayang).

tree of heaven

In India the tree plays an important part in mythological tales. In Indonesia we find the tree of heaven in Java and on Bali, in wayang-kulit and wayang-purwa (kulit = leather, purwa = first, oldest), on a stage-property (gunungan or kekayon), made of parchment, either shaped like a screen (Java) or resembling a leaf (Bali). The dalang (q.v.) uses it to indicate intervals.

tree of life

A very ancient motif, frequently found in Indonesia. It is above all used in textiles, and is formed by a stylized tree, the roots of which are always shown; it is believed to be charged with magic power (cf. tree of heaven).

tumpal

A very ancient motif, in the shape of a triangle, generally ornamented, probably a magic fertility symbol or a human figure which has been so greatly stylized as to be hardly recognizable.

wayang

Literally, 'shadow'. This term indicates all the dramatic plays common in Java and on Bali. In the earliest ones the puppets were made of parchment, in open-work, and were polychrome. The shadows are projected upon a large transparent canvas.

INDEX